# THE COMPLETE PLANT BASED COOKBOOK FOR BEGINNERS

## *By Jordan Worthen*

# Contents

# INTRODUCTION

Five years ago, I was diagnosed with pre-diabetes. I experienced fatigue, frequent urination, frequent infections and other annoying symptoms of high blood sugar levels. I was tired and bloated all the time and I also started finding it hard to focus and concentrate. Plus, I've suffered from eczema (atopic dermatitis) all my life. It is no secret that all these conditions can significantly increase the risk of early death, so it got me worried. Sometimes you win, sometimes you learn!

Despite regular exercise and healthy eating habits, I was unhappy with my weight. I've often experienced the yo-yo effect, since restrictive regimens and perpetual dieting can disrupt hormones, increase appetite and lead to mental problems. All the experts agree on one thing: A wide range of human diseases begin in the gut. Therefore, I decided to find the best diet that works for me. It's time to turn over a new leaf!

Overall, it's not easy to figure out which eating plan will be good for you! With so many diet regimens to choose from, how to decide what to eat? Giving up animal products for myself, animals, and Mother Earth sounds good to me. How about you? I have never regretted my decision – just the op-posite, I love this lifestyle. I enjoy food more than ever! I cured my eczema, lost weight, and solved my health problems. I've learned a lot during this journey so I wanted to collect a large assortment of vegan recipes to help people lose weight and prevent some serious conditions; this collection will help you kick-start your vegan journey or stay on track if you are a long-time vegan. While this depends on your socio-economic background, it is fair to say that starting a new diet may not be the easiest thing in the world. But it is a worthy goal! There are a lot of misconceptions about the vegan diet. They include some commonly held beliefs that the vegan diet is boring, unhealthy, and hard to maintain. This cookbook will hopefully open your eyes to how extraordinary delicious and healthy plant-based meals can be.

# The Vegan Diet:
# Why it's Not Just a Diet, More a Way of Life

I've spent a good portion of my life trying to maintain my healthy weight. I finally realized that there is no instant solution, there is no shortcut or a magic wand! Ultimately, I gave up dieting and decided to find an eating plan that can support my overall wellbeing. And voila! The secret to a healthy diet is simpler than I ever thought! The vegan diet is primarily known for its simplicity; when following this dietary regimen, you should focus on plant-based foods and avoid animal-source food. Whether you are following a vegan diet, or are considering trying this lifestyle, I created this plant-based, budget-friendly food list to make your grocery shopping easier to manage.

VEGETABLES: Try to include different types of vegetables – from above-ground vegetables to root vegetables that grow underground.

FRUITS: Pick up affordable fruits that are on sale/in season. Add frozen fruit to your grocery list since they are just as nutritious as fresh produce. They can be used in smoothies, toppings, compotes or preserves. On the other hand, dried fruit generally contains a lot of antioxidants, especially polyphenols; it has been proven that eating dried fruits can prevent heart disease and some types of cancer.

NUTS & SEEDS: Nuts and seeds offer different dietary benefits. Nuts and seeds do not only ensure essential nutrients but are also a variety of flavors. This "ready to eat" food is a perfect snack with dried fruits and trail mix, essential vegan foods to stockpile for an emergency.

RICE & GRAINS: Rice and grains are versatile foods that're easy to incorporate into the vegan diet. Leftovers reheat wonderfully and can be served at any time of the day, turning simple and inexpensive ingredients into a full-fledged meal. I always make sure my pantry contains a healthy butter such as tahini or peanut butter.

BEANS & LEGUMES: The legumes and beans are highly affordable and there's no end to the variety of tasty dishes you can cook with them. These humble but powerful foods are packed with vitamins, minerals, protein, and dietary fiber. In addition to being super-healthy and versatile, legumes pair very well with other vegan proteins, vegetables, and grains.

HEALTHY FATS: Don't underestimate the importance of quality fats in vegan cooking. Coconut oil, olive oil, and avocado are always good to have on hand.

NON-DAIRY PRODUCTS: Using a plant-based cheese or milk lends flavor, texture, and nutrition to your meals. Although you can find fantastic products on the market, I've included my favorite recipes for vegan feta, vegan ricotta, and plant-based milk in this collection.

HERBS, SPICES & CONDIMENTS: A handful of fresh herbs will add that little something extra to your soups, stews, dips, or casseroles. Vegan condiments such as mustard, ketchup, mayonnaise, and plant-based sauces can be used in salads, casseroles, and spreads. Choosing their distinctive flavors to complement vegetables, grains and legumes will help you to make the most of your vegan dishes. Herbs and spices are naturally plant-based, but play it safe and look for a label that says "Suitable for vegans".

BAKING GOODS & CANNED GOODS: These vegan essentials include all types of flour, baking powder, baking soda, and yeast. Further, cocoa powder, vegan chocolate, and sweeteners are good to have on hand. As for the health vegan sweeteners, opt for fresh or dried fruits, agave syrup, maple syrup, and stevia. When it comes to the canned goods, stock your pantry with cooking essentials such as tomato, sauerkraut, pickles, low sodium chickpeas and beans, coconut milk, green chiles, pumpkin puree, tomato sauce, low sodium corn, and artichoke hearts. Thus, if you want to make sure you have nutritious, delicious and quality meals for you and your family, building a healthy vegan pantry is half success.

# What are the Health Benefits of a Plant-Based Diet?

As it turns out, eating plant-based is one of the healthiest diets in the world. Healthy vegan diets include plenty of fresh products, whole grains, legumes, and healthy fats such as seeds and nuts. They are abundant with antioxidants, minerals, vitamins, and dietary fiber.

Current scientific researches pointed out that higher consumption of plant-based foods is associated with a lower risk of mortality from conditions such as cardiovascular disease, type 2 diabetes, hypertension, and obesity. Vegan eating plans often rely heavily on healthy staples, avoiding animal products that are loaded with antibiotics, additives, and hormones. Plus, consuming a higher proportion of essential amino acids with animal protein can be damaging to human health. Since animal products contain much more fat than plant-based foods, it's not a shocker that studies have shown that meat-eaters have nine times the obesity rate of vegans.

This leads us to the next point, one of the greatest benefits of the vegan diet – weight loss. While many people choose to live a vegan life for ethical reasons, the diet itself can help you achieve your weight loss goals. If you're struggling to shift pounds, you may want to consider trying a plant-based diet. How exactly? As a vegan, you will reduce the number of high-calorie foods such as full-fat dairy products, fatty fish, pork and other cholesterol-containing foods such as eggs. Try replacing such foods with high-fiber and protein-rich alternatives that will keep you fuller longer. The key is focusing on nutrient-dense, clean and natural foods and avoid empty calories such as sugar, saturated fats, and highly-processed foods. Here are a few tricks that help me maintain my weight on the vegan diet for years. I eat vegetables as a main course; I consume good fats in moderation – a good fat such as olive oil does not make you fat; I exercise regularly and cook at home.

# A Few Words about This Recipe Collection

As a long-term vegan, I learned to simplify my diet by planning meals ahead of time and keeping pantry staples at my fingertips. Remember – even if you don't follow a plant-based diet strictly, eating more of the natural foods is an extraordinary accomplishment!

This collection contains the best plant-based recipes I've ever tried. The recipes are selected into categories based on the food group so you can easily plan your meals. If you've always wanted to make your own hummus, tahini, began burgers, spreads, and condiments, I have you covered. This cookbook includes recipes for homemade versions of our favorite vegan substitutes such as peanut butter, cashew cheese, coconut yogurt, chia eggs, flax eggs, plant-based protein sources, and so forth.

Do you still think that vegan products are expensive or difficult to re-create at home? With this cookbook, you can transform any regular meal into a veg-friendly wonder! Making plant-based milk, cheese or burgers at home is really as simple as making any other common recipe. In this regard, I'm sharing my favorite vegan recipe of all times, the ones I return to again and again. I hope you'll enjoy them as much as I do!

# BREAKFAST

# 1. Scrambled Tofu and Avocado Sandwich

(Ready in about 15 minutes | Servings 2)

## Ingredients

1 tablespoon olive oil
5 ounces extra-firm tofu, pressed and crumbled
1/2 teaspoon turmeric powder
4 slices rye bread
1 tablespoon spicy mustard
1/2 medium-sized avocado, pitted, peeled and sliced
1 medium-sized tomato, sliced
1 small-sized cucumber, sliced
salt and ground black pepper, to season

## Directions

Heat the olive oil in a frying pan over medium-high heat. When it's hot, add the tofu and sauté for 8 minutes, stirring occasionally to promote even cooking.

Add in the turmeric powder and continue to sauté an additional minute or so.

Spread the spicy mustard on each piece of bread.

To assemble your sandwiches, divide the tofu scramble between 2 bread pieces; top with avocado, tomatoes and cucumber; season with salt and black pepper to taste.

Close the sandwiches with the remaining bread slices and serve. Enjoy!

**Per serving:** Calories: 363; Fat: 20.3g; Carbs: 35.4g; Protein: 13.6g

# 2. Mixed Berry Bowl

(Ready in about 10 minutes | Servings 2)

## Ingredients

1 ½ cups coconut milk
2 small-sized bananas
1 cup mixed berries, frozen
2 tablespoons almond butter
1 tablespoon chia seeds
2 tablespoons granola

## Directions

Add the coconut milk, bananas, berries, almond butter and chia seeds.

Puree until creamy, uniform and smooth.

Divide the blended mixture between serving bowls and top with granola. Serve immediately.

**Per serving:** Calories: 533; Fat: 42.3g; Carbs: 43.4g; Protein: 6.9g

# 3. Oatmeal with Banana and Figs

(Ready in about 15 minutes | Servings 2)

## Ingredients

1 ½ cups almond milk
1/2 cup rolled oats
A pinch of sea salt
A pinch of grated nutmeg
1/3 teaspoon cinnamon
3 dried figs, chopped
2 bananas, peeled and sliced
1 tablespoon maple syrup

## Directions

In a deep saucepan, bring the milk to a rapid boil. Add in the oats, cover the saucepan and turn the heat to medium.

Add in the salt, nutmeg and cinnamon. Continue to cook for about 12 minutes, stirring periodically.

Spoon the mixture into serving bowls; top with figs and bananas; add a few drizzles of the maple syrup to each serving and serve warm. Bon appétit!

**Per serving:** Calories: 404; Fat: 5.4g; Carbs: 84g; Protein: 9g

# 4. Nutty Granola with Dried Currants

(Ready in about 25 minutes | Servings 12)

## Ingredients

1/2 cup coconut oil
1/3 cup maple syrup
1 teaspoon vanilla paste
1/2 teaspoon ground cardamom
1 teaspoon ground cinnamon
1/3 teaspoon Himalayan salt
4 cups old-fashioned oats
1/2 cup pecans, chopped
1/2 cup walnuts, chopped
1/4 cup pepitas
1 cup dried currants

## Directions

Begin by preheating your oven to 290 degrees F; line a large baking sheet with a piece parchment paper.

Then, thoroughly combine the coconut oil, maple syrup, vanilla paste, cardamom, cinnamon and Himalayan salt.

Gradually add in the oats, nuts and seeds; toss to coat well.

Spread the mixture out onto the prepared baking sheet.

Bake in the middle of the oven, stirring halfway through the cooking time, for about 20 minutes or until golden brown.

Stir in the dried currants and let your granola cool completely before storing. Store in an airtight container.

Serve with your favorite plant-based milk or yogurt. Bon appétit!

**Per serving:** Calories: 374; Fat: 19.1g; Carbs: 43.2g; Protein: 10.5g

# 5. Fruit Salad with Lemon-Ginger Syrup

(Ready in about 10 minutes + chilling time | Servings 4)

## Ingredients

1/2 cup fresh lemon juice
1/4 cup agave syrup
1 teaspoon fresh ginger, grated
1/2 teaspoon vanilla extract
1 banana, sliced
2 cups mixed berries
1 cup seedless grapes
2 cups apples, cored and diced

## Directions

Bring the lemon juice, agave syrup and ginger to a boil over medium-high heat. Then, turn the heat to medium-low and let it simmer for about 6 minutes until it has slightly thickened.

Remove from the heat and stir in the vanilla extract. Allow it to cool.

Layer the fruits in serving bowls. Pour the cooled sauce over the fruit and serve well chilled. Bon appétit!

**Per serving:** Calories: 164; Fat: 0.5g; Carbs: 42g; Protein: 1.4g

## 6. Fluffy Banana Pancakes

(Ready in about 25 minutes | Servings 4)

### Ingredients

2 tablespoons ground flaxseeds
1/2 cup oat flour
1/2 cup coconut flour
1/2 cup instant oats
1 teaspoon baking powder
1/4 teaspoon kosher salt
1/4 teaspoon ground cardamom
1/4 teaspoon ground cinnamon
1/2 teaspoon coconut extract
1 cup banana
2 tablespoons coconut oil, at room temperature

### Directions

To make the "flax" egg, in a small mixing dish, whisk 2 tablespoons of the ground flaxseeds with 4 tablespoons of the water. Let it sit for at least 15 minutes.

In a mixing bowl, thoroughly combine the flour, oats, baking powder and spices. Add in the flax egg and mashed banana. Mix until everything is well incorporated.

Heat 1/2 tablespoon of the coconut oil in a frying pan over medium-low flame. Spoon about 1/4 cup of the batter into the frying pan; fry your pancake for approximately 3 minutes per side.

Repeat until you run out of batter. Serve with your favorite fixings and enjoy!

**Per serving:** Calories: 302; Fat: 15g; Carbs: 37.2g; Protein: 7.1g

## 7. Classic French Toast

(Ready in about 20 minutes | Servings 2)

### Ingredients

1 tablespoon ground flax seeds
1 cup coconut milk
1/2 teaspoon vanilla paste
A pinch of sea salt
A pinch of grated nutmeg
1/2 teaspoon ground cinnamon
1/4 teaspoon ground cloves
1 tablespoon agave syrup
4 slices bread

### Directions

In a mixing bowl, thoroughly combine the flax seeds, coconut milk, vanilla, salt, nutmeg, cinnamon, cloves and agave syrup.

Dredge each slice of bread into the milk mixture until well coated on all sides.

Preheat an electric griddle to medium heat and lightly oil it with a nonstick cooking spray.

Cook each slice of bread on the preheated griddle for about 3 minutes per side until golden brown.

Bon appétit!

**Per serving:** Calories: 233; Fat: 6.5g; Carbs: 35.5g; Protein: 8.2g

## 8. Frybread with Peanut Butter and Jam

(Ready in about 20 minutes | Servings 3)

### Ingredients

1 cup all-purpose flour
1/2 teaspoon baking powder
1/2 teaspoon sea salt
1 teaspoon coconut sugar
1/2 cup warm water
3 teaspoon olive oil
3 tablespoons peanut butter
3 tablespoons raspberry jam

### Directions

Thoroughly combine the flour, baking powder, salt and sugar. Gradually add in the water until the dough comes together.

Divide the dough into three balls; flatten each ball to create circles.

Heat 1 teaspoon of the olive oil in a frying pan over a moderate flame. Fry the first bread for about 9 minutes or until golden brown. Repeat with the remaining oil and dough.

Serve the frybread with the peanut butter and raspberry jam. Enjoy!

**Per serving:** Calories: 293; Fat: 7.8g; Carbs: 50.3g; Protein: 5.5g

## 9. Ciabatta Bread Pudding with Sultanas

(Ready in about 2 hours 10 minutes | Servings 4)

### Ingredients

2 cups coconut milk, unsweetened
1/2 cup agave syrup
1 tablespoon coconut oil
1/2 teaspoon vanilla essence
1/2 teaspoon ground cardamom
1/4 teaspoon ground cloves
1/2 teaspoon ground cinnamon
1/4 teaspoon Himalayan salt
3/4 pound stale ciabatta bread, cubed
1/2 cup sultana raisins

### Directions

In a mixing bowl, combine the coconut milk, agave syrup, coconut oil, vanilla, cardamom, ground cloves, cinnamon and Himalayan salt.

Add the bread cubes to the custard mixture and stir to combine well. Fold in the sultana raisins and allow it to rest for about 1 hour on a counter.

Then, spoon the mixture into a lightly oiled casserole dish.

Bake in the preheated oven at 350 degrees F for about 1 hour or until the top is golden brown.

Place the bread pudding on a wire rack for 10 minutes before slicing and serving. Bon appétit!

**Per serving:** Calories: 458; Fat: 10.4g; Carbs: 81.3g; Protein: 11.4g

# 10. Vegan Banh Mi

(Ready in about 35 minutes | Servings 4)

## Ingredients

1/2 cup rice vinegar
1/4 cup water
1/4 cup white sugar
2 carrots, cut into 1/16-inch-thick matchsticks
1/2 cup white (daikon) radish, cut into 1/16-inch-thick matchsticks
1 white onion, thinly sliced
2 tablespoons olive oil
12 ounces firm tofu, cut into sticks
1/4 cup vegan mayonnaise
1 ½ tablespoons soy sauce
2 cloves garlic, minced
1/4 cup fresh parsley, chopped
Kosher salt and ground black pepper, to taste
2 standard French baguettes, cut into four pieces
4 tablespoons fresh cilantro, chopped
4 lime wedges

## Directions

Bring the rice vinegar, water and sugar to a boil and stir until the sugar has dissolved, about 1 minute. Allow it to cool.

Pour the cooled vinegar mixture over the carrot, daikon radish and onion; allow the vegetables to marinate for at least 30 minutes.

While the vegetables are marinating, heat the olive oil in a frying pan over medium-high heat. Once hot, add the tofu and sauté for 8 minutes, stirring occasionally to promote even cooking.

Then, mix the mayo, soy sauce, garlic, parsley, salt and ground black pepper in a small bowl.

Slice each piece of the baguette in half the long way Then, toast the baguette halves under the preheated broiler for about 3 minutes.

To assemble the banh mi sandwiches, spread each half of the toasted baguette with the mayonnaise mixture; fill the cavity of the bottom half of the bread with the fried tofu sticks, marinated vegetables and cilantro leaves.

Lastly, squeeze the lime wedges over the filling and top with the other half of the baguette. Bon appétit!

**Per serving:** Calories: 372; Fat: 21.9g; Carbs: 29.5g; Protein: 17.6g

# 11. Morning Nutty Oatmeal Muffins

(Ready in about 30 minutes | Servings 9)

## Ingredients

1 ½ cups rolled oats
1/2 cup shredded coconut, unsweetened
3/4 teaspoon baking powder
1/4 teaspoon salt
1/4 teaspoon vanilla extract
1/4 teaspoon coconut extract
1/4 teaspoon grated nutmeg
1/2 teaspoon cardamom
3/4 cup coconut milk
1/3 cup canned pumpkin
1/4 cup agave syrup
1/4 cup golden raisins
1/4 cup pecans, chopped

## Directions

Begin by preheating your oven to 360 degrees F. Spritz a muffin tin with a nonstick cooking oil.

In a mixing bowl, thoroughly combine all the ingredients, except for the raisins and pecans.

Fold in the raisins and pecans and scrape the batter into the prepared muffin tin.

Bake your muffins for about 25 minutes or until the top is set. Bon appétit!

**Per serving:** Calories: 192; Fat: 6g; Carbs: 30.5g; Protein: 5.6g

# 12. Raspberry and Chia Smoothie Bowl

(Ready in about 10 minutes | Servings 2)

## Ingredients

1 cup coconut milk
2 small-sized bananas, peeled
1 ½ cups raspberries, fresh or frozen
2 dates, pitted
1 tablespoon coconut flakes
1 tablespoon pepitas
2 tablespoons chia seeds

## Directions

In your blender or food processor, mix the coconut milk with the bananas, raspberries and dates.

Process until creamy and smooth. Divide the smoothie between two bowls.

Top each smoothie bowl with the coconut flakes, pepitas and chia seeds. Bon appétit!

**Per serving:** Calories: 442; Fat: 10.9g; Carbs: 85g; Protein: 9.6g

# 13. Morning Oats with Walnuts and Currants

(Ready in about 10 minutes | Servings 2)

## Ingredients

1 cup water
1 ½ cups oat milk
1 ½ cups rolled oats
A pinch of salt
A pinch of grated nutmeg
1/4 teaspoon cardamom
1 handful walnuts, roughly chopped
4 tablespoons dried currants

## Directions

In a deep saucepan, bring the water and milk to a rolling boil. Add in the oats, cover the saucepan and turn the heat to medium.

Add in the salt, nutmeg and cardamom. Continue to cook for about 12 to 13 minutes more, stirring occasionally.

Spoon the mixture into serving bowls; top with walnuts and currants. Bon appétit!

**Per serving:** Calories: 442; Fat: 10.9g; Carbs: 85g; Protein: 9.6g

## 14. Classic Applesauce Pancakes with Coconut

(Ready in about 50 minutes | Servings 8)

### Ingredients

1 ¼ cups whole-wheat flour
1 teaspoon baking powder
1/4 teaspoon sea salt
1/2 teaspoon coconut sugar
1/4 teaspoon ground cloves
1/4 teaspoon ground cardamom
1/2 teaspoon ground cinnamon

3/4 cup oat milk
1/2 cup applesauce, unsweetened
2 tablespoons coconut oil
8 tablespoons coconut, shredded
8 tablespoons pure maple syrup

### Directions

In a mixing bowl, thoroughly combine the flour, baking powder, salt, sugar and spices. Gradually add in the milk and applesauce.

Heat a frying pan over a moderately high flame and add a small amount of the coconut oil.

Once hot, pour the batter into the frying pan. Cook for approximately 3 minutes until the bubbles form; flip it and cook on the other side for 3 minutes longer until browned on the underside. Repeat with the remaining oil and batter.

Serve with shredded coconut and maple syrup. Bon appétit!

Per serving: Calories: 208; Fat: 8g; Carbs: 33.2g; Protein: 3.6g

## 15. Cinnamon-Banana French Toast

(Ready in about 25 minutes | Servings 3)

### Ingredients

1/3 cup coconut milk
1/2 cup banana, mashed
2 tablespoons besan (chickpea flour)
1/2 teaspoon baking powder
1/2 teaspoon vanilla paste
A pinch of sea salt
1 tablespoon agave syrup

1/2 teaspoon ground allspice
A pinch of grated nutmeg
6 slices day-old sourdough bread
2 bananas, sliced
2 tablespoons brown sugar
1 teaspoon ground cinnamon

### Directions

To make the batter, thoroughly combine the coconut milk, mashed banana, besan, baking powder, vanilla, salt, agave syrup, allspice and nutmeg.

Dredge each slice of bread into the batter until well coated on all sides.

Preheat an electric griddle to medium heat and lightly oil it with a nonstick cooking spray.

Cook each slice of bread on the preheated griddle for about 3 minutes per side until golden brown.

Garnish the French toast with the bananas, brown sugar and cinnamon. Bon appétit!

Per serving: Calories: 278; Fat: 2.9g; Carbs: 59g; Protein: 6.6g

## 16. Traditional Indian Roti

(Ready in about 30 minutes | Servings 5)

### Ingredients

2 cups bread flour
1 teaspoon baking powder
1/2 teaspoon salt

3/4 warm water
1 cup vegetable oil, for frying

### Directions

Thoroughly combine the flour, baking powder and salt in a mixing bowl. Gradually add in the water until the dough comes together.

Divide the dough into five balls; flatten each ball to create circles.

Heat the olive oil in a frying pan over a moderately high flame. Fry the first bread, turning it over to promote even cooking; fry it for about 10 minutes or until golden brown.

Repeat with the remaining dough. Transfer each roti to a paper towel-lined plate to drain the excess oil. Bon appétit!

Per serving: Calories: 413; Fat: 26g; Carbs: 38.1g; Protein: 5.6g

## 17. Chocolate Chia Pudding

(Ready in about 10 minutes + chilling time | Servings 4)

### Ingredients

4 tablespoons unsweetened cocoa powder
4 tablespoons maple syrup
1 2/3 cups coconut milk
A pinch of grated nutmeg

A pinch of ground cloves
1/2 teaspoon ground cinnamon
1/2 cup chia seeds

### Directions

Add the cocoa powder, maple syrup, milk and spices to a bowl and stir until everything is well incorporated.

Add in the chia seeds and stir again to combine well. Spoon the mixture into four jars, cover and place in your refrigerator overnight.

On the actual day, stir with a spoon and serve. Bon appétit!

Per serving: Calories: 346; Fat: 26.7g; Carbs: 28.1g; Protein: 5.5g

## 18. Easy Morning Polenta

(Ready in about 20 minutes | Servings 2)

### Ingredients

2 cups vegetable broth
1/2 cup cornmeal
1/2 teaspoon sea salt
1/4 teaspoon ground black pepper, to taste

1/4 teaspoon red pepper flakes, crushed
2 tablespoons olive oil

### Directions

In a medium saucepan, bring the vegetable broth to boil over medium-high heat. Now, add in the cornmeal, whisking continuously to prevent lumps.

Season with salt, black pepper and red pepper.

Reduce the heat to a simmer. Continue to simmer, whisking periodically, for about 18 minutes, until the mixture has thickened.

Now, pour the olive oil into a saucepan and stir to combine well. Bon appétit!

Per serving: Calories: 306; Fat: 16g; Carbs: 32.4g; Protein: 7.7g

## 19. Scallion and Pepper Omelet

(Ready in about 15 minutes | Servings 2)

### Ingredients

2 tablespoons olive oil
3 scallions, chopped
2 bell peppers, chopped
6 tablespoons besan (chickpea flour)
10 tablespoons rice milk, unsweetened

Kala namak salt and ground black pepper, to season
1/3 teaspoon red pepper flakes
2 tablespoons fresh Italian parsley, chopped

### Directions

Heat the olive oil in a frying pan over medium-high heat. Once hot, sauté the scallions and peppers for about 3 minutes until tender and aromatic.

Meanwhile, whisk the chickpea flour with the milk, salt, black pepper and red pepper flakes.

Then, pour the mixture into the frying pan.

Cook for about 4 minutes. Turn it over and cook for an additional 3 to 4 minutes until set. Serve with fresh parsley. Bon appétit!

**Per serving:** Calories: 269; Fat: 17g; Carbs: 22.4g; Protein: 8.1g

## 20. Classic Tofu Scramble

(Ready in about 15 minutes | Servings 2)

### Ingredients

1 tablespoon olive oil
6 ounces extra-firm tofu, pressed and crumbled
1 cup baby spinach
Sea salt and ground black pepper to taste

1/2 teaspoon turmeric powder
1/4 teaspoon cumin powder
1/2 teaspoon garlic powder
1 handful fresh chives, chopped

### Directions

Heat the olive oil in a frying skillet over medium heat. When it's hot, add the tofu and sauté for 8 minutes, stirring occasionally to promote even cooking.

Add in the baby spinach and aromatics and continue sautéing an additional 1 to 2 minutes.

Garnish with fresh chives and serve warm. Bon appétit!

**Per serving:** Calories: 202; Fat: 14.3g; Carbs: 7.5g; Protein: 14.6g

## 21. Mixed Berry and Almond Butter Swirl Bowl

(Ready in about 10 minutes | Servings 3)

### Ingredients

1 ½ cups almond milk
2 small bananas
2 cups mixed berries, fresh or frozen
3 dates, pitted

3 scoops hemp protein powder
3 tablespoons smooth almond butter
2 tablespoons pepitas

### Directions

In your blender or food processor, mix the almond milk with the bananas, berries and dates.

Process until everything is well combined. Divide the smoothie between three bowls.

Top each smoothie bowl with almond butter and use a butter knife to swirl the almond butter into the top of each smoothie bowl.

Afterwards, garnish each smoothie bowl with pepitas, serve well-chilled and enjoy!

**Per serving:** Calories: 397; Fat: 16.3g; Carbs: 48.5g; Protein: 19.6g

## 22. Everyday Oats with Coconut and Strawberries

(Ready in about 15 minutes | Servings 2)

### Ingredients

1/2 tablespoon coconut oil
1 cup rolled oats
A pinch of flaky sea salt
1/8 teaspoon grated nutmeg
1/4 teaspoon cardamom
1 tablespoon coconut sugar

1 cup coconut milk, sweetened
1 cup water
2 tablespoons coconut flakes
4 tablespoons fresh strawberries

### Directions

In a saucepan, melt the coconut oil over a moderate flame. Then, toast the oats for about 3 minutes, stirring continuously.

Add in the salt, nutmeg, cardamom, coconut sugar, milk and water; continue to cook for 12 minutes more or until cooked through.

Spoon the mixture into serving bowls; top with coconut flakes and fresh strawberries. Bon appétit!

**Per serving:** Calories: 457; Fat: 14.4g; Carbs: 66.3g; Protein: 17.3g

## 23. The Best Chocolate Granola Ever

(Ready in about 1 hour | Servings 10)

### Ingredients

1/2 cup coconut oil
1/2 cup agave syrup
1 teaspoon vanilla paste
3 cups rolled oats
1/2 cup hazelnuts, chopped
1/2 cup pumpkin seeds

1/2 teaspoon ground cardamom
1 teaspoon ground cinnamon
1/4 teaspoon ground cloves
1 teaspoon Himalayan salt
1/2 cup dark chocolate, cut into chunks

### Directions

Begin by preheating your oven to 260 degrees F; line two rimmed baking sheets with a piece parchment paper.

Then, thoroughly combine the coconut oil, agave syrup and vanilla in a mixing bowl.

Gradually add in the oats, hazelnuts, pumpkin seeds and spices; toss to coat well. Spread the mixture out onto the prepared baking sheets.

Bake in the middle of the oven, stirring halfway through the cooking time, for about 1 hour or until golden brown.

Stir in the dark chocolate and let your granola cool completely before storing. Store in an airtight container. Bon appétit!

**Per serving:** Calories: 428; Fat: 23.4g; Carbs: 46.4g; Protein: 11.3g

## 24. Autumn Pumpkin Griddle Cakes

(Ready in about 30 minutes | Servings 4)

### Ingredients

1/2 cup oat flour
1/2 cup whole-wheat white flour
1 teaspoon baking powder
1/4 teaspoon Himalayan salt
1 teaspoon sugar
1/2 teaspoon ground allspice
1/2 teaspoon ground cinnamon
1/2 teaspoon crystalized ginger
1 teaspoon lemon juice, freshly squeezed
1/2 cup almond milk
1/2 cup pumpkin puree
2 tablespoons coconut oil

### Directions

In a mixing bowl, thoroughly combine the flour, baking powder, salt, sugar and spices. Gradually add in the lemon juice, milk and pumpkin puree.

Heat an electric griddle on medium and lightly slick it with the coconut oil.

Cook your cake for approximately 3 minutes until the bubbles form; flip it and cook on the other side for 3 minutes longer until browned on the underside.

Repeat with the remaining oil and batter. Serve dusted with cinnamon sugar, if desired. Bon appétit!

**Per serving:** Calories: 198; Fat: 9.4g; Carbs: 24.5g; Protein: 5.2g

## 25. English Muffins with Tofu

(Ready in about 15 minutes | Servings 4)

### Ingredients

2 tablespoons olive oil
16 ounces extra-firm tofu
1 tablespoon nutritional yeast
1/4 teaspoon turmeric powder
2 handfuls fresh kale, chopped
Kosher salt and ground black pepper, to taste
4 English muffins, cut in half
4 tablespoons ketchup
4 slices vegan cheese

### Directions

Heat the olive oil in a frying skillet over medium heat. When it's hot, add the tofu and sauté for 8 minutes, stirring occasionally to promote even cooking.

Add in the nutritional yeast, turmeric and kale and continue sautéing an additional 2 minutes or until the kale wilts. Season with salt and pepper to taste.

Meanwhile, toast the English muffins until crisp.

To assemble the sandwiches, spread the bottom halves of the English muffins with ketchup; top them with the tofu mixture and vegan cheese; place the bun topper on, close the sandwiches and serve warm. Bon appétit!

**Per serving:** Calories: 452; Fat: 24.3g; Carbs: 38g; Protein: 25.6g

## 26. Cinnamon Semolina Porridge

(Ready in about 20 minutes | Servings 3)

### Ingredients

3 cups almond milk
3 tablespoons maple syrup
3 teaspoons coconut oil
1/4 teaspoon kosher salt
1/2 teaspoon ground cinnamon
1 ¼ cups semolina

### Directions

In a saucepan, heat the almond milk, maple syrup, coconut oil, salt and cinnamon over a moderate flame.

Once hot, gradually stir in the semolina flour. Turn the heat to a simmer and continue cooking until the porridge reaches your preferred consistency.

Garnish with your favorite toppings and serve warm. Bon appétit!

**Per serving:** Calories: 491; Fat: 13.2g; Carbs: 76g; Protein: 16.6g

## 27. Decadent Applesauce French Toast

(Ready in about 15 minutes | Servings 1)

### Ingredients

1/4 cup oat milk, sweetened
2 tablespoons applesauce, sweetened
1/2 teaspoon vanilla paste
A pinch of salt
A pinch of grated nutmeg
1/4 teaspoon ground cloves
1/4 teaspoon ground cinnamon
2 slices rustic day-old bread slices
1 tablespoon coconut oil
1 tablespoon maple syrup

### Directions

In a mixing bowl, thoroughly combine the oat milk, applesauce, vanilla, salt, nutmeg, cloves and cinnamon.

Dip each slice of bread into the custard mixture until well coated on all sides.

Preheat the coconut oil in a frying pan over medium-high heat. Cook for about 3 minutes on each side, until golden brown.

Drizzle the French toast with maple syrup and serve immediately. Bon appétit!

**Per serving:** Calories: 333; Fat: 16.9g; Carbs: 40.3g; Protein: 5.6g

## 28. Nutty Morning Bread Pudding

(Ready in about 2 hours 10 minutes | Servings 6)

### Ingredients

1 ½ cups almond milk
1/2 cup maple syrup
2 tablespoons almond butter
1/2 teaspoon vanilla extract
1/2 teaspoon almond extract
1/2 teaspoon ground cinnamon
1/2 teaspoon ground cloves
1/3 teaspoon kosher salt
1/2 cup almonds, roughly chopped
4 cups day-old white bread, cubed

### Directions

In a mixing bowl, combine the almond milk, maple syrup, almond butter, vanilla extract, almond extract and spices.

Add the bread cubes to the custard mixture and stir to combine well. Fold in the almonds and allow it to rest for about 1 hour.

Then, spoon the mixture into a lightly oiled casserole dish.

Bake in the preheated oven at 350 degrees F for about 1 hour or until the top is golden brown.

Place the bread pudding on a wire rack for 10 minutes before slicing and serving. Bon appétit!

**Per serving:** Calories: 463; Fat: 6.2g; Carbs: 83g; Protein: 11.4g

## 29. Omelet with Mushrooms and Peppers

(Ready in about 30 minutes | Servings 4)

### Ingredients

4 tablespoons olive oil
1 red onion, minced
1 red bell pepper, sliced
1 teaspoon garlic, finely chopped
1 pound button mushrooms, sliced
Sea salt and ground black pepper, to taste
1/2 teaspoon dried oregano
1/2 teaspoon dried dill
16 ounces tofu, drained and crumbled
2 tablespoons nutritional yeast
1/2 teaspoon turmeric powder
4 tablespoons corn flour
1/3 cup oat milk, unsweetened

### Directions

Preheat 2 tablespoons of the olive oil in a nonstick skillet over medium-high heat. Then, cook the onion and pepper for about 4 minutes until tender and fragrant.

Add in the garlic and mushrooms and continue to sauté an additional 2 to 3 minutes or until aromatic. Season with salt, black pepper, oregano and dill. Reserve.

In your blender or food processor, mix the tofu, nutritional yeast, turmeric powder, corn flour and milk. Process until you have a smooth and uniform paste.

In the same skillet, heat 1 tablespoon of the olive oil until sizzling. Pour in 1/2 of the tofu mixture and spread it with a spatula.

Cook for about 6 minutes or until set; flip and cook it for another 3 minutes. Slide the omelet onto a serving plate.

Spoon 1/2 of the mushroom filling over half of the omelet. Fold the unfilled half of omelet over the filling.

Repeat with another omelet. Cut them into halves and serve warm. Bon appétit!

**Per serving:** Calories: 390; Fat: 26.2g; Carbs: 22.4g; Protein: 22.1g

## 30. Frosty Hemp and Blackberry Smoothie Bowl

(Ready in about 10 minutes | Servings 2)

### Ingredients

2 tablespoons hemp seeds
1/2 cup coconut milk
1 cup coconut yogurt
1 cup blackberries, frozen
2 small-sized bananas, frozen
4 tablespoons granola

### Directions

In your blender, mix all ingredients, trying to keep the liquids at the bottom of the blender to help it break up the fruits.

Divide your smoothie between serving bowls.

Garnish each bowl with granola and some extra frozen berries, if desired. Serve immediately!

**Per serving:** Calories: 362; Fat: 9.1g; Carbs: 52.1g; Protein: 22.1g

## 31. Chocolate and Walnut Steel-Cut Oats

(Ready in about 30 minutes | Servings 3)

### Ingredients

2 cups oat milk
1/3 cup steel-cut oats
1 tablespoon coconut oil
1/4 cup coconut sugar
A pinch of grated nutmeg
A pinch of flaky sea salt
1/4 teaspoon cinnamon powder
1/4 teaspoon vanilla extract
4 tablespoons cocoa powder
1/3 cup English walnut halves
4 tablespoons chocolate chips

### Directions

Bring the oat milk and oats to a boil over a moderately high heat. Then, turn the heat to low and add in the coconut oil, sugar and spices; let it simmer for about 25 minutes, stirring periodically.

Add in the cocoa powder and continue simmering an additional 3 minutes.

Spoon the oatmeal into serving bowls. Top each bowl with the walnut halves and chocolate chips.

Bon appétit!

**Per serving:** Calories: 452; Fat: 18.1g; Carbs: 67g; Protein: 11g

## 32. Buckwheat Porridge with Apples and Almonds

(Ready in about 20 minutes | Servings 3)

### Ingredients

1 cup buckwheat groats, toasted
3/4 cup water
1 cup rice milk
1/4 teaspoon sea salt
3 tablespoons agave syrup
1 cup apples, cored and diced
3 tablespoons almonds, slivered
2 tablespoons coconut flakes
2 tablespoons hemp seeds

### Directions

In a saucepan, bring the buckwheat groats, water, milk and salt to a boil. Immediately turn the heat to a simmer; let it simmer for about 13 minutes until it has softened.

Stir in the agave syrup. Divide the porridge between three serving bowls.

Garnish each serving with the apples, almonds, coconut and hemp seeds. Bon appétit!

**Per serving:** Calories: 377; Fat: 8.8g; Carbs: 70g; Protein: 10.6g

## 33. Traditional Spanish Tortilla

(Ready in about 35 minutes | Servings 2)

### Ingredients

3 tablespoons olive oil
2 medium potatoes, peeled and diced
1/2 white onion, chopped
8 tablespoons gram flour

8 tablespoons water
Sea salt and ground black pepper, to season
1/2 teaspoon Spanish paprika

### Directions

Heat 2 tablespoons of the olive oil in a frying pan over a moderate flame. Now, cook the potatoes and onion; cook for about 20 minutes or until tender; reserve.

In a mixing bowl, thoroughly combine the flour, water, salt, black pepper and paprika. Add in the potato/onion mixture.

Heat the remaining 1 tablespoon of the olive oil in the same frying pan. Pour 1/2 of the batter into the frying pan. Cook your tortilla for about 11 minutes, turning it once or twice to promote even cooking.

Repeat with the remaining batter and serve warm.

**Per serving:** Calories: 379; Fat: 20.6g; Carbs: 45.2g; Protein: 5.6g

## 34. Gingerbread Belgian Waffles

(Ready in about 25 minutes | Servings 3)

### Ingredients

1 cup all-purpose flour
1 teaspoon baking powder
1 tablespoon brown sugar
1 teaspoon ground ginger

1 cup almond milk
1 teaspoon vanilla extract
2 olive oil

### Directions

Preheat a waffle iron according to the manufacturer's instructions.

In a mixing bowl, thoroughly combine the flour, baking powder, brown sugar, ground ginger, almond milk, vanilla extract and olive oil.

Beat until everything is well blended.

Ladle 1/3 of the batter into the preheated waffle iron and cook until the waffles are golden and crisp. Repeat with the remaining batter.

Serve your waffles with blackberry jam, if desired. Bon appétit!

**Per serving:** Calories: 299; Fat: 12.6g; Carbs: 38.5g; Protein: 6.8g

## 35. Porridge with Banana and Walnuts

(Ready in about 15 minutes | Servings 4)

### Ingredients

1 cup rolled oats
1 cup spelt flakes
2 cups unsweetened almond milk

4 tablespoons agave nectar
4 tablespoons walnuts, chopped
2 bananas, sliced

### Directions

In a nonstick skillet, fry the oats and spelt flakes until fragrant, working in batches.

Bring the milk to a boil and add in the oats, spelt flakes and agave nectar.

Turn the heat to a simmer and let it cook for 6 to 7 minutes, stirring occasionally. Top with walnuts and bananas and serve warm. Bon appétit!

**Per serving:** Calories: 389; Fat: 11.6g; Carbs: 67.7g; Protein: 16.8g

## 36. Kid-Friendly Cereal

(Ready in about 15 minutes | Servings 5)

Ingredients

1 ½ cups spelt flour
1/2 teaspoon baking powder
1 teaspoon cinnamon
1/2 teaspoon cardamom

1/4 teaspoon ground cloves
1/2 cup brown sugar
1/3 cup almond milk
2 teaspoons coconut oil, melted

### Directions

Begin by preheating your oven to 350 degrees F.

In a mixing bowl, thoroughly combine all the dry ingredients. Gradually, pour in the milk and coconut oil and mix to combine well.

Fill the pastry bag with the batter. Now, pipe 1/4-inch balls onto parchment-lined cookie sheets.

Bake in the preheated oven for about 13 minutes. Serve with your favorite plant-based milk.

Store in an air-thigh container for about 1 month. Bon appétit!

**Per serving:** Calories: 203; Fat: 2.7g; Carbs: 39.7g; Protein: 4.4g

## 37. Classic Breakfast Burrito

(Ready in about 15 minutes | Servings 4)

### Ingredients

1 tablespoon olive oil
16 ounces tofu, pressed
4 (6-inch) whole-wheat tortillas
1 ½ cups canned chickpeas, drained
1 medium-sized avocado, pitted and sliced

1 tablespoon lemon juice
1 teaspoon garlic, pressed
2 bell peppers, sliced
Sea salt and ground black pepper, to taste
1/2 teaspoon red pepper flakes

### Directions

Heat the olive oil in a frying skillet over medium heat. When it's hot, add the tofu and sauté for about 10 minutes, stirring occasionally to promote even cooking.

Divide the fried tofu between warmed tortillas; place the remaining ingredients on your tortillas, roll them up and serve immediately.

Bon appétit!

**Per serving:** Calories: 593; Fat: 23.7g; Carbs: 71.7g; Protein: 30.4g

# 38. Homemade Toast Crunch

(Ready in about 15 minutes | Servings 8)

## Ingredients

1 cup almond flour
1 cup coconut flour
1/2 cup all-purpose flour
1 cup sugar
1 teaspoon kosher salt
1 teaspoon cardamom

1/4 teaspoon grated nutmeg
1 tablespoon cinnamon
3 tablespoons flax seeds, ground
1/2 cup coconut oil, melted
8 tablespoons coconut milk

## Directions

Begin by preheating the oven to 340 degrees F. In a mixing bowl, thoroughly combine all the dry ingredients.

Gradually pour in the oil and milk; mix to combine well.

Shape the dough into a ball and roll out between 2 sheets of a parchment paper. Cut into small squares and prick them with a fork to prevent air bubbles.

Bake in the preheated oven for about 15 minutes. They will continue to crisp as they cool. Bon appétit!

**Per serving:** Calories: 330; Fat: 25.7g; Carbs: 24.7g; Protein: 4.8g

# 39. Autumn Cinnamon and Apple Oatmeal Cups

(Ready in about 30 minutes | Servings 9)

## Ingredients

2 cups old-fashioned oats
1/2 teaspoon baking powder
1 teaspoon cinnamon
1/4 teaspoon grated nutmeg
1/4 teaspoon sea salt
1 cup almond milk

1/4 cup agave syrup
1/2 cup applesauce
2 tablespoons coconut oil
2 tablespoons peanut butter
1 tablespoon chia seeds
1 small apple, cored and diced

## Directions

Begin by preheating your oven to 360 degrees F. Spritz a muffin tin with a nonstick cooking oil.

In a mixing bowl, thoroughly combine all the ingredients, except for the apples.

Fold in the apples and scrape the batter into the prepared muffin tin.

Bake your muffins for about 25 minutes or until a toothpick comes out dry and clean. Bon appétit!

**Per serving:** Calories: 232; Fat: 7.1g; Carbs: 36.3g; Protein: 7.1g

# 40. Spicy Vegetable and Chickpea Tofu Scramble

(Ready in about 15 minutes | Servings 2)

## Ingredients

2 tablespoons oil
1 bell pepper, seeded and sliced
2 tablespoons scallions, chopped
6 ounces cremini button mushrooms, sliced
1/2 teaspoon garlic, minced

1 jalapeno pepper, seeded and chopped
6 ounces firm tofu, pressed
1 tablespoon nutritional yeast
1/4 teaspoon turmeric powder
Kala namak and ground black pepper, to taste
6 ounces chickpeas, drained

## Directions

Heat the olive oil in a nonstick skillet over a moderate flame. Once hot, sauté the pepper for about 2 minutes.

Now, add in the scallions, mushrooms and continue sautéing for a further 3 minutes or until the mushrooms release the liquid.

Then, add in the garlic, jalapeno and tofu and sauté for 5 minutes more, crumbling the tofu with a fork.

Add in the nutritional yeast, turmeric, salt, pepper and chickpeas; continue sautéing an additional 2 minutes or until cooked through. Bon appétit!

**Per serving:** Calories: 422; Fat: 23.8g; Carbs: 33g; Protein: 25.3g

# 41. Coconut Granola with Prunes

(Ready in about 1 hour | Servings 10)

## Ingredients

1/3 cup coconut oil
1/2 cup maple syrup
1 teaspoon sea salt
1/4 teaspoon grated nutmeg
1/2 teaspoon cinnamon powder

1/2 teaspoon vanilla extract
4 cups old-fashioned oats
1/2 cup almonds, chopped
1/2 cup pecans, chopped
1/2 coconut, shredded
1 cup prunes, chopped

## Directions

Begin by preheating your oven to 260 degrees F; line two rimmed baking sheets with a piece of parchment paper.

Then, thoroughly combine the coconut oil, maple syrup, salt, nutmeg, cinnamon and vanilla.

Gradually add in the oats, almonds, pecans and coconut; toss to coat well.

Spread the mixture out onto the prepared baking sheets.

Bake in the middle of the oven, stirring halfway through the cooking time, for about 1 hour or until golden brown.

Stir in the prunes and let your granola cool completely before storing. Store in an airtight container.

Bon appétit!

**Per serving:** Calories: 420; Fat: 15.2g; Carbs: 64.3g; Protein: 11.6g

## 42. Yogurt Carrot Griddle Cakes

(Ready in about 25 minutes | Servings 4)

### Ingredients

1/2 cup oat flour
1/2 teaspoon baking powder
1 teaspoon coconut sugar
1/4 teaspoon ground allspice
1/4 teaspoon vanilla extract
1 large-sized carrot, trimmed and grated
1 cup banana, mashed
1/2 cup coconut yogurt
4 teaspoons coconut oil, at room temperature
4 tablespoons icing sugar
1 teaspoon ground cinnamon

### Directions

In a mixing bowl, thoroughly combine the flour, baking powder, coconut sugar, ground allspice and vanilla.

Gradually add in the carrot, banana and coconut yogurt.

Heat an electric griddle on medium and lightly slick it with the coconut oil.

Spoon about 1/4 of the batter onto the preheated griddle. Cook your cake for approximately 3 minutes until the bubbles form; flip it and cook on the other side for 3 minutes longer until browned on the underside.

Repeat with the remaining oil and batter. In a small bowl, mix the icing sugar and ground cinnamon.

Dust each griddle cake with the cinnamon sugar and serve hot. Enjoy!

**Per serving:** Calories: 254; Fat: 13.1g; Carbs: 34g; Protein: 3.4g

## 43. Raw Morning Pudding

(Ready in about 10 minutes + chilling time | Servings 3)

### Ingredients

2 ½ cups almond milk
3 tablespoons agave syrup
1/2 teaspoon vanilla essence
A pinch of flaky salt
A pinch of grated nutmeg
1/4 teaspoon ground cardamom
1/4 teaspoon crystalized ginger
1/2 cup instant oats
1/2 cup chia seeds

### Directions

Add the milk, agave syrup and spices to a bowl and stir until everything is well incorporated.

Fold in the instant oats and chia seeds and stir again to combine well. Spoon the mixture into three jars, cover and place in your refrigerator overnight.

On the actual day, stir with a spoon and serve. Bon appétit!

**Per serving:** Calories: 364; Fat: 10.5g; Carbs: 61.4g; Protein: 9g

## 44. Baked Apple Pie Oatmeal

(Ready in about 45 minutes | Servings 5)

### Ingredients

1 ½ cups old-fashioned oats
1/2 teaspoon cinnamon
1/4 teaspoon grated nutmeg
1/4 teaspoon ground cloves
1/4 teaspoon sea salt
1 cup oat milk
1/2 cup canned applesauce
1/4 cup agave syrup
1 tablespoon chia seeds
1 tablespoon coconut oil
1/2 teaspoon almond extract
1/3 cup walnuts, chopped

### Directions

Start by preheating your oven to 370 degrees F. Spritz a casserole dish with a nonstick cooking spray.

In a mixing bowl, thoroughly combine all ingredients until everything is well incorporated.

Next, spoon the oatmeal mixture into the prepared casserole dish.

Bake in the preheated oven for about 35 minutes, until the center is set. Allow it to cool for 10 minutes before cutting and serving. Bon appétit!

**Per serving:** Calories: 345; Fat: 12g; Carbs: 51.4g; Protein: 10.8g

## 45. Easy Omelet with Tomato and Hummus

(Ready in about 20 minutes | Servings 2)

### Ingredients

10 ounces silken tofu, pressed
4 tablespoons water
1 teaspoon balsamic vinegar
3 tablespoons nutritional yeast
2 teaspoons arrowroot powder
1/2 teaspoon turmeric powder
Kala namak salt and black pepper
2 tablespoons olive oil
Topping:
2 tablespoons hummus
1 medium tomato, sliced
1 teaspoon garlic, minced
2 scallions, chopped

### Directions

In your blender or food processor, mix the tofu, water, balsamic vinegar, nutritional yeast, arrowroot powder, turmeric powder, salt and black pepper. Process until you have a smooth and uniform paste.

In a nonstick skillet, heat the olive oil until sizzling. Pour in 1/2 of the tofu mixture and spread it with a spatula.

Cook for about 6 minutes or until set; flip and cook it for another 3 minutes. Slide the omelet onto a serving plate.

Repeat with the remaining batter. Place the topping ingredients over half of each omelet. Fold unfilled half of your omelet over the filling. Bon appétit!

**Per serving:** Calories: 324; Fat: 20.3g; Carbs: 18.4g; Protein: 18g

# 46. Grandma's Breakfast Waffles

(Ready in about 20 minutes | Servings 4)

## Ingredients

1 cup all-purpose flour
1/2 cup spelt flour
1 teaspoon baking powder
A pinch of salt
1/4 teaspoon ground cinnamon
1/4 teaspoon grated nutmeg
1/2 teaspoon vanilla extract

1 cup almond milk, unsweetened
2 tablespoons blackstrap molasses
2 tablespoons coconut oil, melted
1 tablespoon fresh lime juice

## Directions

Preheat a waffle iron according to the manufacturer's instructions.

In a mixing bowl, thoroughly combine the flour, baking powder, salt, cinnamon, nutmeg and vanilla extract.

In another bowl, mix the liquid ingredients. Then, gradually add in the wet mixture to the dry mixture.

Beat until everything is well blended.

Ladle 1/4 of the batter into the preheated waffle iron and cook until the waffles are golden and crisp. Repeat with the remaining batter.

Serve your waffles with a fruit compote or coconut cream, if desired. Bon appétit!

**Per serving:** Calories: 316; Fat: 9.9g; Carbs: 50.4g; Protein: 8.3g

# 47. Crunch Cereal with Almonds

(Ready in about 35 minutes | Servings 8)

## Ingredients

1 cup spelt flakes
1 cup old-fashioned oats
1 ½ cups almonds, roughly chopped

1/4 cup date syrup
7 tablespoons coconut oil, melted

## Directions

Start by preheating your oven to 330 degrees F. Line a baking sheet with parchment paper or a Silpat mat.

In a mixing bowl, thoroughly combine all the ingredients until everything is well incorporated. Now, spread the cereal mixture onto the prepared baking sheet.

Bake for about 33 minutes or until crunchy. Allow it to cool fully before breaking up into clumps. Serve with a plant-based milk of choice. Bon appétit!

**Per serving:** Calories: 286; Fat: 14.7g; Carbs: 34.4g; Protein: 6.6g

# 48. Grits with Fried Tofu and Avocado

(Ready in about 30 minutes | Servings 3)

## Ingredients

3 teaspoons sesame oil
12 ounces firm tofu, cubed
1 small white onion, chopped
1/2 teaspoon turmeric
1/2 teaspoon red pepper flakes
3 cups water
1 cup stone-ground corn grits

1 thyme sprig
1 rosemary sprig
1 bay leaf
1/4 cup nutritional yeast
1 medium tomato, sliced
1 medium avocado, pitted, peeled and sliced

## Directions

Heat the sesame oil in a wok over a moderately high heat. Now, fry your tofu for about 6 minutes.

Add in the onion, turmeric and red pepper and continue cooking until the tofu is crisp on all sides and the onion is tender and translucent.

In a saucepan, place the water, grits, thyme sprig, rosemary sprig and bay leaf and bring to a boil. Tun the heat to a simmer, cover and let it cook for approximately 20 minutes or until the most of the water is absorbed.

Add in the nutritional yeast and stir to combine well.

Divide the grits between serving bowls and top with the fried tofu/ onion mixture. Top with tomato and avocado, salt to taste and serve immediately. Bon appétit!

**Per serving:** Calories: 466; Fat: 27g; Carbs: 29.4g; Protein: 26.6g

# 49. Morning Kasha with Mushrooms

(Ready in about 30 minutes | Servings 2)

## Ingredients

1 cup water
1/2 cup buckwheat groats, toasted
Sea salt and ground black pepper, to taste
2 tablespoons olive oil
1 cup button mushrooms, sliced

2 tablespoons scallions, chopped
1 garlic clove, minced
1 small avocado, pitted, peeled and sliced
1 tablespoon fresh lemon juice

## Directions

In a saucepan, bring the water and buckwheat to a boil. Immediately turn the heat to a simmer and continue to cook for about 20 minutes. Season with sea salt and ground black pepper to taste.

Then, heat the olive oil in a nonstick skillet, over medium-high heat. Sauté the mushrooms, scallions and garlic for about 4 minutes or until they've softened.

Spoon the kasha into two serving bowls; top each serving with the sautéed mushroom mixture.

Garnish with avocado, add a few drizzles of fresh lemon juice and serve immediately. Bon appétit!

**Per serving:** Calories: 446; Fat: 29g; Carbs: 43.1g; Protein: 9.6g

## 50. Tomato Tofu Scramble

(Ready in about 15 minutes | Servings 3)

### Ingredients

2 tablespoons olive oil
2 garlic cloves, minced
12 ounces extra-firm tofu
1 medium-sized tomato, diced
2 tablespoons nutritional yeast
Kosher salt and ground black pepper, to taste
1/2 teaspoon red pepper flakes, crushed
A pinch of seaweed flakes
3 tablespoons soy milk, unsweetened
1 medium-sized avocado, pitted, peeled and sliced

### Directions

Heat the olive oil in a nonstick skillet over a moderate flame. Then, sauté the garlic, tofu and tomato, crumbling the tofu with a fork, for about 8 minutes

Add in the nutritional yeast, salt, black pepper, red pepper, seaweed flakes and soy milk. Continue to sauté an additional 2 minutes.

Divide the scramble between three serving plates, garnish with avocado and serve. Bon appétit!

**Per serving:** Calories: 399; Fat: 29.4g; Carbs: 17.3g; Protein: 23.3g

## 51. Spring Onion Flat Bread

(Ready in about 30 minutes | Servings 3)

### Ingredients

1 cup all-purpose flour
1/2 teaspoon baking powder
1/4 teaspoon sea salt
1/2 cup warm water
1 cup spring onions, chopped
Sea salt and ground black pepper, to taste
1/2 teaspoon garlic powder
1/2 teaspoon cayenne pepper
1/2 teaspoon dried thyme
3 teaspoons olive oil

### Directions

Thoroughly combine the flour, baking powder and salt in a mixing bowl. Gradually add in the water until the dough comes together.

Add in the spring onions and spices and knead the dough one more time.

Divide the dough into three balls; flatten each ball to create circles.

Heat 1 teaspoon of the olive oil in a frying pan over a moderately high flame. Fry the first bread, turning it over to promote even cooking; fry it for about 9 minutes or until golden brown.

Repeat with the remaining oil and dough. Bon appétit!

**Per serving:** Calories: 219; Fat: 5g; Carbs: 36.2g; Protein: 5.3g

## 52. Chocolate Granola Bars

(Ready in about 40 minutes | Servings 12)

### Ingredients

1 1/3 cups old-fashioned oats
1/2 cup fresh dates, pitted and mashed
1/2 cup dried cherries
1/3 cup agave syrup
1/3 cup almond butter, room temperature
2 tablespoons coconut oil, melted
1/2 cup almonds
1/2 cup walnuts
1/4 cup pecans
1/2 teaspoon allspice
A pinch of salt
A pinch of grated nutmeg
1/2 cup dark chocolate chunks

### Directions

In a mixing bowl, thoroughly combine the oats, dates and dried cherries.

Add in the agave syrup, almond butter and coconut oil. Stir in the nuts, spices and chocolate.

Press the mixture into a lightly greased baking dish. Transfer it to your refrigerator for about 30 minutes.

Slice into 12 even bars and store in airtight containers. Enjoy!

**Per serving:** Calories: 229; Fat: 13.4g; Carbs: 27.9g; Protein: 3.1g

## 53. Mexican-Style Omelet

(Ready in about 15 minutes | Servings 2)

### Ingredients

2 tablespoons olive oil
1 small onion, chopped
2 Spanish peppers, deseeded and chopped
1/2 cup chickpea flour
1/2 cup water
3 tablespoons rice milk, unsweetened
2 tablespoons nutritional yeast
Kala namak salt and ground black pepper, to taste
1/2 teaspoon dried Mexican oregano
1/4 cup salsa

### Directions

Heat the olive oil in a frying pan over medium-high flame. Once hot, sauté the onion and peppers for about 3 minutes until tender and aromatic.

Meanwhile, whisk the chickpea flour with the water, milk, nutritional yeast, salt, black pepper and dried Mexican oregano.

Then, pour the mixture into the frying pan.

Cook for about 4 minutes. Turn it over and cook for an additional 3 to 4 minutes until set. Serve with salsa and enjoy!

**Per serving:** Calories: 329; Fat: 16.4g; Carbs: 35.2g; Protein: 12.9g

## 54. Breakfast Cranberry and Coconut Crisp

(Ready in about 30 minutes | Servings 10)

### Ingredients

1/2 cup rye flakes
1/2 cup rolled oats
1/2 cup spelt flakes
1/2 cup walnut halves
1 cup flaked coconut
1/3 teaspoon salt
1/2 teaspoon ground cloves
1/2 teaspoon ground cardamom
1 teaspoon cinnamon
1 teaspoon vanilla extract
1/3 cup coconut oil, at room temperature
1/2 cup maple syrup
3 cups cranberries

### Directions

Begin by preheating your oven to 340 degrees. Spritz a baking pan with a nonstick oil. Arrange the cranberries in the bottom of your pan.

Mix the remaining ingredients until everything is well incorporated. Spread the mixture over the cranberries.

Bake in the preheated oven for about 35 minutes or until the top is golden brown.

Serve at room temperature. Bon appétit!

**Per serving:** Calories: 209; Fat: 13.5g; Carbs: 26.2g; Protein: 3.5g

## 55. Authentic French Toast with Strawberries

(Ready in about 20 minutes | Servings 5)

### Ingredients

1 cup coconut milk
1/4 teaspoon sea salt
1/2 teaspoon ground cinnamon
1 teaspoon vanilla extract
1/2 teaspoon ground cardamom

1 French baguette, sliced
2 tablespoons peanut oil
2 ounces fresh strawberries, hulled and sliced
4 tablespoons confectioners' sugar

### Directions

In a mixing bowl, thoroughly combine the milk, salt, cinnamon, vanilla and cardamom.

Dip each slice of bread into the milk mixture until well coated on all sides.

Preheat the peanut oil in a frying pan over medium-high heat. Cook for about 3 minutes on each side, until golden brown.

Serve the French toast with the strawberries and confectioners' sugar. Bon appétit!

**Per serving:** Calories: 296; Fat: 8.9g; Carbs: 45.3g; Protein: 8.9g

## 56. Easy Breakfast Wafers

(Ready in about 30 minutes | Servings 8)

### Ingredients

1 ¼ cups rice flour
1/4 cup tapioca flour
1/2 cup potato starch
1/2 cup instant oats
1 teaspoon baking powder
1/2 teaspoon baking soda
1 pinch sea salt

1/2 teaspoon vanilla essence
1/2 teaspoon cinnamon
1 ½ cups oat milk
1 teaspoon apple cider vinegar
1/3 cup coconut oil, softened
1/3 cup maple syrup

### Directions

Preheat a waffle iron according to the manufacturer's instructions.

In a mixing bowl, thoroughly combine the flour, potato starch, instant oats, baking powder, baking soda, salt, vanilla and cinnamon.

Gradually add in the milk, whisking continuously to avoid lumps. Add in the apple cider vinegar, coconut oil and maple syrup. Whisk again to combine well.

Beat until everything is well blended.

Ladle 1/2 cup of the batter into the preheated iron and cook according to manufacturer instructions, until your wafers are golden. Repeat with the remaining batter.

Serve with toppings of choice. Bon appétit!

**Per serving:** Calories: 288; Fat: 11.1g; Carbs: 45.3g; Protein: 4.4g

## 57. Traditional Ukrainian Blinis

(Ready in about 1 hour | Servings 6)

### Ingredients

1 teaspoon yeast
1 teaspoon brown sugar
3/4 cup oat milk
1 cup all-purpose flour

A pinch of salt
A pinch of grated nutmeg
A pinch of ground cloves
2 tablespoons olive oil

### Directions

Place the yeast, sugar and 2 tablespoons of the lukewarm milk in a small mixing bowl; whisk to combine and let it dissolve and ferment for about 10 minutes.

In a mixing bowl, combine the flour with the salt, nutmeg and cloves; add in the yeast mixture and stir to combine well.

Gradually pour in the milk and stir until everything is well incorporated. Let the batter sit for about 30 minutes at a warm place.

Heat a small amount of the oil in a nonstick skillet over a moderate flame. Drop the batter, 1/4 cup at a time, onto the preheated skillet. Fry until bubbles form or about 2 minutes.

Flip your blini and continue frying until brown, about 2 minutes more. Repeat with the remaining oil and batter,

Serve with toppings of choice. Bon appétit!

**Per serving:** Calories: 138; Fat: 5.7g; Carbs: 17.9g; Protein: 3.4g

## 58. Old-Fashioned Cornbread

(Ready in about 50 minutes | Servings 10)

### Ingredients

2 tablespoons chia seeds
1 ½ cups plain flour
1 cup cornmeal
1 teaspoon baking powder
1 teaspoon baking soda

1 teaspoon kosher salt
1/3 cup sugar
1 ½ cups oat milk
1/3 cup olive oil

### Directions

Start by preheating your oven to 420 degrees F. Now, spritz a baking pan with a nonstick cooking spray.

To make the chia "egg", mix 2 tablespoons of the chia seeds with 4 tablespoons of the water. Stir and let it sit for about 15 minutes.

In a mixing bowl, thoroughly combine the flour, cornmeal, baking powder, baking soda, salt and sugar.

Gradually add in the chia "egg", oat milk and olive oil, whisking constantly to avoid lumps. Scrape the batter into the prepared baking pan.

Bake your cornbread for about 25 minutes or until a tester inserted in the middle comes out dry and clean.

Let it stand for about 10 minutes before slicing and serving. Bon appétit!

**Per serving:** Calories: 388; Fat: 23.7g; Carbs: 39g; Protein: 4.7g

## 59. Breakfast Banana Muffins with Pecans

(Ready in about 30 minutes | Servings 9)

### Ingredients

2 ripe bananas
4 tablespoons coconut oil, room temperature
2 tablespoons maple syrup
1/2 cup brown sugar
1 ½ cups all-purpose flour
1/2 teaspoon baking powder
1/2 teaspoon baking soda
1/2 teaspoon salt
1/4 teaspoon grated nutmeg
1/4 teaspoon ground cardamom
1/3 teaspoon ground cinnamon
1/2 cup pecans, chopped

### Directions

Begin by preheating your oven to 350 degrees F. Coat 9-cup muffin tin with muffin liners.

In a mixing bowl, mash the bananas; stir in the coconut oil, maple syrup and sugar. Gradually stir in the flour, followed by the baking powder, baking soda and spices.

Stir to combine well and fold in the pecans. Scrape the mixture into the prepared muffin tin.

Bake your muffins in the preheated oven for about 27 minutes, or until a tester comes out dry and clean. Bon appétit!

**Per serving:** Calories: 258; Fat: 10.7g; Carbs: 37.8g; Protein: 3.1g

## 60. Grandma's Breakfast Gallete

(Ready in about 40 minutes | Servings 5)

### Ingredients

1 cup all-purpose flour
1/2 cup oat flour
1 teaspoon baking powder
1 teaspoon baking soda
1/2 teaspoon kosher salt
1 teaspoon brown sugar
1/4 teaspoon ground allspice
1 cup water
1/2 cup rice milk
2 tablespoons olive oil

### Directions

Mix the flour, baking powder, baking soda, salt, sugar and ground allspice using an electric mixer.

Gradually pour in the water, milk and oil and continue mixing until everything is well incorporated.

Heat a lightly greased griddle over medium-high heat.

Ladle 1/4 of the batter into the preheated griddle and cook until your galette is golden and crisp. Repeat with the remaining batter.

Serve your galette with a homemade jelly, if desired. Bon appétit!

**Per serving:** Calories: 208; Fat: 7.7g; Carbs: 27.7g; Protein: 4.8g

## 61. Homemade Chocolate Crunch

(Ready in about 35 minutes | Servings 9)

### Ingredients

1/2 cup rye flakes
1/2 cup buckwheat flakes
1 cup rolled oats
1/2 cup pecans, chopped
1/2 cup hazelnuts, chopped
1 cup coconut, shredded
1/2 cup date syrup
1 teaspoon vanilla paste
1/2 teaspoon pumpkin spice mix
1/4 cup coconut oil, softened
1/2 cup chocolate chunks

### Directions

Start by preheating your oven to 330 degrees F. Line a baking sheet with parchment paper or a Silpat mat.

In a mixing bowl, thoroughly combine all the ingredients, except for the chocolate chunks. Then, spread the cereal mixture onto the prepared baking sheet.

Bake for about 33 minutes or until crunchy. Fold the chocolate chunks into the warm cereal mixture.

Allow it to cool fully before breaking up into clumps. Serve with a plant-based milk of choice. Bon appétit!

**Per serving:** Calories: 372; Fat: 19.9g; Carbs: 43.7g; Protein: 8.2g

# SOUPS & SALADS

## 62. Classic Lentil Soup with Swiss Chard

(Ready in about 25 minutes | Servings 5)

### Ingredients

2 tablespoons olive oil
1 white onion, chopped
1 teaspoon garlic, minced
2 large carrots, chopped
1 parsnip, chopped
2 stalks celery, chopped
2 bay leaves
1/2 teaspoon dried thyme
1/4 teaspoon ground cumin
5 cups roasted vegetable broth
1 ¼ cups brown lentils, soaked overnight and rinsed
2 cups Swiss chard, torn into pieces

### Directions

In a heavy-bottomed pot, heat the olive oil over a moderate heat. Now, sauté the vegetables along with the spices for about 3 minutes until they are just tender.

Add in the vegetable broth and lentils, bringing it to a boil. Immediately turn the heat to a simmer and add in the bay leaves. Let it cook for about 15 minutes or until lentils are tender.

Add in the Swiss chard, cover and let it simmer for 5 minutes more or until the chard wilts.

Serve in individual bowls and enjoy!

**Per serving:** Calories: 148; Fat: 7.2g; Carbs: 14.6g; Protein: 7.7g

## 63. Spicy Winter Farro Soup

(Ready in about 30 minutes | Servings 4)

### Ingredients

2 tablespoons olive oil
1 medium-sized leek, chopped
1 medium-sized turnip, sliced
2 Italian peppers, seeded and chopped
1 jalapeno pepper, minced
2 potatoes, peeled and diced
4 cups vegetable broth
1 cup farro, rinsed
1/2 teaspoon granulated garlic
1/2 teaspoon turmeric powder
1 bay laurel
2 cups spinach, turn into pieces

### Directions

In a heavy-bottomed pot, heat the olive oil over a moderate heat. Now, sauté the leek, turnip, peppers and potatoes for about 5 minutes until they are crisp-tender.

Add in the vegetable broth, farro, granulated garlic, turmeric and bay laurel; bring it to a boil.

Immediately turn the heat to a simmer. Let it cook for about 25 minutes or until farro and potatoes have softened.

Add in the spinach and remove the pot from the heat; let the spinach sit in the residual heat until it wilts. Bon appétit!

**Per serving:** Calories: 298; Fat: 8.9g; Carbs: 44.6g; Protein: 11.7g

## 64. Rainbow Chickpea Salad

(Ready in about 30 minutes | Servings 4)

### Ingredients

16 ounces canned chickpeas, drained
1 medium avocado, sliced
1 bell pepper, seeded and sliced
1 large tomato, sliced
2 cucumber, diced
1 red onion, sliced
1/2 teaspoon garlic, minced
1/4 cup fresh parsley, chopped
1/4 cup olive oil
2 tablespoons apple cider vinegar
1/2 lime, freshly squeezed
Sea salt and ground black pepper, to taste

### Directions

Toss all the ingredients in a salad bowl.

Place the salad in your refrigerator for about 1 hour before serving.

Bon appétit!

**Per serving:** Calories: 378; Fat: 24g; Carbs: 34.2g; Protein: 10.1g

## 65. Mediterranean-Style Lentil Salad

(Ready in about 20 minutes + chilling time | Servings 5)

### Ingredients

1 ½ cups red lentil, rinsed
1 teaspoon deli mustard
1/2 lemon, freshly squeezed
2 tablespoons tamari sauce
2 scallion stalks, chopped
1/4 cup extra-virgin olive oil
2 garlic cloves, minced
1 cup butterhead lettuce, torn into pieces
2 tablespoons fresh parsley, chopped
2 tablespoons fresh cilantro, chopped
1 teaspoon fresh basil
1 teaspoon fresh oregano
1 ½ cups cherry tomatoes, halved
3 ounces Kalamata olives, pitted and halved

### Directions

In a large-sized saucepan, bring 4 ½ cups of the water and the red lentils to a boil.

Immediately turn the heat to a simmer and continue to cook your lentils for about 15 minutes or until tender. Drain and let it cool completely.

Transfer the lentils to a salad bowl; toss the lentils with the remaining ingredients until well combined.

Serve chilled or at room temperature. Bon appétit!

**Per serving:** Calories: 348; Fat: 15g; Carbs: 41.6g; Protein: 15.8g

# 66. Roasted Asparagus and Avocado Salad

(Ready in about 20 minutes + chilling time | Servings 4)

## Ingredients

1 pound asparagus, trimmed, cut into bite-sized pieces
1 white onion, chopped
2 garlic cloves, minced
1 Roma tomato, sliced
1/4 cup olive oil
1/4 cup balsamic vinegar
1 tablespoon stone-ground mustard
2 tablespoons fresh parsley, chopped
1 tablespoon fresh cilantro, chopped
1 tablespoon fresh basil, chopped
Sea salt and ground black pepper, to taste
1 small avocado, pitted and diced
1/2 cup pine nuts, roughly chopped

## Directions

Begin by preheating your oven to 420 degrees F.

Toss the asparagus with 1 tablespoon of the olive oil and arrange them on a parchment-lined roasting pan.

Bake for about 15 minutes, rotating the pan once or twice to promote even cooking. Let it cool completely and place in your salad bowl.

Toss the asparagus with the vegetables, olive oil, vinegar, mustard and herbs. Salt and pepper to taste.

Toss to combine and top with avocado and pine nuts. Bon appétit!

**Per serving:** Calories: 378; Fat: 33.2g; Carbs: 18.6g; Protein: 7.8g

# 67. Creamed Green Bean Salad with Pine Nuts

(Ready in about 10 minutes + chilling time | Servings 5)

## Ingredients

1 ½ pounds green beans, trimmed
2 medium tomatoes, diced
2 bell peppers, seeded and diced
4 tablespoons shallots, chopped
1/2 cup pine nuts, roughly chopped
1/2 cup vegan mayonnaise
1 tablespoon deli mustard
2 tablespoons fresh basil, chopped
2 tablespoons fresh parsley, chopped
1/2 teaspoon red pepper flakes, crushed
Sea salt and freshly ground black pepper, to taste

## Directions

Boil the green beans in a large saucepan of salted water until they are just tender or about 2 minutes.

Drain and let the beans cool completely; then, transfer them to a salad bowl. Toss the beans with the remaining ingredients.

Taste and adjust the seasonings. Bon appétit!

**Per serving:** Calories: 308; Fat: 26.2g; Carbs: 16.6g; Protein: 5.8g

# 68. Cannellini Bean Soup with Kale

(Ready in about 25 minutes | Servings 5)

## Ingredients

1 tablespoon olive oil
1/2 teaspoon ginger, minced
1/2 teaspoon cumin seeds
1 red onion, chopped
1 carrot, trimmed and chopped
1 parsnip, trimmed and chopped
2 garlic cloves, minced
5 cups vegetable broth
12 ounces Cannellini beans, drained
2 cups kale, torn into pieces
Sea salt and ground black pepper, to taste

## Directions

In a heavy-bottomed pot, heat the olive over medium-high heat. Now, sauté the ginger and cumin for 1 minute or so.

Now, add in the onion, carrot and parsnip; continue sautéing an additional 3 minutes or until the vegetables are just tender.

Add in the garlic and continue to sauté for 1 minute or until aromatic.

Then, pour in the vegetable broth and bring to a boil. Immediately reduce the heat to a simmer and let it cook for 10 minutes.

Fold in the Cannellini beans and kale; continue to simmer until the kale wilts and everything is thoroughly heated. Season with salt and pepper to taste.

Ladle into individual bowls and serve hot. Bon appétit!

**Per serving:** Calories: 188; Fat: 4.7g; Carbs: 24.5g; Protein: 11.1g

# 69. Hearty Cream of Mushroom Soup

(Ready in about 15 minutes | Servings 5)

## Ingredients

2 tablespoons soy butter
1 large shallot, chopped
20 ounces Cremini mushrooms, sliced
2 cloves garlic, minced
4 tablespoons flaxseed meal
5 cups vegetable broth
1 1/3 cups full-fat coconut milk
1 bay leaf
Sea salt and ground black pepper, to taste

## Directions

In a stockpot, melt the vegan butter over medium-high heat. Once hot, cook the shallot for about 3 minutes until tender and fragrant.

Add in the mushrooms and garlic and continue cooking until the mushrooms have softened. Add in the flaxseed meal and continue to cook for 1 minute or so.

Add in the remaining ingredients. Let it simmer, covered and continue to cook for 5 to 6 minutes more until your soup has thickened slightly.

Bon appétit!

**Per serving:** Calories: 308; Fat: 25.5g; Carbs: 11.8g; Protein: 11.6g

# 70. Authentic Italian Panzanella Salad

(Ready in about 35 minutes | Servings 3)

## Ingredients

3 cups artisan bread, broken into 1-inch cubes

3/4 pound asparagus, trimmed and cut into bite-sized pieces

4 tablespoons extra-virgin olive oil

1 red onion, chopped

2 tablespoons fresh lime juice

1 teaspoon deli mustard

2 medium heirloom tomatoes, diced

2 cups arugula

2 cups baby spinach

2 Italian peppers, seeded and sliced

Sea salt and ground black pepper, to taste

## Directions

Arrange the bread cubes on a parchment-lined baking sheet. Bake in the preheated oven at 310 degrees F for about 20 minutes, rotating the baking sheet twice during the baking time; reserve.

Turn the oven to 420 degrees F and toss the asparagus with 1 tablespoon of olive oil. Roast the asparagus for about 15 minutes or until crisp-tender.

Toss the remaining ingredients in a salad bowl; top with the roasted asparagus and toasted bread.

Bon appétit!

**Per serving:** Calories: 334; Fat: 20.4g; Carbs: 33.3g; Protein: 8.3g

# 71. Quinoa and Black Bean Salad

(Ready in about 15 minutes + chilling time | Servings 4)

## Ingredients

2 cups water

1 cup quinoa, rinsed

16 ounces canned black beans, drained

2 Roma tomatoes, sliced

1 red onion, thinly sliced

1 cucumber, seeded and chopped

2 cloves garlic, pressed or minced

2 Italian peppers, seeded and sliced

2 tablespoons fresh parsley, chopped

2 tablespoons fresh cilantro, chopped

1/4 cup olive oil

1 lemon, freshly squeezed

1 tablespoon apple cider vinegar

1/2 teaspoon dried dill weed

1/2 teaspoon dried oregano

Sea salt and ground black pepper, to taste

## Directions

Place the water and quinoa in a saucepan and bring it to a rolling boil. Immediately turn the heat to a simmer.

Let it simmer for about 13 minutes until the quinoa has absorbed all of the water; fluff the quinoa with a fork and let it cool completely. Then, transfer the quinoa to a salad bowl.

Add the remaining ingredients to the salad bowl and toss to combine well. Bon appétit!

**Per serving:** Calories: 433; Fat: 17.3g; Carbs: 57g; Protein: 15.1g

# 72. Rich Bulgur Salad with Herbs

(Ready in about 20 minutes + chilling time | Servings 4)

## Ingredients

2 cups water

1 cup bulgur

12 ounces canned chickpeas, drained

1 Persian cucumber, thinly sliced

2 bell peppers, seeded and thinly sliced

1 jalapeno pepper, seeded and thinly sliced

2 Roma tomatoes, sliced

1 onion, thinly sliced

2 tablespoons fresh basil, chopped

2 tablespoons fresh parsley, chopped

2 tablespoons fresh mint, chopped

2 tablespoons fresh chives, chopped

4 tablespoons olive oil

1 tablespoon balsamic vinegar

1 tablespoon lemon juice

1 teaspoon fresh garlic, pressed

Sea salt and freshly ground black pepper, to taste

2 tablespoons nutritional yeast

1/2 cup Kalamata olives, sliced

## Directions

In a saucepan, bring the water and bulgur to a boil. Immediately turn the heat to a simmer and let it cook for about 20 minutes or until the bulgur is tender and water is almost absorbed. Fluff with a fork and spread on a large tray to let cool.

Place the bulgur in a salad bowl followed by the chickpeas, cucumber, peppers, tomatoes, onion, basil, parsley, mint and chives.

In a small mixing dish, whisk the olive oil, balsamic vinegar, lemon juice, garlic, salt and black pepper. Dress the salad and toss to combine.

Sprinkle nutritional yeast over the top, garnish with olives and serve at room temperature. Bon appétit!

**Per serving:** Calories: 408; Fat: 18.3g; Carbs: 51.8g; Protein: 13.1g

# 73. Classic Roasted Pepper Salad

(Ready in about 15 minutes + chilling time | Servings 3)

## Ingredients

6 bell peppers

3 tablespoons extra-virgin olive oil

3 teaspoons red wine vinegar

3 garlic cloves, finely chopped

2 tablespoons fresh parsley, chopped

Sea salt and freshly cracked black pepper, to taste

1/2 teaspoon red pepper flakes

6 tablespoons pine nuts, roughly chopped

## Directions

Broil the peppers on a parchment-lined baking sheet for about 10 minutes, rotating the pan halfway through the cooking time, until they are charred on all sides.

Then, cover the peppers with a plastic wrap to steam. Discard the skin, seeds and cores.

Slice the peppers into strips and toss them with the remaining ingredients. Place in your refrigerator until ready to serve. Bon appétit!

**Per serving:** Calories: 178; Fat: 14.4g; Carbs: 11.8g; Protein: 2.4g

## 74. Hearty Winter Quinoa Soup

(Ready in about 25 minutes | Servings 4)

### Ingredients

2 tablespoons olive oil
1 onion, chopped
2 carrots, peeled and chopped
1 parsnip, chopped
1 celery stalk, chopped
1 cup yellow squash, chopped
4 garlic cloves, pressed or minced
4 cups roasted vegetable broth
2 medium tomatoes, crushed
1 cup quinoa
Sea salt and ground black pepper, to taste
1 bay laurel
2 cup Swiss chard, tough ribs removed and torn into pieces
2 tablespoons Italian parsley, chopped

### Directions

In a heavy-bottomed pot, heat the olive over medium-high heat. Now, sauté the onion, carrot, parsnip, celery and yellow squash for about 3 minutes or until the vegetables are just tender.

Add in the garlic and continue to sauté for 1 minute or until aromatic.

Then, stir in the vegetable broth, tomatoes, quinoa, salt, pepper and bay laurel; bring to a boil. Immediately reduce the heat to a simmer and let it cook for 13 minutes.

Fold in the Swiss chard; continue to simmer until the chard wilts.

Ladle into individual bowls and serve garnished with the fresh parsley. Bon appétit!

**Per serving:** Calories: 328; Fat: 11.1g; Carbs: 44.1g; Protein: 13.3g

## 75. Green Lentil Salad

(Ready in about 20 minutes + chilling time | Servings 5)

### Ingredients

1 ½ cups green lentils, rinsed
2 cups arugula
2 cups Romaine lettuce, torn into pieces
1 cup baby spinach
1/4 cup fresh basil, chopped
1/2 cup shallots, chopped
2 garlic cloves, finely chopped
1/4 cup oil-packed sun-dried tomatoes, rinsed and chopped
5 tablespoons extra-virgin olive oil
3 tablespoons fresh lemon juice
Sea salt and ground black pepper, to taste

### Directions

In a large-sized saucepan, bring 4 ½ cups of the water and red lentils to a boil.

Immediately turn the heat to a simmer and continue to cook your lentils for a further 15 to 17 minutes or until they've softened but not mushy. Drain and let it cool completely.

Transfer the lentils to a salad bowl; toss the lentils with the remaining ingredients until well combined.

Serve chilled or at room temperature. Bon appétit!

**Per serving:** Calories: 349; Fat: 15.1g; Carbs: 40.9g; Protein: 15.4g

## 76. Acorn Squash, Chickpea and Couscous Soup

(Ready in about 20 minutes | Servings 4)

### Ingredients

2 tablespoons olive oil
1 shallot, chopped
1 carrot, trimmed and chopped
2 cups acorn squash, chopped
1 stalk celery, chopped
1 teaspoon garlic, finely chopped
1 teaspoon dried rosemary, chopped
1 teaspoon dried thyme, chopped
2 cups cream of onion soup
2 cups water
1 cup dry couscous
Sea salt and ground black pepper, to taste
1/2 teaspoon red pepper flakes
6 ounces canned chickpeas, drained
2 tablespoons fresh lemon juice

### Directions

In a heavy-bottomed pot, heat the olive over medium-high heat. Now, sauté the shallot, carrot, acorn squash and celery for about 3 minutes or until the vegetables are just tender.

Add in the garlic, rosemary and thyme and continue to sauté for 1 minute or until aromatic.

Then, stir in the soup, water, couscous, salt, black pepper and red pepper flakes; bring to a boil. Immediately reduce the heat to a simmer and let it cook for 12 minutes.

Fold in the canned chickpeas; continue to simmer until heated through or about 5 minutes more.

Ladle into individual bowls and drizzle with the lemon juice over the top. Bon appétit!

**Per serving:** Calories: 378; Fat: 11g; Carbs: 60.1g; Protein: 10.9g

## 77. Cabbage Soup with Garlic Crostini

(Ready in about 1 hour | Servings 4)

### Ingredients

Soup:
2 tablespoons olive oil
1 medium leek, chopped
1 cup turnip, chopped
1 parsnip, chopped
1 carrot, chopped
2 cups cabbage, shredded
2 garlic cloves, finely chopped
4 cups vegetable broth
2 bay leaves
Sea salt and ground black pepper, to taste
1/4 teaspoon cumin seeds
1/2 teaspoon mustard seeds
1 teaspoon dried basil
2 tomatoes, pureed
Crostini:
8 slices of baguette
2 heads garlic
4 tablespoons extra-virgin olive oil

### Directions

In a soup pot, heat 2 tablespoons of the olive over medium-high heat. Now, sauté the leek, turnip, parsnip and carrot for about 4 minutes or until the vegetables are crisp-tender.

Add in the garlic and cabbage and continue to sauté for 1 minute or until aromatic.

Then, stir in the vegetable broth, bay leaves, salt, black pepper, cumin seeds, mustard seeds, dried basil and pureed tomatoes; bring to a boil. Immediately reduce the heat to a simmer and let it cook for about 20 minutes.

Meanwhile, preheat your oven to 375 degrees F. Now, roast the garlic and baguette slices for about 15 minutes. Remove the crostini from the oven.

Continue baking the garlic for 45 minutes more or until very tender. Allow the garlic to cool.

Now, cut each head of the garlic using a sharp serrated knife in order to separate all the cloves.

Squeeze the roasted garlic cloves out of their skins. Mash the garlic pulp with 4 tablespoons of the extra-virgin olive oil.

Spread the roasted garlic mixture evenly on the tops of the crostini. Serve with the warm soup. Bon appétit!

**Per serving:** Calories: 408; Fat: 23.1g; Carbs: 37.6g; Protein: 11.8g

# 78. Cream of Green Bean Soup

(Ready in about 35 minutes | Servings 4)

## Ingredients

1 tablespoon sesame oil
1 onion, chopped
1 green pepper, seeded and chopped
2 russet potatoes, peeled and diced

2 garlic cloves, chopped
4 cups vegetable broth
1 pound green beans, trimmed
Sea salt and ground black pepper, to season
1 cup full-fat coconut milk

## Directions

In a heavy-bottomed pot, heat the sesame over medium-high heat. Now, sauté the onion, peppers and potatoes for about 5 minutes, stirring periodically.

Add in the garlic and continue sautéing for 1 minute or until fragrant.

Then, stir in the vegetable broth, green beans, salt and black pepper; bring to a boil. Immediately reduce the heat to a simmer and let it cook for 20 minutes.

Puree the green bean mixture using an immersion blender until creamy and uniform.

Return the pureed mixture to the pot. Fold in the coconut milk and continue to simmer until heated through or about 5 minutes longer.

Ladle into individual bowls and serve hot. Bon appétit!

**Per serving:** Calories: 410; Fat: 19.6g; Carbs: 50.6g; Protein: 13.3g

# 79. Traditional French Onion Soup

(Ready in about 1 hour 30 minutes | Servings 4)

## Ingredients

2 tablespoons olive oil
2 large yellow onions, thinly sliced
2 thyme sprigs, chopped
2 rosemary sprigs, chopped

2 teaspoons balsamic vinegar
4 cups vegetable stock
Sea salt and ground black pepper, to taste

## Directions

In a or Dutch oven, heat the olive oil over a moderate heat. Now, cook the onions with thyme, rosemary and 1 teaspoon of the sea salt for about 2 minutes.

Now, turn the heat to medium-low and continue cooking until the onions caramelize or about 50 minutes.

Add in the balsamic vinegar and continue to cook for a further 15 more. Add in the stock, salt and black pepper and continue simmering for 20 to 25 minutes.

Serve with toasted bread and enjoy!

**Per serving:** Calories: 129; Fat: 8.6g; Carbs: 7.4g; Protein: 6.3g

# 80. Roasted Carrot Soup

(Ready in about 50 minutes | Servings 4)

## Ingredients

1 ½ pounds carrots
4 tablespoons olive oil
1 yellow onion, chopped
2 cloves garlic, minced
1/3 teaspoon ground cumin
Sea salt and white pepper, to taste

1/2 teaspoon turmeric powder
4 cups vegetable stock
2 teaspoons lemon juice
2 tablespoons fresh cilantro, roughly chopped

## Directions

Start by preheating your oven to 400 degrees F. Place the carrots on a large parchment-lined baking sheet; toss the carrots with 2 tablespoons of the olive oil.

Roast the carrots for about 35 minutes or until they've softened.

In a heavy-bottomed pot, heat the remaining 2 tablespoons of the olive oil. Now, sauté the onion and garlic for about 3 minutes or until aromatic.

Add in the cumin, salt, pepper, turmeric, vegetable stock and roasted carrots. Continue to simmer for 12 minutes more.

Puree your soup with an immersion blender. Drizzle lemon juice over your soup and serve garnished with fresh cilantro leaves. Bon appétit!

**Per serving:** Calories: 264; Fat: 18.6g; Carbs: 20.1g; Protein: 7.4g

# 81. Italian Penne Pasta Salad

(Ready in about 15 minutes + chilling time | Servings 3)

## Ingredients

9 ounces penne pasta
9 ounces canned Cannellini bean, drained
1 small onion, thinly sliced
1/3 cup Niçoise olives, pitted and sliced
2 Italian peppers, sliced
1 cup cherry tomatoes, halved
3 cups arugula

Dressing:
3 tablespoons extra-virgin olive oil
1 teaspoon lemon zest
1 teaspoon garlic, minced
3 tablespoons balsamic vinegar
1 teaspoon Italian herb mix
Sea salt and ground black pepper, to taste

## Directions

Cook the penne pasta according to the package directions. Drain and rinse the pasta. Let it cool completely and then, transfer it to a salad bowl.

Then, add the beans, onion, olives, peppers, tomatoes and arugula to the salad bowl.

Mix all the dressing ingredients until everything is well incorporated. Dress your salad and serve well-chilled. Bon appétit!

**Per serving:** Calories: 614; Fat: 18.1g; Carbs: 101g; Protein: 15.4g

## 82. Indian Chana Chaat Salad

(Ready in about 45 minutes + chilling time | Servings 4)

### Ingredients

1 pound dry chickpeas, soaked overnight
2 San Marzano tomatoes, diced
1 Persian cucumber, sliced
1 onion, chopped
1 bell pepper, seeded and thinly sliced
1 green chili, seeded and thinly sliced
2 handfuls baby spinach
1/2 teaspoon Kashmiri chili powder
4 curry leaves, chopped
1 tablespoon chaat masala
2 tablespoons fresh lemon juice, or to taste
4 tablespoons olive oil
1 teaspoon agave syrup
1/2 teaspoon mustard seeds
1/2 teaspoon coriander seeds
2 tablespoons sesame seeds, lightly toasted
2 tablespoons fresh cilantro, roughly chopped

### Directions

Drain the chickpeas and transfer them to a large saucepan. Cover the chickpeas with water by 2 inches and bring it to a boil.

Immediately turn the heat to a simmer and continue to cook for approximately 40 minutes.

Toss the chickpeas with the tomatoes, cucumber, onion, peppers, spinach, chili powder, curry leaves and chaat masala.

In a small mixing dish, thoroughly combine the lemon juice, olive oil, agave syrup, mustard seeds and coriander seeds.

Garnish with sesame seeds and fresh cilantro. Bon appétit!

**Per serving:** Calories: 604; Fat: 23.1g; Carbs: 80g; Protein: 25.3g

## 83. Thai-Style Tempeh and Noodle Salad

(Ready in about 45 minutes | Servings 3)

### Ingredients

6 ounces tempeh
4 tablespoons rice vinegar
4 tablespoons soy sauce
2 garlic cloves, minced
1 small-sized lime, freshly juiced
5 ounces rice noodles
1 carrot, julienned
1 shallot, chopped
3 handfuls Chinese cabbage, thinly sliced
3 handfuls kale, torn into pieces
1 bell pepper, seeded and thinly sliced
1 bird's eye chili, minced
1/4 cup peanut butter
2 tablespoons agave syrup

### Directions

Place the tempeh, 2 tablespoons of the rice vinegar, soy sauce, garlic and lime juice in a ceramic dish; let it marinate for about 40 minutes.

Meanwhile, cook the rice noodles according to the package directions. Drain your noodles and transfer them to a salad bowl.

Add the carrot, shallot, cabbage, kale and peppers to the salad bowl. Add in the peanut butter, the remaining 2 tablespoons of the rice vinegar and agave syrup and toss to combine well.

Top with the marinated tempeh and serve immediately. Enjoy!

**Per serving:** Calories: 494; Fat: 14.5g; Carbs: 75g; Protein: 18.7g

## 84. Classic Cream of Broccoli Soup

(Ready in about 35 minutes | Servings 4)

### Ingredients

2 tablespoons olive oil
1 pound broccoli florets
1 onion, chopped
1 celery rib, chopped
1 parsnip, chopped
1 teaspoon garlic, chopped
3 cups vegetable broth
1/2 teaspoon dried dill
1/2 teaspoon dried oregano
Sea salt and ground black pepper, to taste
2 tablespoons flaxseed meal
1 cup full-fat coconut milk

### Directions

In a heavy-bottomed pot, heat the olive oil over medium-high heat. Now, sauté the broccoli onion, celery and parsnip for about 5 minutes, stirring periodically.

Add in the garlic and continue sautéing for 1 minute or until fragrant.

Then, stir in the vegetable broth, dill, oregano, salt and black pepper; bring to a boil. Immediately reduce the heat to a simmer and let it cook for about 20 minutes.

Puree the soup using an immersion blender until creamy and uniform.

Return the pureed mixture to the pot. Fold in the flaxseed meal and coconut milk; continue to simmer until heated through or about 5 minutes.

Ladle into four serving bowls and enjoy!

**Per serving:** Calories: 334; Fat: 24.5g; Carbs: 22.5g; Protein: 10.2g

## 85. Moroccan Lentil and Raisin Salad

(Ready in about 20 minutes + chilling time | Servings 4)

### Ingredients

1 cup red lentils, rinsed
1 large carrot, julienned
1 Persian cucumber, thinly sliced
1 sweet onion, chopped
1/2 cup golden raisins
1/4 cup fresh mint, snipped
1/4 cup fresh basil, snipped
1/4 cup extra-virgin olive oil
1/4 cup lemon juice, freshly squeezed
1 teaspoon grated lemon peel
1/2 teaspoon fresh ginger root, peeled and minced
1/2 teaspoon granulated garlic
1 teaspoon ground allspice
Sea salt and ground black pepper, to taste

### Directions

In a large-sized saucepan, bring 3 cups of the water and 1 cup of the lentils to a boil.

Immediately turn the heat to a simmer and continue to cook your lentils for a further 15 to 17 minutes or until they've softened but are not mushy yet. Drain and let it cool completely.

Transfer the lentils to a salad bowl; add in the carrot, cucumber and sweet onion. Then, add the raisins, mint and basil to your salad.

In a small mixing dish, whisk the olive oil, lemon juice, lemon peel, ginger, granulated garlic, allspice, salt and black pepper.

Dress your salad and serve well-chilled. Bon appétit!

**Per serving:** Calories: 418; Fat: 15g; Carbs: 62.9g; Protein: 12.4g

# 86. Asparagus and Chickpea Salad

(Ready in about 10 minutes + chilling time | Servings 5)

## Ingredients

1 ¼ pounds asparagus, trimmed and cut into bite-sized pieces

5 ounces canned chickpeas, drained and rinsed

1 chipotle pepper, seeded and chopped

1 Italian pepper, seeded and chopped

1/4 cup fresh basil leaves, chopped

1/4 cup fresh parsley leaves, chopped

2 tablespoons fresh mint leaves

2 tablespoons fresh chives, chopped

1 teaspoon garlic, minced

1/4 cup extra-virgin olive oil

1 tablespoon balsamic vinegar

1 tablespoon fresh lime juice

2 tablespoons soy sauce

1/4 teaspoon ground allspice

1/4 teaspoon ground cumin

Sea salt and freshly cracked peppercorns, to taste

## Directions

Bring a large pot of salted water with the asparagus to a boil; let it cook for 2 minutes; drain and rinse.

Transfer the asparagus to a salad bowl.

Toss the asparagus with the chickpeas, peppers, herbs, garlic, olive oil, vinegar, lime juice, soy sauce and spices.

Toss to combine and serve immediately. Bon appétit!

**Per serving:** Calories: 198; Fat: 12.9g; Carbs: 17.5g; Protein: 5.5g

# 87. Old-Fashioned Green Bean Salad

(Ready in about 10 minutes + chilling time | Servings 4)

## Ingredients

1 ½ pounds green beans, trimmed

1/2 cup scallions, chopped

1 teaspoon garlic, minced

1 Persian cucumber, sliced

2 cups grape tomatoes, halved

1/4 cup olive oil

1 teaspoon deli mustard

2 tablespoons tamari sauce

2 tablespoons lemon juice

1 tablespoon apple cider vinegar

1/4 teaspoon cumin powder

1/2 teaspoon dried thyme

Sea salt and ground black pepper, to taste

## Directions

Boil the green beans in a large saucepan of salted water until they are just tender or about 2 minutes.

Drain and let the beans cool completely; then, transfer them to a salad bowl. Toss the beans with the remaining ingredients.

Bon appétit!

**Per serving:** Calories: 240; Fat: 14.1g; Carbs: 29g; Protein: 4.4g

# 88. Winter Bean Soup

(Ready in about 25 minutes | Servings 4)

## Ingredients

1 tablespoon olive oil

2 tablespoons shallots, chopped

1 carrot, chopped

1 parsnip, chopped

1 celery stalk, chopped

1 teaspoon fresh garlic, minced

4 cups vegetable broth

2 bay leaves

1 rosemary sprig, chopped

16 ounces canned navy beans

Flaky sea salt and ground black pepper, to taste

## Directions

In a heavy-bottomed pot, heat the olive over medium-high heat. Now, sauté the shallots, carrot, parsnip and celery for approximately 3 minutes or until the vegetables are just tender.

Add in the garlic and continue to sauté for 1 minute or until aromatic.

Then, add in the vegetable broth, bay leaves and rosemary and bring to a boil. Immediately reduce the heat to a simmer and let it cook for 10 minutes.

Fold in the navy beans and continue to simmer for about 5 minutes longer until everything is thoroughly heated. Season with salt and black pepper to taste.

Ladle into individual bowls, discard the bay leaves and serve hot. Bon appétit!

**Per serving:** Calories: 234; Fat: 5.5g; Carbs: 32.3g; Protein: 14.4g

# 89. Italian-Style Cremini Mushrooms Soup

(Ready in about 15 minutes | Servings 3)

## Ingredients

3 tablespoons vegan butter

1 white onion, chopped

1 red bell pepper, chopped

1/2 teaspoon garlic, pressed

3 cups Cremini mushrooms, chopped

2 tablespoons almond flour

3 cups water

1 teaspoon Italian herb mix

Sea salt and ground black pepper, to taste

1 heaping tablespoon fresh chives, roughly chopped

## Directions

In a stockpot, melt the vegan butter over medium-high heat. Once hot, sauté the onion and pepper for about 3 minutes until they have softened.

Add in the garlic and Cremini mushrooms and continue sautéing until the mushrooms have softened. Sprinkle almond meal over the mushrooms and continue to cook for 1 minute or so.

Add in the remaining ingredients. Let it simmer, covered and continue to cook for 5 to 6 minutes more until the liquid has thickened slightly.

Ladle into three soup bowls and garnish with fresh chives. Bon appétit!

**Per serving:** Calories: 154; Fat: 12.3g; Carbs: 9.6g; Protein: 4.4g

# 90. Creamed Potato Soup with Herbs

(Ready in about 40 minutes | Servings 4)

**Per serving:** Calories: 400; Fat: 9g; Carbs: 68.7g; Protein: 13.4g

## Ingredients

2 tablespoons olive oil
1 onion, chopped
1 celery stalk, chopped
4 large potatoes, peeled and chopped
2 garlic cloves, minced
1 teaspoon fresh basil, chopped
1 teaspoon fresh parsley, chopped

1 teaspoon fresh rosemary, chopped
1 bay laurel
1 teaspoon ground allspice
4 cups vegetable stock
Salt and fresh ground black pepper, to taste
2 tablespoons fresh chives chopped

## Directions

In a heavy-bottomed pot, heat the olive oil over medium-high heat. Once hot, sauté the onion, celery and potatoes for about 5 minutes, stirring periodically.

Add in the garlic, basil, parsley, rosemary, bay laurel and allspice and continue sautéing for 1 minute or until fragrant.

Now, add in the vegetable stock, salt and black pepper and bring to a rapid boil. Immediately reduce the heat to a simmer and let it cook for about 30 minutes.

Puree the soup using an immersion blender until creamy and uniform.

Reheat your soup and serve with fresh chives. Bon appétit!

# 91. Quinoa and Avocado Salad

(Ready in about 15 minutes + chilling time | Servings 4)

**Per serving:** Calories: 399; Fat: 24.3g; Carbs: 38.5g; Protein: 8.4g

## Ingredients

1 cup quinoa, rinsed
1 onion, chopped
1 tomato, diced
2 roasted peppers, cut into strips
2 tablespoons parsley, chopped
2 tablespoons basil, chopped
1/4 cup extra-virgin olive oil

2 tablespoons red wine vinegar
2 tablespoons lemon juice
1/4 teaspoon cayenne pepper
Sea salt and freshly ground black pepper, to season
1 avocado, peeled, pitted and sliced
1 tablespoon sesame seeds, toasted

## Directions

Place the water and quinoa in a saucepan and bring it to a rolling boil. Immediately turn the heat to a simmer.

Let it simmer for about 13 minutes until the quinoa has absorbed all of the water; fluff the quinoa with a fork and let it cool completely. Then, transfer the quinoa to a salad bowl.

Add the onion, tomato, roasted peppers, parsley and basil to the salad bowl. In another small bowl, whisk the olive oil, vinegar, lemon juice, cayenne pepper, salt and black pepper.

Dress your salad and toss to combine well. Top with avocado slices and garnish with toasted sesame seeds.

Bon appétit!

# 92. Tabbouleh Salad with Tofu

(Ready in about 20 minutes + chilling time | Servings 4)

## Ingredients

1 cup bulgur wheat
2 San Marzano tomatoes, sliced
1 Persian cucumber, thinly sliced
2 tablespoons basil, chopped
2 tablespoons parsley, chopped
4 scallions, chopped
2 cups arugula

2 cups baby spinach, torn into pieces
4 tablespoons tahini
4 tablespoons lemon juice
1 tablespoon soy sauce
1 teaspoon fresh garlic, pressed
Sea salt and ground black pepper, to taste
12 ounces smoked tofu, cubed

## Directions

In a saucepan, bring 2 cups of water and the bulgur to a boil. Immediately turn the heat to a simmer and let it cook for about 20 minutes or until the bulgur is tender and the water is almost absorbed. Fluff with a fork and spread on a large tray to let cool.

Place the bulgur in a salad bowl followed by the tomatoes, cucumber, basil, parsley, scallions, arugula and spinach.

In a small mixing dish, whisk the tahini, lemon juice, soy sauce, garlic, salt and black pepper. Dress the salad and toss to combine.

Top your salad with the smoked tofu and serve at room temperature. Bon appétit!

**Per serving:** Calories: 379; Fat: 18.3g; Carbs: 40.7g; Protein: 19.9g

# 93. Garden Pasta Salad

(Ready in about 10 minutes + chilling time | Servings 4)

## Ingredients

12 ounces rotini pasta
1 small onion, thinly sliced
1 cup cherry tomatoes, halved
1 bell pepper, chopped
1 jalapeno pepper, chopped
1 tablespoon capers, drained
2 cups Iceberg lettuce, torn into pieces
2 tablespoons fresh parsley, chopped
2 tablespoons fresh cilantro, chopped

2 tablespoons fresh basil, chopped
1/4 cup olive oil
2 tablespoons apple cider vinegar
1 teaspoon garlic, pressed
Kosher salt and ground black pepper, to taste
2 tablespoons nutritional yeast
2 tablespoons pine nuts, toasted and chopped

## Directions

Cook the pasta according to the package directions. Drain and rinse the pasta. Let it cool completely and then, transfer it to a salad bowl.

Then, add in the onion, tomatoes, peppers, capers, lettuce, parsley, cilantro and basil to the salad bowl.

Whisk the olive oil, vinegar, garlic, salt, black pepper and nutritional yeast. Dress your salad and top with toasted pine nuts. Bon appétit!

**Per serving:** Calories: 479; Fat: 15g; Carbs: 71.1g; Protein: 14.9g

# 94. Traditional Ukrainian Borscht

(Ready in about 40 minutes | Servings 4)

## Ingredients

2 tablespoons sesame oil
1 red onion, chopped
2 carrots, trimmed and sliced
2 large beets, peeled and sliced
2 large potatoes, peeled and diced
4 cups vegetable stock
2 garlic cloves, minced
1/2 teaspoon caraway seeds
1/2 teaspoon celery seeds
1/2 teaspoon fennel seeds
1 pound red cabbage, shredded
1/2 teaspoon mixed peppercorns, freshly cracked
Kosher salt, to taste
2 bay leaves
2 tablespoons wine vinegar

## Directions

In a Dutch oven, heat the sesame oil over a moderate flame. Once hot, sauté the onions until tender and translucent, about 6 minutes.

Add in the carrots, beets and potatoes and continue to sauté an additional 10 minutes, adding the vegetable stock periodically.

Next, stir in the garlic, caraway seeds, celery seeds, fennel seeds and continue sautéing for another 30 seconds.

Add in the cabbage, mixed peppercorns, salt and bay leaves. Add in the remaining stock and bring to boil.

Immediately turn the heat to a simmer and continue to cook for 20 to 23 minutes longer until the vegetables have softened.

Ladle into individual bowls and drizzle wine vinegar over it. Serve and enjoy!

**Per serving:** Calories: 367; Fat: 9.3g; Carbs: 62.7g; Protein: 12.1g

# 95. Beluga Lentil Salad

(Ready in about 20 minutes + chilling time | Servings 4)

## Ingredients

1 cup Beluga lentils, rinsed
1 Persian cucumber, sliced
1 large-sized tomatoes, sliced
1 red onion, chopped
1 bell pepper, sliced
1/4 cup fresh basil, chopped
1/4 cup fresh Italian parsley, chopped
2 ounces green olives, pitted and sliced
1/4 cup olive oil
4 tablespoons lemon juice
1 teaspoon deli mustard
1/2 teaspoon garlic, minced
1/2 teaspoon red pepper flakes, crushed
Sea salt and ground black pepper, to taste

## Directions

In a large-sized saucepan, bring 3 cups of the water and 1 cup of the lentils to a boil.

Immediately turn the heat to a simmer and continue to cook your lentils for a further 15 to 17 minutes or until they've softened but not mushy. Drain and let it cool completely.

Transfer the lentils to a salad bowl; add in the cucumber, tomatoes, onion, pepper, basil, parsley and olives.

In a small mixing dish, whisk the olive oil, lemon juice, mustard, garlic, red pepper, salt and black pepper.

Dress the salad, toss to combine and serve well-chilled. Bon appétit!

**Per serving:** Calories: 338; Fat: 16.3g; Carbs: 37.2g; Protein: 13g

# 96. Indian-Style Naan Salad

(Ready in about 10 minutes | Servings 3)

## Ingredients

3 tablespoons sesame oil
1 teaspoon ginger, peeled and minced
1/2 teaspoon cumin seeds
1/2 teaspoon mustard seeds
1/2 teaspoon mixed peppercorns
1 tablespoon curry leaves
3 naan breads, broken into bite-sized pieces
1 shallot, chopped
2 tomatoes, chopped
Himalayan salt, to taste
1 tablespoon soy sauce

## Directions

Heat 2 tablespoons of the sesame oil in a nonstick skillet over a moderately high heat.

Sauté the ginger, cumin seeds, mustard seeds, mixed peppercorns and curry leaves for 1 minute or so, until fragrant.

Stir in the naan breads and continue to cook, stirring periodically, until golden-brown and well coated with the spices.

Place the shallot and tomatoes in a salad bowl; toss them with the salt, soy sauce and the remaining 1 tablespoon of the sesame oil.

Place the toasted naan on the top of your salad and serve at room temperature. Enjoy!

**Per serving:** Calories: 328; Fat: 17.3g; Carbs: 36.6g; Protein: 6.9g

# 97. Greek-Style Roasted Pepper Salad

(Ready in about 10 minutes | Servings 2)

## Ingredients

2 red bell peppers
2 yellow bell peppers
2 garlic cloves, pressed
4 teaspoons extra-virgin olive oil
1 tablespoon capers, rinsed and drained
2 tablespoons red wine vinegar
Seas salt and ground pepper, to taste
1 teaspoon fresh dill weed, chopped
1 teaspoon fresh oregano, chopped
1/4 cup Kalamata olives, pitted and sliced

## Directions

Broil the peppers on a parchment-lined baking sheet for about 10 minutes, rotating the pan halfway through the cooking time, until they are charred on all sides.

Then, cover the peppers with a plastic wrap to steam. Discard the skin, seeds and cores.

Slice the peppers into strips and place them in a salad bowl. Add in the remaining ingredients and toss to combine well.

Place in your refrigerator until ready to serve. Bon appétit!

**Per serving:** Calories: 185; Fat: 11.5g; Carbs: 20.6g; Protein: 3.7g

# 98. Kidney Bean and Potato Soup

(Ready in about 30 minutes | Servings 4)

## Ingredients

2 tablespoons olive oil
1 onion, chopped
1 pound potatoes, peeled and diced
1 medium celery stalks, chopped
2 garlic cloves, minced
1 teaspoon paprika
4 cups water
2 tablespoons vegan bouillon powder
16 ounces canned kidney beans, drained
2 cups baby spinach
Sea salt and ground black pepper, to taste

## Directions

In a heavy-bottomed pot, heat the olive over medium-high heat. Now, sauté the onion, potatoes and celery for approximately 5 minutes or until the onion is translucent and tender.

Add in the garlic and continue to sauté for 1 minute or until aromatic.

Then, add in the paprika, water and vegan bouillon powder and bring to a boil. Immediately reduce the heat to a simmer and let it cook for 15 minutes.

Fold in the navy beans and spinach; continue to simmer for about 5 minutes until everything is thoroughly heated. Season with salt and black pepper to taste.

Ladle into individual bowls and serve hot. Bon appétit!

**Per serving:** Calories: 266; Fat: 7.7g; Carbs: 41.3g; Protein: 9.3g

# 99. Winter Quinoa Salad with Pickles

(Ready in about 20 minutes + chilling time | Servings 4)

## Ingredients

1 cup quinoa
4 garlic cloves, minced
2 pickled cucumber, chopped
10 ounces canned red peppers, chopped
1/2 cup green olives, pitted and sliced
2 cups green cabbages, shredded
2 cups Iceberg lettuce, torn into pieces
4 pickled chilies, chopped
4 tablespoons olive oil
1 tablespoon lemon juice
1 teaspoon lemon zest
1/2 teaspoon dried marjoram
Sea salt and ground black pepper, to taste
1/4 cup fresh chives, coarsely chopped

## Directions

Place two cups of water and the quinoa in a pot and bring it to a boil. Immediately turn the heat to a simmer.

Let it simmer for about 13 minutes until the quinoa has absorbed all of the water; fluff the quinoa with a fork and let it cool completely. Then, transfer the quinoa to a salad bowl.

Add the garlic, pickled cucumber, peppers, olives, cabbage, lettuce and pickled chilies to the salad bowl and toss to combine.

In a small mixing bowl, make the dressing by whisking the remaining ingredients. Dress the salad, toss to combine well and serve immediately. Bon appétit!

**Per serving:** Calories: 346; Fat: 16.7g; Carbs: 42.6g; Protein: 9.3g

# 100. Roasted Wild Mushroom Soup

(Ready in about 55 minutes | Servings 3)

## Ingredients

3 tablespoons sesame oil
1 pound mixed wild mushrooms, sliced
1 white onion, chopped
3 cloves garlic, minced and divided
2 sprigs thyme, chopped
2 sprigs rosemary, chopped
1/4 cup flaxseed meal
1/4 cup dry white wine
3 cups vegetable broth
1/2 teaspoon red chili flakes
Garlic salt and freshly ground black pepper, to seasoned

## Directions

Start by preheating your oven to 395 degrees F.

Place the mushrooms in a single layer onto a parchment-lined baking pan. Drizzle the mushrooms with 1 tablespoon of the sesame oil.

Roast the mushrooms in the preheated oven for about 25 minutes, or until tender.

Heat the remaining 2 tablespoons of the sesame oil in a stockpot over medium heat. Then, sauté the onion for about 3 minutes or until tender and translucent.

Then, add in the garlic, thyme and rosemary and continue to sauté for 1 minute or so until aromatic. Sprinkle flaxseed meal over everything.

Add in the remaining ingredients and continue to simmer for 10 to 15 minutes longer or until everything is cooked through.

Stir in the roasted mushrooms and continue simmering for a further 12 minutes. Ladle into soup bowls and serve hot. Enjoy!

**Per serving:** Calories: 313; Fat: 23.5g; Carbs: 14.5g; Protein: 14.5g

# 101. Mediterranean-Style Green Bean Soup

(Ready in about 25 minutes | Servings 5)

## Ingredients

2 tablespoons olive oil
1 onion, chopped
1 celery with leaves, chopped
1 carrot, chopped
2 garlic cloves, minced
1 zucchini, chopped
5 cups vegetable broth
1 ¼ pounds green beans, trimmed and cut into bite-sized chunks
2 medium-sized tomatoes, pureed
Sea salt and freshly ground black pepper, to taste
1/2 teaspoon cayenne pepper
1 teaspoon oregano
1/2 teaspoon dried dill
1/2 cup Kalamata olives, pitted and sliced

## Directions

In a heavy-bottomed pot, heat the olive over medium-high heat. Now, sauté the onion, celery and carrot for about 4 minutes or until the vegetables are just tender.

Add in the garlic and zucchini and continue to sauté for 1 minute or until aromatic.

Then, stir in the vegetable broth, green beans, tomatoes, salt, black pepper, cayenne pepper, oregano and dried dill; bring to a boil. Immediately reduce the heat to a simmer and let it cook for about 15 minutes.

Ladle into individual bowls and serve with sliced olives. Bon appétit!

**Per serving:** Calories: 313; Fat: 23.5g; Carbs: 14.5g; Protein: 14.5g

# 102. Cream of Carrot Soup

(Ready in about 30 minutes | Servings 4)

## Ingredients

2 tablespoons sesame oil
1 onion, chopped
1 ½ pounds carrots, trimmed and chopped
1 parsnip, chopped
2 garlic cloves, minced
1/2 teaspoon curry powder
Sea salt and cayenne pepper, to taste
4 cups vegetable broth
1 cup full-fat coconut milk

## Directions

In a heavy-bottomed pot, heat the sesame oil over medium-high heat. Now, sauté the onion, carrots and parsnip for about 5 minutes, stirring periodically.

Add in the garlic and continue sautéing for 1 minute or until fragrant.

Then, stir in the curry powder, salt, cayenne pepper and vegetable broth; bring to a rapid boil. Immediately reduce the heat to a simmer and let it cook for 18 to 20 minutes.

Puree the soup using an immersion blender until creamy and uniform.

Return the pureed mixture to the pot. Fold in the coconut milk and continue to simmer until heated through or about 5 minutes longer.

Ladle into four bowls and serve hot. Bon appétit!

**Per serving:** Calories: 333; Fat: 23g; Carbs: 26g; Protein: 8.5g

# 103. Italian Nonna's Pizza Salad

(Ready in about 15 minutes + chilling time | Servings 4)

## Ingredients

1 pound macaroni
1 cup marinated mushrooms, sliced
1 cup grape tomatoes, halved
4 tablespoons scallions, chopped
1 teaspoon garlic, minced
1 Italian pepper, sliced
1/4 cup extra-virgin olive oil
1/4 cup balsamic vinegar
1 teaspoon dried oregano
1 teaspoon dried basil
1/2 teaspoon dried rosemary
Sea salt and cayenne pepper, to taste
1/2 cup black olives, sliced

## Directions

Cook the pasta according to the package directions. Drain and rinse the pasta. Let it cool completely and then, transfer it to a salad bowl.

Then, add in the remaining ingredients and toss until the macaroni are well coated.

Taste and adjust the seasonings; place the pizza salad in your refrigerator until ready to use. Bon appétit!

**Per serving:** Calories: 595; Fat: 17.2g; Carbs: 93g; Protein: 16g

# 104. Creamy Golden Veggie Soup

(Ready in about 45 minutes | Servings 4)

## Ingredients

2 tablespoons avocado oil
1 yellow onion, chopped
2 Yukon Gold potatoes, peeled and diced
2 pounds butternut squash, peeled, seeded and diced
1 parsnip, trimmed and sliced
1 teaspoon ginger-garlic paste
1 teaspoon turmeric powder
1 teaspoon fennel seeds
1/2 teaspoon chili powder
1/2 teaspoon pumpkin pie spice
Kosher salt and ground black pepper, to taste
3 cups vegetable stock
1 cup full-fat coconut milk
2 tablespoons pepitas

## Directions

In a heavy-bottomed pot, heat the oil over medium-high heat. Now, sauté the onion, potatoes, butternut squash and parsnip for about 10 minutes, stirring periodically to ensure even cooking.

Add in the ginger-garlic paste and continue sautéing for 1 minute or until aromatic.

Then, stir in the turmeric powder, fennel seeds, chili powder, pumpkin pie spice, salt, black pepper and vegetable stock; bring to a boil. Immediately reduce the heat to a simmer and let it cook for about 25 minutes.

Puree the soup using an immersion blender until creamy and uniform.

Return the pureed mixture to the pot. Fold in the coconut milk and continue to simmer until heated through or about 5 minutes longer.

Ladle into individual bowls and serve garnished with pepitas. Bon appétit!

**Per serving:** Calories: 550; Fat: 27.2g; Carbs: 70.4g; Protein: 13.2g

# 105. Roasted Cauliflower Soup

(Ready in about 1 hour | Servings 4)

## Ingredients

1 ½ pounds cauliflower florets
4 tablespoons olive oil
1 onion, chopped
2 cloves garlic, minced
1/2 teaspoon ginger, peeled and minced
1 teaspoon fresh rosemary, chopped
2 tablespoons fresh basil, chopped
2 tablespoons fresh parsley, chopped
4 cups vegetable stock
Sea salt and ground black pepper, to taste
1/2 teaspoon ground sumac
1/4 cup tahini
1 lemon, freshly squeezed

## Directions

Begin by preheating the oven to 425 degrees F. Toss the cauliflower with 2 tablespoons of the olive oil and arrange them on a parchment-lined roasting pan.

Then, roast the cauliflower florets for about 30 minutes stirring, them once or twice to promote even cooking.

Meanwhile, in a heavy-bottomed pot, heat the remaining 2 tablespoons of the olive oil over medium-high heat. Now, sauté the onion for about 4 minutes until tender and translucent.

Add in the garlic, ginger, rosemary, basil and parsley and continue sautéing for 1 minute or until fragrant.

Then, stir in the vegetable stock, salt, black pepper and sumac and bring it to a boil. Immediately reduce the heat to a simmer and let it cook for about 20 to 22 minutes.

Puree the soup using an immersion blender until creamy and uniform.

Return the pureed mixture to the pot. Fold in the tahini and continue to simmer for about 5 minutes or until everything is thoroughly cooked.

Ladle into individual bowls, garnish with lemon juice and serve hot. Enjoy!

**Per serving:** Calories: 310; Fat: 24g; Carbs: 16.8g; Protein: 11.8g

## 106. Classic Vegan Coleslaw

(Ready in about 10 minutes | Servings 4)

### Ingredients

1 pound red cabbage, shredded
2 carrots, trimmed and grated
4 tablespoons onion, chopped
1 garlic clove, minced
1/2 cup fresh Italian parsley, roughly chopped
1 cup vegan mayo

1 teaspoon brown mustard
1 teaspoon lemon zest
2 tablespoons apple cider vinegar
Sea salt and ground black pepper, to taste
2 tablespoons sunflower seeds

### Directions

Toss the cabbage, carrots, onion, garlic and parsley in a salad bowl.

In a mixing bowl, whisk the mayo, mustard, lemon zest, apple cider vinegar, salt and black pepper.

Dress your salad and serve garnished with the sunflower seeds.

**Per serving:** Calories: 293; Fat: 25.8g; Carbs: 14g; Protein: 3.5g

## 107. Indian-Style Turnip Soup

(Ready in about 30 minutes | Servings 4)

### Ingredients

2 tablespoons olive oil
1 onion, chopped
3/4 pound turnip, trimmed and sliced
1/4 pound carrot, trimmed and sliced
1/4 cup parsnip, trimmed and sliced
1 tablespoon ginger-garlic paste
3 cups water

1/2 teaspoon coriander seeds
1/2 teaspoon celery seeds
1/2 teaspoon fennel seeds
1 teaspoon curry powder
Sea salt and ground black pepper
1 tablespoon bouillon granules
1/2 cup raw cashews, soaked
1 cup water, divided
1 tablespoon lemon juice

### Directions

In a heavy-bottomed pot, heat the olive oil over medium-high heat. Now, sauté the onion, turnip, carrot and parsnip for about 5 minutes, stirring periodically.

Add in the ginger-garlic paste and continue sautéing for 1 minute or until fragrant.

Then, stir in the water, coriander seeds, celery seeds, fennel seeds, curry powder, salt, black pepper and bouillon granules; bring to a boil. Immediately reduce the heat to a simmer and let it cook for about 20 to 22 minutes.

Puree the soup using an immersion blender until creamy and uniform.

Drain the cashews and add them to the bowl of your blender or food processor; add in the water, lemon juice and salt to taste. Blend into a cream.

Return the pureed mixture to the pot. Fold in the cashew cream and continue simmering until heated through or about 5 minutes longer.

Ladle into serving bowls and serve hot. Bon appétit!

**Per serving:** Calories: 225; Fat: 14g; Carbs: 20.2g; Protein: 4.9g

## 108. Winter Root Vegetable Soup

(Ready in about 40 minutes | Servings 4)

### Ingredients

4 tablespoons avocado oil
1 large leek, sliced
2 carrots, diced
2 parsnips, diced
2 cups turnip, diced
2 celery stalks, diced
1 pound sweet potatoes, diced
1 teaspoon ginger-garlic paste
1 habanero pepper, seeded and chopped

1/2 teaspoon caraway seeds
1/2 teaspoon fennel seeds
2 bay leaves
Sea salt and ground black pepper, to season
1 teaspoon cayenne pepper
4 cups vegetable broth
4 tablespoons tahini

### Directions

In a stockpot, heat the oil over medium-high heat. Now, sauté the leeks, carrots, parsnip, turnip, celery and sweet potatoes for about 5 minutes, stirring periodically.

Add in the ginger-garlic paste and habanero peppers and continue sautéing for 1 minute or until fragrant.

Then, stir in the caraway seeds, fennel seeds, bay leaves, salt, black pepper, cayenne pepper and vegetable broth; bring to a boil. Immediately turn the heat to a simmer and let it cook for approximately 25 minutes.

Puree the soup using an immersion blender until creamy and uniform.

Return the pureed mixture to the pot. Fold in the tahini and continue to simmer until heated through or about 5 minutes longer.

Ladle into individual bowls and serve hot. Bon appétit!

**Per serving:** Calories: 427; Fat: 24.2g; Carbs: 41.4g; Protein: 13.7g

## 109. Greek Orzo and Bean Salad

(Ready in about 15 minutes + chilling time | Servings 4)

### Ingredients

10 ounces orzo
1 cup canned green beans, drained
1 cup canned kidney beans, drained
1 cup canned sweet corn, drained
1 small red onion, thinly sliced
1 small sweet onion, thinly sliced
1 cup grape tomatoes, halved
2 bell peppers, seeded and diced
1 green chili pepper, seeded and diced
1 tablespoon capers, drained
1 tablespoon fresh oregano, chopped

1 tablespoon fresh parsley, chopped
1 tablespoon fresh chervil, chopped
1 tablespoon fresh basil, chopped
4 tablespoons extra-virgin olive oil
Sea salt and ground black pepper, to season
1/2 teaspoon red pepper flakes, crushed
2 tablespoons fresh lemon juice
1 teaspoon garlic powder
1 cup figs, sliced

### Directions

Cook the orzo according to the package directions. Drain and rinse the pasta. Let it cool completely and then, transfer it to a salad bowl.

Then, add in the beans, corn, onions, tomatoes, peppers, capers and herbs to the salad bowl.

Whisk the olive oil, salt, black pepper, red pepper, lemon juice and garlic powder. Dress your salad and top with sliced figs. Bon appétit!

**Per serving:** Calories: 565; Fat: 15.4g; Carbs: 93g; Protein: 17.5g

## 110. Greek-Style Pinto Bean and Tomato Soup

(Ready in about 30 minutes | Servings 4)

### Ingredients

2 tablespoons olive oil
1 carrot, chopped
1 parsnip, chopped
1 red onion, chopped
1 chili pepper, minced
2 garlic cloves, minced
3 cups vegetable broth
1 cup canned tomatoes, crushed
1/2 teaspoon cumin
Sea salt and ground black pepper, to taste

1 teaspoon cayenne pepper
1 teaspoon Greek herb mix
20 ounces canned pinto beans
12 ounces canned corn, drained
2 tablespoons fresh cilantro, chopped
2 tablespoons fresh parsley, chopped
2 tablespoons Kalamata olives, pitted and sliced

### Directions

In a heavy-bottomed pot, heat the olive over medium-high heat. Now, sauté the carrot, parsnip and onion for approximately 3 minutes or until the vegetables are just tender.

Add in the chili pepper and garlic and continue to sauté for 1 minute or until aromatic.

Then, add in the vegetable broth, canned tomatoes, cumin, salt, black pepper, cayenne pepper and Greek herb mix and bring to a boil. Immediately reduce the heat to a simmer and let it cook for 10 minutes.

Fold in the beans and corn and continue simmering for about 10 minutes longer until everything is thoroughly heated. Taste and adjust the seasonings.

Ladle into individual bowls and garnish with cilantro, parsley and olives. Bon appétit!

**Per serving:** Calories: 363; Fat: 10.3g; Carbs: 55.2g; Protein: 17g

## 111. The Best Cauliflower Salad Ever

(Ready in about 10 minutes + chilling time | Servings 4)

### Ingredients

1 ½ pounds cauliflower florets
1/4 cup extra-virgin olive oil
1 teaspoon garlic, minced
1 teaspoon lemon zest
2 tablespoons lemon juice
Sea salt and ground black pepper, to taste

1/4 teaspoon dried dill
1/2 teaspoon dried oregano
1 teaspoon dried mint
10 ounces canned chickpeas, drained
1/4 cup fresh cilantro, chopped

### Directions

In a saucepan, bring about 1/4 inch of water to a boil. Add in the cauliflower florets. Cover and steam the cauliflower until crisp-tender or about 4 minutes.

Let the cauliflower florets cool completely and place them in a salad bowl.

Add the remaining ingredients, except for the cilantro, to the salad bowl and toss to combine well. Garnish with fresh cilantro leaves and serve well-chilled. Bon appétit!

**Per serving:** Calories: 270; Fat: 16g; Carbs: 26.5g; Protein: 8.7g

## 112. Sicilian Eggplant and Pasta Salad

(Ready in about 15 minutes | Servings 4)

### Ingredients

1 tablespoon olive oil
1 pound eggplant, cut into rounds
4 tablespoons dry white wine
1 teaspoon Italian seasoning blend
12 ounces shell pasta
2 Roma tomatoes, diced

1 cup radicchio, sliced
1/2 cup olives, pitted and halved
4 tablespoons extra-virgin olive oil
2 tablespoons balsamic vinegar
1/2 teaspoon lemon zest
Sea salt and ground black pepper, to taste

### Directions

Heat 2 tablespoons of the olive oil in a cast-iron skillet over a moderate flame. Once hot, fry the eggplant for about 10 minutes until browned on all sides.

Meanwhile, cook the pasta according to the package directions. Drain and rinse the pasta. Let it cool completely and then, transfer it to a salad bowl.

Then, add in the remaining ingredients, including the cooked eggplant; toss until well combined.

Taste and adjust the seasonings; serve at room temperature or well-chilled. Bon appétit!

**Per serving:** Calories: 559; Fat: 20.3g; Carbs: 85.5g; Protein: 15.3g

## 113. Autumn Squash Soup

(Ready in about 35 minutes | Servings 4)

### Ingredients

2 tablespoons olive oil
1 onion, chopped
1 large carrot, trimmed and chopped
1 bell pepper, chopped
2 pounds acorn squash, peeled, seeded and cubed
4 garlic cloves, pressed
1 teaspoon fresh ginger, peeled and minced
1 tablespoon fresh coriander, chopped

1 tablespoon fresh Italian parsley, chopped
1 teaspoon curry powder
1 tablespoon brown sugar
1/2 teaspoon chili powder
Kosher salt and ground black pepper, to taste
1/2 teaspoon paprika
4 cups vegetable broth
1 cup full-fat coconut milk
1 lemon, cut into wedges
2 tablespoons fresh chervil, for garnish

### Directions

In a heavy-bottomed pot, heat the olive oil over medium-high heat. Now, sauté the onion, carrot, pepper and acorn squash for about 5 minutes, stirring periodically.

Add in the garlic, ginger, coriander and parsley and continue sautéing for 1 minute or until fragrant.

Then, stir in the curry powder, brown sugar, chili powder, salt, black pepper, paprika and vegetable broth; bring to a boil. Immediately reduce the heat to a simmer and let it cook for about 20 to 22 minutes.

Puree the soup using an immersion blender until creamy and uniform.

Return the pureed mixture to the pot. Fold in the coconut milk and continue to simmer until heated through or about 5 minutes longer.

Ladle into four bowls and serve garnished with lemon wedges and fresh chervil. Bon appétit!

**Per serving:** Calories: 376; Fat: 23.1g; Carbs: 39.2g; Protein: 9.6g

## 114. Broccoli Coleslaw with Coconut Bacon

(Ready in about 15 minutes | Servings 4)

### Ingredients

2 pounds broccoli florets, frozen and thawed
1 large carrot, shredded
1 shallot, chopped
1 teaspoon garlic, minced
4 tablespoons cashew butter
2 tablespoons rice vinegar

2 tablespoons soy sauce
Sea salt and ground black pepper, to taste
1/2 cup coconut bacon
2 tablespoons sesame seeds, lightly toasted

### Directions

In a salad bowl, toss the broccoli florets, carrot, shallot and garlic.

In a small bowl, whisk the cashew butter, vinegar, soy sauce, salt and black pepper until everything is well incorporated.

Dress your salad and top with coconut bacon and toasted sesame seeds. Enjoy!

**Per serving:** Calories: 298; Fat: 21.6g; Carbs: 22g; Protein: 10.3g

## 115. Creamy Roasted Beet Soup

(Ready in about 1 hour 25 minutes | Servings 4)

### Ingredients

2 tablespoons olive oil
1 pound beets, trimmed and scrubbed
1 large red onion, chopped
1 teaspoon garlic, chopped
1/4 teaspoon ground cumin
1/4 teaspoon dried dill
1/2 teaspoon dried oregano

1 bay laurel
4 cups vegetable broth
Sea salt and ground black pepper
1 teaspoon red pepper flakes
1 tablespoon red wine vinegar
1 cup full-fat coconut milk

### Directions

Begin by preheating the oven to 400 degrees F. Toss the beets with 1 tablespoon of the olive oil and wrap them loosely in aluminum foil.

Then, roast the beets for about 1 hour, checking them every 20 minutes. Cut the roasted beets into wedges and set them aside.

Meanwhile, in a heavy-bottomed pot, heat the remaining 1 tablespoon of the olive oil over medium-high heat. Now, sauté the onion for about 4 minutes until tender and translucent.

Add in the garlic, cumin, dill, oregano and bay leaf and continue sautéing for 1 minute or until fragrant.

Then, stir in the vegetable broth, salt, black pepper, red pepper flakes and roasted beets; bring it to a rolling boil. Immediately reduce the heat to a simmer and let it cook for about 20 to 22 minutes.

Puree the soup using an immersion blender until creamy and uniform.

Return the pureed mixture to the pot. Fold in the coconut milk and continue to simmer for about 5 minutes or until everything is thoroughly cooked.

Ladle into individual bowls and serve hot. Bon appétit!

**Per serving:** Calories: 308; Fat: 22.8g; Carbs: 20.2g; Protein: 8.8g

## 116. Creamy Rutabaga Soup

(Ready in about 35 minutes | Servings 4)

### Ingredients

2 tablespoons olive oil
1 onion, chopped
1/2 pound rutabaga, peeled and chopped
1/2 pound sweet potatoes, peeled and chopped
1/2 cup carrots, chopped
1/2 cup parsnip, chopped
1 teaspoon ginger-garlic paste
3 cups vegetable broth
Salt and ground black pepper, to taste

1/4 teaspoon dried dill
1/2 teaspoon dried oregano
1 teaspoon dried basil
1 teaspoon dried parsley flakes
1 teaspoon paprika
1/2 cup raw cashews, soaked
1 cup water, divided
1 tablespoon lemon juice
2 tablespoons fresh cilantro, chopped

### Directions

In a heavy-bottomed pot, heat the olive oil over medium-high heat. Now, sauté the onion, rutabaga, sweet potatoes, carrot and parsnip for about 5 minutes, stirring periodically.

Add in the ginger-garlic paste and continue sautéing for 1 minute or until fragrant.

Then, stir in the vegetable broth, salt, black pepper, dried dill, oregano, basil, parsley and paprika; bring to a boil. Immediately reduce the heat to a simmer and let it cook for about 20 to 22 minutes.

Puree the soup using an immersion blender until creamy and uniform.

Drain the cashews and add them to the bowl of your blender or food processor; add in the water, lemon juice and salt to taste. Blend into a cream.

Return the pureed mixture to the pot. Fold in the cashew cream and continue simmering until heated through or about 5 minutes longer.

Ladle into serving bowls and serve garnished with the fresh cilantro. Bon appétit!

**Per serving:** Calories: 385; Fat: 25.2g; Carbs: 33.8g; Protein: 10.3g

## 117. Mom's Cauliflower Coleslaw

(Ready in about 10 minutes + chilling time | Servings 4)

### Ingredients

2 cups small cauliflower florets, frozen and thawed
2 cups red cabbage, shredded
1 cup carrots, trimmed and shredded
1 medium onion, chopped
1/2 cup vegan mayonnaise

4 tablespoons coconut yogurt, unsweetened
1 tablespoon yellow mustard
1 tablespoon fresh lemon juice
1/2 teaspoon cayenne pepper
Sea salt and ground black pepper, to taste

### Directions

In a salad bowl, toss the vegetables until well combined.

In a small mixing bowl, thoroughly combine the remaining ingredients. Add the mayo dressing to the vegetables and toss to combine well.

Place the coleslaw in your refrigerator until ready to serve. Bon appétit!

**Per serving:** Calories: 280; Fat: 24.6g; Carbs: 13.8g; Protein: 3.3g

# 118. Decadent Broccoli Salad

(Ready in about 10 minutes + chilling time | Servings 4)

## Ingredients

2 pounds broccoli florets
1/4 cup sunflower seeds
1/4 cup pine nuts
1 shallot, chopped
2 garlic cloves, finely chopped
1 cup vegan mayonnaise
1 tablespoon balsamic vinegar
1 tablespoon fresh lime juice
1 teaspoon mustard
Sea salt and freshly ground black pepper, to taste
1/2 cup pomegranate seeds

## Directions

In a saucepan, bring about 1/4 inch of water to a boil. Add in the broccoli florets. Cover and steam the broccoli until crisp-tender or about 5 minutes.

Let the broccoli florets cool completely and place them in a salad bowl.

Add in the sunflower seeds, pine nuts, shallot, garlic, mayo, balsamic vinegar, lime juice, mustard, salt and black pepper. Toss to combine well.

Garnish with pomegranate seeds and serve well-chilled. Bon appétit!

**Per serving:** Calories: 417; Fat: 30.6g; Carbs: 28.3g; Protein: 13.7g

# 119. Creamed Cavatappi and Cauliflower Salad

(Ready in about 15 minutes + chilling time | Servings 4)

## Ingredients

12 ounces cavatappi pasta
1 cup cauliflower florets
1/2 cup vegan mayonnaise
1 tablespoon fresh lemon juice
1 onion, chopped
2 garlic cloves, finely chopped
1 teaspoon deli mustard
2 medium tomatoes, sliced
2 cups arugula, torn into pieces

## Directions

Bring a large pot of salted water to a boil. Now, cook the pasta and cauliflower florets for about 6 minutes.

Remove the cauliflower with a slotted spoon from the water. Continue to cook your pasta for a further 6 minutes until al dente.

Allow the pasta and cauliflower to cool completely; then, transfer them to a salad bowl.

Then, add in the remaining ingredients and toss until well combined.

Taste and adjust the seasonings; place the salad in your refrigerator until ready to use. Bon appétit!

**Per serving:** Calories: 523; Fat: 22.2g; Carbs: 69g; Protein: 12.6g

# 120. French Green Bean Salad with Sesame and Mint

(Ready in about 10 minutes + chilling time | Servings 5)

## Ingredients

1 ½ pounds French green beans, trimmed
1 white onion, thinly sliced
2 garlic cloves, minced
Himalayan salt and ground black pepper, to taste
1/4 cup extra-virgin olive oil
2 tablespoons fresh lime juice
2 tablespoons tamari sauce
1 tablespoon mustard
2 tablespoons sesame seeds, lightly toasted
2 tablespoons fresh mint leaves, roughly chopped

## Directions

Boil the green beans in a large saucepan of salted water until they are just tender or about 2 minutes.

Drain and let the beans cool completely; then, transfer them to a salad bowl. Add in the onion, garlic, salt, black pepper, olive oil, lime juice, tamari sauce and mustard.

Top your salad with the sesame seeds and mint leaves.

Bon appétit!

**Per serving:** Calories: 338; Fat: 16.3g; Carbs: 37.2g; Protein: 13g

# 121. Grandma's Creamy Soup

(Ready in about 40 minutes | Servings 4)

## Ingredients

2 tablespoons olive oil
1 shallot, chopped
4 large carrots, trimmed and sliced
4 large potatoes, peeled and sliced
2 garlic cloves, minced
1/2 teaspoon ground cumin
1/2 teaspoon mustard powder
1/2 teaspoon fennel seeds
Kosher salt and cayenne pepper, to taste
3 ½ cups vegetable broth
1 cup coconut milk

## Directions

In a heavy-bottomed pot, heat the olive oil over medium-high heat. Once hot, sauté the shallot, carrots and potatoes for about 5 minutes, stirring periodically.

Add in the garlic and continue sautéing for 1 minute or until fragrant.

Then, stir in the ground cumin, mustard powder, fennel seeds, salt, cayenne pepper and vegetable broth; bring to a rapid boil. Immediately reduce the heat to a simmer and let it cook for about 30 minutes.

Puree the soup using an immersion blender until creamy and uniform.

Return the pureed soup to the pot. Fold in the coconut milk and continue to simmer until heated through or about 5 minutes longer.

Ladle into four bowls and serve hot. Bon appétit!

**Per serving:** Calories: 400; Fat: 9.3g; Carbs: 72.5g; Protein: 9.3g

# 122. Mexican-Style Chili Soup

(Ready in about 1 hour 15 minutes | Servings 4)

**Per serving:** Calories: 498; Fat: 10.4g; Carbs: 74.9g; Protein: 28.3g

## Ingredients

2 cups dry red beans, soaked overnight and drained

2 tablespoons olive oil

1 medium-sized leek, chopped

2 red bell peppers, chopped

1 chipotle chili pepper, chopped

2 cloves garlic, chopped

4 cups vegetable broth

1 bay laurel

1/2 teaspoon fennel seeds

1/2 teaspoon mustard seeds

1/2 teaspoon cumin seeds

Kosher salt and ground black pepper, to taste

1/2 cup salsa

3 heaping tablespoons fresh cilantro, chopped

2 ounces tortilla chips

## Directions

Place the soaked beans in a soup pot; cover with a fresh change of the water and bring to a boil over medium-high heat. Let it boil for about 10 minutes.

Next, turn the heat to a simmer and continue to cook for 45 minutes; reserve.

In the same pot, heat the olive over medium-high heat. Now, sauté the leek and peppers for approximately 3 minutes or until the vegetables have softened.

Add in the chipotle chili pepper and garlic and continue to sauté for 1 minute or until aromatic.

Then, add in the vegetable broth, bay laurel, fennel seeds, mustard seeds, cumin seeds, salt and black pepper and bring to a boil. Immediately reduce the heat to a simmer and let it cook for 10 minutes.

Fold in the reserved beans and continue to simmer for about 10 minutes longer until everything is thoroughly heated.

Ladle into individual bowls and serve with salsa, cilantro and tortilla chips. Bon appétit!

# VEGETABLES & SIDE DISHES

# 123. Wine and Lemon Braised Artichokes

(Ready in about 35 minutes | Servings 4)

## Ingredients

1 large lemon, freshly squeezed
1 ½ pounds artichokes, trimmed, tough outer leaves and chokes removed
2 tablespoons mint leaves, finely chopped
2 tablespoons cilantro leaves, finely chopped

2 tablespoons basil leaves, finely chopped
2 cloves garlic, minced
1/4 cup dry white wine
1/4 cup extra-virgin olive oil, plus more for drizzling
Sea salt and freshly ground black pepper, to taste

## Directions

Fill a bowl with water and add in the lemon juice. Place the cleaned artichokes in the bowl, keeping them completely submerged.

In another small bowl, thoroughly combine the herbs and garlic. Rub your artichokes with the herb mixture.

Pour the wine and olive oil in a saucepan; add the artichokes to the saucepan. Turn the heat to a simmer and continue to cook, covered, for about 30 minutes until the artichokes are crisp-tender.

To serve, drizzle the artichokes with the cooking juices, season them with the salt and black pepper and enjoy!

**Per serving:** Calories: 228; Fat: 15.4g; Carbs: 19.3g; Protein: 7.2g

# 124. Roasted Carrots with Herbs

(Ready in about 25 minutes | Servings 4)

## Ingredients

2 pounds carrots, trimmed and halved lengthwise
4 tablespoons olive oil
1 teaspoon granulated garlic
1 teaspoon paprika
Sea salt and freshly ground black pepper

2 tablespoons fresh cilantro, chopped
2 tablespoons fresh parsley, chopped
2 tablespoons fresh chives, chopped

## Directions

Start by preheating your oven to 400 degrees F.

Toss the carrots with the olive oil, granulated garlic, paprika, salt and black pepper. Arrange them in a single layer on a parchment-lined roasting sheet.

Roast the carrots in the preheated oven for about 20 minutes, until fork-tender.

Toss the carrots with the fresh herbs and serve immediately. Bon appétit!

**Per serving:** Calories: 217; Fat: 14.4g; Carbs: 22.4g; Protein: 2.3g

# 125. Easy Braised Green Beans

(Ready in about 15 minutes | Servings 4)

**Per serving:** Calories: 207; Fat: 14.5g; Carbs: 16.5g; Protein: 5.3g

## Ingredients

4 tablespoons olive oil
1 carrot, cut into matchsticks
1 ½ pounds green beans, trimmed
4 garlic cloves, peeled

1 bay laurel
1 ½ cups vegetable broth
Sea salt and ground black pepper, to taste
1 lemon, cut into wedges

## Directions

Heat the olive oil in a saucepan over medium flame. Once hot, fry the carrots and green beans for about 5 minutes, stirring periodically to promote even cooking.

Add in the garlic and bay laurel and continue sautéing an additional 1 minute or until fragrant.

Add in the broth, salt and black pepper and continue to simmer, covered, for about 9 minutes or until the green beans are tender.

Taste, adjust the seasonings and serve with lemon wedges. Bon appétit!

# 126. Braised Kale with Sesame Seeds

(Ready in about 10 minutes | Servings 4)

## Ingredients

1 cup vegetable broth
1 pound kale, cleaned, tough stems removed, torn into pieces
4 tablespoons olive oil
6 garlic cloves, chopped

1 teaspoon paprika
Kosher salt and ground black pepper, to taste
4 tablespoons sesame seeds, lightly toasted

## Directions

In a saucepan, bring the vegetable broth to a boil; add in the kale leaves and turn the heat to a simmer. Cook for about 5 minutes until kale has softened; reserve.

Heat the oil in the same saucepan over medium heat. Once hot, sauté the garlic for about 30 seconds or until aromatic.

Add in the reserved kale, paprika, salt and black pepper and let it cook for a few minutes more or until heated through.

Garnish with lightly toasted sesame seeds and serve immediately. Bon appétit!

**Per serving:** Calories: 247; Fat: 19.9g; Carbs: 13.9g; Protein: 8.3g

## 127. Winter Roasted Vegetables

(Ready in about 45 minutes | Servings 4)

### Ingredients

1/2 pound carrots, slice into 1-inch chunks
1/2 pound parsnips, slice into 1-inch chunks
1/2 pound celery, slice into 1-inch chunks
1/2 pound sweet potatoes, slice into 1-inch chunks
1 large onion, slice into wedges
1/4 cup olive oil
1 teaspoon red pepper flakes
1 teaspoon dried basil
1 teaspoon dried oregano
1 teaspoon dried thyme
Sea salt and freshly ground black pepper

### Directions

Start by preheating your oven to 420 degrees F.

Toss the vegetables with the olive oil and spices. Arrange them on a parchment-lined roasting pan.

Roast for about 25 minutes. Stir the vegetables and continue to cook for 20 minutes more. Bon appétit!

**Per serving:** Calories: 255; Fat: 14g; Carbs: 31g; Protein: 3g

## 128. Traditional Moroccan Tagine

(Ready in about 30 minutes | Servings 4)

### Ingredients

3 tablespoons olive oil
1 large shallot, chopped
1 teaspoon ginger, peeled and minced
4 garlic cloves, chopped
2 medium carrots, trimmed and chopped
2 medium parsnips, trimmed and chopped
2 medium sweet potatoes, peeled and cubed
Sea salt and ground black pepper, to taste
1 teaspoon hot sauce
1 teaspoon fenugreek
1/2 teaspoon saffron
1/2 teaspoon caraway
2 large tomatoes, pureed
4 cups vegetable broth
1 lemon, cut into wedges

### Directions

In a Dutch Oven, heat the olive oil over medium heat. Once hot, sauté the shallots for 4 to 5 minutes, until tender.

Then, sauté the ginger and garlic for about 40 seconds or until aromatic.

Add in the remaining ingredients, except for the lemon and bring to a boil. Immediately turn the heat to a simmer.

Let it simmer for about 25 minutes or until the vegetables have softened. Serve with fresh lemon wedges and enjoy!

**Per serving:** Calories: 258; Fat: 12.2g; Carbs: 31g; Protein: 8.1g

## 129. Chinese Cabbage Stir-Fry

(Ready in about 10 minutes | Servings 3)

### Ingredients

3 tablespoons sesame oil
1 pound Chinese cabbage, sliced
1/2 teaspoon Chinese five-spice powder
Kosher salt, to taste
1/2 teaspoon Szechuan pepper
2 tablespoons soy sauce
3 tablespoons sesame seeds, lightly toasted

### Directions

In a wok, heat the sesame oil until sizzling. Stir fry the cabbage for about 5 minutes.

Stir in the spices and soy sauce and continue to cook, stirring frequently, for about 5 minutes more, until the cabbage is crisp-tender and aromatic.

Sprinkle sesame seeds over the top and serve immediately.

**Per serving:** Calories: 228; Fat: 20.7g; Carbs: 9.2g; Protein: 4.4g

## 130. Sautéed Cauliflower with Sesame Seeds

(Ready in about 15 minutes | Servings 4)

### Ingredients

1 cup vegetable broth
1 ½ pounds cauliflower florets
4 tablespoons olive oil
2 scallion stalks, chopped
4 garlic cloves, minced
Sea salt and freshly ground black pepper, to taste
2 tablespoons sesame seeds, lightly toasted

### Directions

In a large saucepan, bring the vegetable broth to a boil; then, add in the cauliflower and cook for about 6 minutes or until fork-tender; reserve.

Then, heat the olive oil until sizzling; now, sauté the scallions and garlic for about 1 minute or until tender and aromatic.

Add in the reserved cauliflower, followed by salt and black pepper; continue to simmer for about 5 minutes or until heated through

Garnish with toasted sesame seeds and serve immediately. Bon appétit!

**Per serving:** Calories: 217; Fat: 17g; Carbs: 13.2g; Protein: 7.1g

## 131. Sweet Mashed Carrots

(Ready in about 25 minutes | Servings 4)

### Ingredients

1 ½ pounds carrots, trimmed
3 tablespoons vegan butter
1 cup scallions, sliced
1 tablespoon maple syrup
1/2 teaspoon garlic powder
1/2 teaspoon ground allspice
Sea salt, to taste
1/2 cup soy sauce
2 tablespoons fresh cilantro, chopped

### Directions

Steam the carrots for about 15 minutes until they are very tender; drain well.

In a sauté pan, melt the butter until sizzling. Now, turn the heat down to maintain an insistent sizzle.

Now, cook the scallions until they've softened. Add in the maple syrup, garlic powder, ground allspice, salt and soy sauce for about 10 minutes or until they are caramelized.

Add the caramelized scallions to your food processor; add in the carrots and puree the ingredients until everything is well blended.

Serve garnished with the fresh cilantro. Enjoy!

**Per serving:** Calories: 270; Fat: 14.8g; Carbs: 29.2g; Protein: 4.5g

## 132. Sautéed Turnip Greens

(Ready in about 15 minutes | Servings 4)

### Ingredients

2 tablespoons olive oil
1 onion, sliced
2 garlic cloves, sliced
1 ½ pounds turnip greens
cleaned and chopped
1/4 cup vegetable broth

1/4 cup dry white wine
1/2 teaspoon dried oregano
1 teaspoon dried parsley flakes
Kosher salt and ground black
pepper, to taste

### Directions

In a sauté pan, heat the olive oil over a moderately high heat.

Now, sauté the onion for 3 to 4 minutes or until tender and translucent. Add in the garlic and continue to cook for 30 seconds more or until aromatic.

Stir in the turnip greens, broth, wine, oregano and parsley; continue sautéing an additional 6 minutes or until they have wilted completely.

Season with salt and black pepper to taste and serve warm. Bon appétit!

**Per serving:** Calories: 140; Fat: 8.8g; Carbs: 13g; Protein: 4.4g

## 133. Yukon Gold Mashed Potatoes

(Ready in about 25 minutes | Servings 5)

### Ingredients

2 pounds Yukon Gold potatoes,
peeled and diced
1 clove garlic, pressed
Sea salt and red pepper flakes,
to taste

3 tablespoons vegan butter
1/2 cup soy milk
2 tablespoons scallions, sliced

### Directions

Cover the potatoes with an inch or two of cold water. Cook the potatoes in gently boiling water for about 20 minutes.

Then, puree the potatoes, along with the garlic, salt, red pepper, butter and milk, to your desired consistency.

Serve garnished with fresh scallions. Bon appétit!

**Per serving:** Calories: 221; Fat: 7.9g; Carbs: 34.1g; Protein: 4.7g

## 134. Aromatic Sautéed Swiss Chard

(Ready in about 15 minutes | Servings 4)

### Ingredients

2 tablespoons vegan butter
1 onion, chopped
2 cloves garlic, sliced
Sea salt and ground black
pepper, to season
1 ½ pounds Swiss chard,
torn into pieces, tough stalks
removed

1 cup vegetable broth
1 bay leaf
1 thyme sprig
2 rosemary sprigs
1/2 teaspoon mustard seeds
1 teaspoon celery seeds

### Directions

In a saucepan, melt the vegan butter over medium-high heat.

Then, sauté the onion for about 3 minutes or until tender and translucent; sauté the garlic for about 1 minute until aromatic.

Add in the remaining ingredients and turn the heat to a simmer; let it simmer, covered, for about 10 minutes or until everything is cooked through. Bon appétit!

**Per serving:** Calories: 124; Fat: 6.7g; Carbs: 11.1g; Protein: 5g

## 135. Classic Sautéed Bell Peppers

(Ready in about 15 minutes | Servings 2)

### Ingredients

3 tablespoons olive oil
4 bell peppers, seeded and
slice into strips
2 cloves garlic, minced
Salt and freshly ground black
pepper, to taste

1 teaspoon cayenne pepper
4 tablespoons dry white wine
2 tablespoons fresh cilantro,
roughly chopped

### Directions

In a saucepan, heat the oil over medium-high heat.

Once hot, sauté the peppers for about 4 minutes or until tender and fragrant. Then, sauté the garlic for about 1 minute until aromatic.

Add in the salt, black pepper and cayenne pepper; continue to sauté, adding the wine, for about 6 minutes more until tender and cooked through.

Taste and adjust the seasonings. Top with fresh cilantro and serve. Bon appétit!

**Per serving:** Calories: 154; Fat: 13.7g; Carbs: 2.9g; Protein: 0.5g

## 136. Mashed Root Vegetables

(Ready in about 25 minutes | Servings 5)

### Ingredients

1 pound russet potatoes,
peeled and cut into chunks
1/2 pound parsnips, trimmed
and diced
1/2 pound carrots, trimmed
and diced

4 tablespoons vegan butter
1 teaspoon dried oregano
1/2 teaspoon dried dill weed
1/2 teaspoon dried marjoram
1 teaspoon dried basil

### Directions

Cover the vegetables with the water by 1 inch. Bring to a boil and cook for about 25 minutes until they've softened; drain.

Mash the vegetables with the remaining ingredients, adding cooking liquid, as needed.

Serve warm and enjoy!

**Per serving:** Calories: 207; Fat: 9.5g; Carbs: 29.1g; Protein: 3g

## 137. Roasted Butternut Squash

(Ready in about 25 minutes | Servings 4)

### Ingredients

4 tablespoons olive oil
1/2 teaspoon ground cumin
1/2 teaspoon ground allspice
1 ½ pounds butternut squash, peeled, seeded and diced
1/4 cup dry white wine

2 tablespoons dark soy sauce
1 teaspoon mustard seeds
1 teaspoon paprika
Sea salt and ground black pepper, to taste

### Directions

Start by preheating your oven to 420 degrees F. Toss the squash with the remaining ingredients.

Roast the butternut squash for about 25 minutes or until tender and caramelized.

Serve warm and enjoy!

**Per serving:** Calories: 247; Fat: 16.5g; Carbs: 23.8g; Protein: 4.3g

## 138. Sautéed Cremini Mushrooms

(Ready in about 10 minutes | Servings 4)

### Ingredients

4 tablespoons olive oil
4 tablespoons shallots, chopped
2 cloves garlic, minced

1 ½ pounds Cremini mushrooms, sliced
1/4 cup dry white wine
Sea salt and ground black pepper, to taste

### Directions

In a sauté pan, heat the olive oil over a moderately high heat.

Now, sauté the shallot for 3 to 4 minutes or until tender and translucent. Add in the garlic and continue to cook for 30 seconds more or until aromatic.

Stir in the Cremini mushrooms, wine, salt and black pepper; continue sautéing an additional 6 minutes, until your mushrooms are lightly browned.

Bon appétit!

**Per serving:** Calories: 197; Fat: 15.5g; Carbs: 8.8g; Protein: 7.3g

## 139. Roasted Asparagus with Sesame Seeds

(Ready in about 25 minutes | Servings 4)

### Ingredients

1 ½ pounds asparagus, trimmed
4 tablespoons extra-virgin olive oil
Sea salt and ground black pepper, to taste
1/2 teaspoon dried oregano

1/2 teaspoon dried basil
1 teaspoon red pepper flakes, crushed
4 tablespoons sesame seeds
2 tablespoons fresh chives, roughly chopped

### Directions

Start by preheating the oven to 400 degrees F. Then, line a baking sheet with parchment paper.

Toss the asparagus with the olive oil, salt, black pepper, oregano, basil and red pepper flakes. Now, arrange your asparagus in a single layer on the prepared baking sheet.

Roast your asparagus for approximately 20 minutes.

Sprinkle sesame seeds over your asparagus and continue to bake an additional 5 minutes or until the asparagus spears are crisp-tender and the sesame seeds are lightly toasted.

Garnish with fresh chives and serve warm. Bon appétit!

**Per serving:** Calories: 215; Fat: 19.1g; Carbs: 8.8g; Protein: 5.6g

## 140. Greek-Style Eggplant Skillet

(Ready in about 15 minutes | Servings 4)

### Ingredients

4 tablespoons olive oil
1 ½ pounds eggplant, peeled and sliced
1 teaspoon garlic, minced
1 tomato, crushed
Sea salt and ground black pepper, to taste

1 teaspoon cayenne pepper
1/2 teaspoon dried oregano
1/4 teaspoon ground bay leaf
2 ounces Kalamata olives, pitted and sliced

### Directions

Heat the oil in a sauté pan over medium-high flame.

Then, sauté the eggplant for about 9 minutes or until just tender.

Add in the remaining ingredients, cover and continue to cook for 2 to 3 minutes more or until thoroughly cooked. Serve warm.

**Per serving:** Calories: 195; Fat: 16.1g; Carbs: 13.4g; Protein: 2.4g

## 141. Keto Cauliflower Rice

(Ready in about 10 minutes | Servings 5)

### Ingredients

2 medium heads cauliflower, stems and leaves removed
4 tablespoons extra-virgin olive oil
4 garlic cloves, pressed

1/2 teaspoon red pepper flakes, crushed
Sea salt and ground black pepper, to taste
1/4 cup flat-leaf parsley, roughly chopped

### Directions

Pulse the cauliflower in a food processor with the S-blade until they're broken into "rice".

Heat the olive oil in a saucepan over medium-high heat. Once hot, cook the garlic until fragrant or about 1 minute.

Add in the cauliflower rice, red pepper, salt and black pepper and continue sautéing for a further 7 to 8 minutes.

Taste, adjust the seasonings and garnish with fresh parsley. Bon appétit!

**Per serving:** Calories: 135; Fat: 11.5g; Carbs: 7.2g; Protein: 2.4g

## 142. Easy Garlicky Kale

(Ready in about 10 minutes | Servings 4)

### Ingredients

4 tablespoons olive oil
4 cloves garlic, chopped
1 ½ pounds fresh kale, tough stems and ribs removed, torn into pieces
1 cup vegetable broth
1/2 teaspoon cumin seeds
1/2 teaspoon dried oregano
1/2 teaspoon paprika
1 teaspoon onion powder
Sea salt and ground black pepper, to taste

### Directions

In a saucepan, heat the olive oil over a moderately high heat. Now, sauté the garlic for about 1 minute or until aromatic.

Add in the kale in batches, gradually adding the vegetable broth; stir to promote even cooking.

Turn the heat to a simmer, add in the spices and let it cook for 5 to 6 minutes, until the kale leaves wilt.

Serve warm and enjoy!

**Per serving:** Calories: 217; Fat: 15.4g; Carbs: 16.1g; Protein: 8.6g

## 143. Artichokes Braised in Lemon and Olive Oil

(Ready in about 35 minutes | Servings 4)

### Ingredients

1 ½ cups water
2 lemons, freshly squeezed
2 pounds artichokes, trimmed, tough outer leaves and chokes removed
1 handful fresh Italian parsley
2 thyme sprigs
2 rosemary sprigs
2 bay leaves
2 garlic cloves, chopped
1/3 cup olive oil
Sea salt and ground black pepper, to taste
1/2 teaspoon red pepper flakes

### Directions

Fill a bowl with water and add in the lemon juice. Place the cleaned artichokes in the bowl, keeping them completely submerged.

In another small bowl, thoroughly combine the herbs and garlic. Rub your artichokes with the herb mixture.

Pour the lemon water and olive oil in a saucepan; add the artichokes to the saucepan. Turn the heat to a simmer and continue to cook, covered, for about 30 minutes until the artichokes are crisp-tender.

To serve, drizzle the artichokes with cooking juices, season them with the salt, black pepper and red pepper flakes. Bon appétit!

**Per serving:** Calories: 278; Fat: 18.2g; Carbs: 27g; Protein: 7.8g

## 144. Rosemary and Garlic Roasted Carrots

(Ready in about 25 minutes | Servings 4)

### Ingredients

2 pounds carrots, trimmed and halved lengthwise
4 tablespoons olive oil
2 tablespoons champagne vinegar
4 cloves garlic, minced
2 sprigs rosemary, chopped
Sea salt and ground black pepper, to taste
4 tablespoons pine nuts, chopped

### Directions

Begin by preheating your oven to 400 degrees F.

Toss the carrots with the olive oil, vinegar, garlic, rosemary, salt and black pepper. Arrange them in a single layer on a parchment-lined roasting sheet.

Roast the carrots in the preheated oven for about 20 minutes, until fork-tender.

Garnish the carrots with the pine nuts and serve immediately. Bon appétit!

**Per serving:** Calories: 228; Fat: 14.2g; Carbs: 23.8g; Protein: 2.8g

## 145. Mediterranean-Style Green Beans

(Ready in about 20 minutes | Servings 4)

### Ingredients

2 tablespoons olive oil
1 red bell pepper, seeded and diced
1 ½ pounds green beans
4 garlic cloves, minced
1/2 teaspoon mustard seeds
1/2 teaspoon fennel seeds
1 teaspoon dried dill weed
2 tomatoes, pureed
1 cup cream of celery soup
1 teaspoon Italian herb mix
1 teaspoon cayenne pepper
Salt and freshly ground black pepper

### Directions

Heat the olive oil in a saucepan over medium flame. Once hot, fry the peppers and green beans for about 5 minutes, stirring periodically to promote even cooking.

Add in the garlic, mustard seeds, fennel seeds and dill and continue sautéing an additional 1 minute or until fragrant.

Add in the pureed tomatoes, cream of celery soup, Italian herb mix, cayenne pepper, salt and black pepper. Continue to simmer, covered, for about 9 minutes or until the green beans are tender.

Taste, adjust the seasonings and serve warm. Bon appétit!

**Per serving:** Calories: 159; Fat: 8.8g; Carbs: 18.8g; Protein: 4.8g

## 146. Roasted Garden Vegetables

(Ready in about 45 minutes | Servings 4)

### Ingredients

1 pound butternut squash, peeled and cut into 1-inch pieces
4 sweet potatoes, peeled and cut into 1-inch pieces
1/2 cup carrots, peeled and cut into 1-inch pieces
2 medium onions, cut into wedges
4 tablespoons olive oil
1 teaspoon granulated garlic
1 teaspoon paprika
1 teaspoon dried rosemary
1 teaspoon mustard seeds
Kosher salt and freshly ground black pepper, to taste

### Directions

Start by preheating your oven to 420 degrees F.

Toss the vegetables with the olive oil and spices. Arrange them on a parchment-lined roasting pan.

Roast for about 25 minutes. Stir the vegetables and continue to cook for 20 minutes more. Bon appétit!

**Per serving:** Calories: 311; Fat: 14.1g; Carbs: 45.2g; Protein: 3.9g

## 147. Easy Roasted Kohlrabi

(Ready in about 30 minutes | Servings 4)

### Ingredients

1 pound kohlrabi bulbs, peeled and sliced
4 tablespoons olive oil
1/2 teaspoon mustard seeds
1 teaspoon celery seeds
1 teaspoon dried marjoram

1 teaspoon granulated garlic, minced
Sea salt and ground black pepper, to taste
2 tablespoons nutritional yeast

### Directions

Start by preheating your oven to 450 degrees F.

Toss the kohlrabi with the olive oil and spices until well coated. Arrange the kohlrabi in a single layer on a parchment-lined roasting pan.

Bake the kohlrabi in the preheated oven for about 15 minutes; stir them and continue to cook an additional 15 minutes.

Sprinkle nutritional yeast over the warm kohlrabi and serve immediately. Bon appétit!

**Per serving:** Calories: 177; Fat: 14g; Carbs: 10.5g; Protein: 4.5g

## 148. Cauliflower with Tahini Sauce

(Ready in about 10 minutes | Servings 4)

### Ingredients

1 cup water
2 pounds cauliflower florets
Sea salt and ground black pepper, to taste

3 tablespoons soy sauce
5 tablespoons tahini
2 cloves garlic, minced
2 tablespoons lemon juice

### Directions

In a large saucepan, bring the water to a boil; then, add in the cauliflower and cook for about 6 minutes or until fork-tender; drain, season with salt and pepper and reserve.

In a mixing bowl, thoroughly combine the soy sauce, tahini, garlic and lemon juice. Spoon the sauce over the cauliflower florets and serve.

Bon appétit!

**Per serving:** Calories: 217; Fat: 13g; Carbs: 20.3g; Protein: 8.7g

## 149. Herb Cauliflower Mash

(Ready in about 25 minutes | Servings 4)

### Ingredients

1 ½ pounds cauliflower florets
4 tablespoons vegan butter
4 cloves garlic, sliced
Sea salt and ground black pepper, to taste

1/4 cup plain oat milk, unsweetened
2 tablespoons fresh parsley, roughly chopped

### Directions

Steam the cauliflower florets for about 20 minutes; set it aside to cool.

In a saucepan, melt the vegan butter over a moderately high heat; now, sauté the garlic for about 1 minute or until aromatic.

Add the cauliflower florets to your food processor followed by the sautéed garlic, salt, black pepper and oat milk. Puree until everything is well incorporated.

Garnish with fresh parsley leaves and serve hot. Bon appétit!

**Per serving:** Calories: 167; Fat: 13g; Carbs: 11.3g; Protein: 4.4g

## 150. Garlic and Herb Mushroom Skillet

(Ready in about 10 minutes | Servings 4)

### Ingredients

4 tablespoons vegan butter
1 ½ pounds oyster mushrooms halved
3 cloves garlic, minced
1 teaspoon dried oregano
1 teaspoon dried rosemary

1 teaspoon dried parsley flakes
1 teaspoon dried marjoram
1/2 cup dry white wine
Kosher salt and ground black pepper, to taste

### Directions

In a sauté pan, heat the olive oil over a moderately high heat.

Now, sauté the mushrooms for 3 minutes or until they release the liquid. Add in the garlic and continue to cook for 30 seconds more or until aromatic.

Stir in the spices and continue sautéing an additional 6 minutes, until your mushrooms are lightly browned.

Bon appétit!

**Per serving:** Calories: 207; Fat: 15.2g; Carbs: 12.7g; Protein: 9.1g

## 151. Pan-Fried Asparagus

(Ready in about 10 minutes | Servings 4)

### Ingredients

4 tablespoons vegan butter
1 ½ pounds asparagus spears, trimmed
1/2 teaspoon cumin seeds, ground

1/4 teaspoon bay leaf, ground
Sea salt and ground black pepper, to taste
1 teaspoon fresh lime juice

### Directions

Melt the vegan butter in a saucepan over medium-high heat.

Sauté the asparagus for about 3 to 4 minutes, stirring periodically to promote even cooking.

Add in the cumin seeds, bay leaf, salt and black pepper and continue to cook the asparagus for 2 minutes more until crisp-tender.

Drizzle lime juice over the asparagus and serve warm. Bon appétit!

**Per serving:** Calories: 142; Fat: 11.8g; Carbs: 7.7g; Protein: 5.1g

# 152. Gingery Carrot Mash

(Ready in about 25 minutes | Servings 4)

## Ingredients

2 pounds carrots, cut into rounds
2 tablespoons olive oil
1 teaspoon ground cumin
Salt ground black pepper, to taste
1/2 teaspoon cayenne pepper
1/2 teaspoon ginger, peeled and minced
1/2 cup whole milk

## Directions

Begin by preheating your oven to 400 degrees F.

Toss the carrots with the olive oil, cumin, salt, black pepper and cayenne pepper. Arrange them in a single layer on a parchment-lined roasting sheet.

Roast the carrots in the preheated oven for about 20 minutes, until crisp-tender.

Add the roasted carrots, ginger and milk to your food processor; puree the ingredients until everything is well blended. Bon appétit!

**Per serving:** Calories: 187; Fat: 8.4g; Carbs: 27.1g; Protein: 3.4g

# 153. Mediterranean-Style Roasted Artichokes

(Ready in about 50 minutes | Servings 4)

## Ingredients

4 artichokes, trimmed, tough outer leaves and chokes removed, halved
2 lemons, freshly squeezed
4 tablespoons extra-virgin olive oil
4 cloves garlic, chopped
1 teaspoon fresh rosemary
1 teaspoon fresh basil
1 teaspoon fresh parsley
1 teaspoon fresh oregano
Flaky sea salt and ground black pepper, to taste
1 teaspoon red pepper flakes
1 teaspoon paprika

## Directions

Start by preheating your oven to 395 degrees F. Rub the lemon juice all over the entire surface of your artichokes.

In a small mixing bowl, thoroughly combine the garlic with herbs and spices

Place the artichoke halves in a parchment-lined baking dish, cut-side-up. Brush the artichokes evenly with the olive oil. Fill the cavities with the garlic/herb mixture.

Bake for about 20 minutes. Now, cover them with aluminum foil and bake for a further 30 minutes. Serve warm and enjoy!

**Per serving:** Calories: 218; Fat: 13g; Carbs: 21.4g; Protein: 5.8g

# 154. Thai-Style Braised Kale

(Ready in about 10 minutes | Servings 4)

## Ingredients

1 cup water
1 ½ pounds kale, tough stems and ribs removed, torn into pieces
2 tablespoons sesame oil
1 teaspoon fresh garlic, pressed
1 teaspoon ginger, peeled and minced
1 Thai chili, chopped
1/2 teaspoon turmeric powder
1/2 cup coconut milk
Kosher salt and ground black pepper, to taste

## Directions

In a large saucepan, bring the water to a rapid boil. Add in the kale and let it cook until bright, about 3 minutes. Drain, rinse and squeeze dry.

Wipe the saucepan with paper towels and preheat the sesame oil over a moderate heat. Once hot, cook the garlic, ginger and chili for approximately 1 minute or so, until fragrant.

Add in the kale and turmeric powder and continue to cook for a further 1 minute or until heated through.

Gradually pour in the coconut milk, salt and black pepper; continue to simmer until the liquid has thickened. Taste, adjust the seasonings and serve hot. Bon appétit!

**Per serving:** Calories: 165; Fat: 9.3g; Carbs: 16.5g; Protein: 8.3g

# 155. Silky Kohlrabi Puree

(Ready in about 30 minutes | Servings 4)

## Ingredients

1 ½ pounds kohlrabi, peeled and cut into pieces
4 tablespoons vegan butter
Sea salt and freshly ground black pepper, to taste
1/2 teaspoon cumin seeds
1/2 teaspoon coriander seeds
1/2 cup soy milk
1 teaspoon fresh dill
1 teaspoon fresh parsley

## Directions

Cook the kohlrabi in boiling salted water until soft, about 30 minutes; drain.

Puree the kohlrabi with the vegan butter, salt, black pepper, cumin seeds and coriander seeds.

Puree the ingredients with an immersion blender, gradually adding the milk. Top with fresh dill and parsley. Bon appétit!

**Per serving:** Calories: 175; Fat: 12.8g; Carbs: 12.5g; Protein: 4.1g

# 156. Creamed Sautéed Spinach

(Ready in about 15 minutes | Servings 4)

## Ingredients

2 tablespoons vegan butter
1 onion, chopped
1 teaspoon garlic, minced
1 ½ cups vegetable broth
2 pounds spinach, torn into pieces
Sea salt and ground black pepper, to taste
1/4 teaspoon dried dill
1/4 teaspoon mustard seeds
1/2 teaspoon celery seeds
1 teaspoon cayenne pepper
1/2 cup oat milk

## Directions

In a saucepan, melt the vegan butter over medium-high heat.

Then, sauté the onion for about 3 minutes or until tender and translucent. Then, sauté the garlic for about 1 minute until aromatic.

Add in the broth and spinach and bring to a boil.

Turn the heat to a simmer. Add in the spices and continue to cook for 5 minutes longer.

Add in the milk and continue to cook for 5 minutes more. Bon appétit!

**Per serving:** Calories: 146; Fat: 7.8g; Carbs: 15.1g; Protein: 8.3g

## 157. Aromatic Sautéed Kohlrabi

(Ready in about 10 minutes | Servings 4)

### Ingredients

3 tablespoons sesame oil
1 ½ pounds kohlrabi, peeled and cubed
1 teaspoon garlic, minced

1/2 teaspoon dried basil
1/2 teaspoon dried oregano
Sea salt and ground black pepper, to taste

### Directions

In a nonstick skillet, heat the sesame oil. Once hot, sauté the kohlrabi for about 6 minutes.

Add in the garlic, basil, oregano, salt and black pepper. Continue to cook for 1 to 2 minutes more.

Serve warm. Bon appétit!

**Per serving:** Calories: 137; Fat: 10.3g; Carbs: 10.7g; Protein: 2.9g

## 158. Classic Braised Cabbage

(Ready in about 20 minutes | Servings 4)

### Ingredients

4 tablespoons sesame oil
1 shallot, chopped
2 garlic cloves, minced
2 bay leaves
1 cup vegetable broth

1 ½ pounds purple cabbage, cut into wedges
1 teaspoon red pepper flakes
Sea salt and black pepper, to taste

### Directions

Heat the sesame oil in a saucepan over medium flame. Once hot, fry the shallot for 3 to 4 minutes, stirring periodically to promote even cooking.

Add in the garlic and bay laurel and continue sautéing an additional 1 minute or until fragrant.

Add in the broth, cabbage red pepper flakes, salt and black pepper and continue to simmer, covered, for about 12 minutes or until the cabbage has softened.

Taste, adjust the seasonings and serve hot. Bon appétit!

**Per serving:** Calories: 197; Fat: 14.3g; Carbs: 14.8g; Protein: 4g

## 159. Sautéed Carrots with Sesame Seeds

(Ready in about 10 minutes | Servings 4)

### Ingredients

1/3 cup vegetable broth
2 pounds carrots, trimmed and cut into sticks
4 tablespoons sesame oil
1 teaspoon garlic, chopped

Himalayan salt and freshly ground black pepper, to taste
1 teaspoon cayenne pepper
2 tablespoons fresh parsley, chopped
2 tablespoons sesame seeds

### Directions

In a large saucepan, bring the vegetable broth to a boil. Turn the heat to medium-low. Add in the carrots and continue to cook, covered, for about 8 minutes, until the carrots are crisp-tender.

Heat the sesame oil over medium-high heat; now, sauté the garlic for 30 seconds or until aromatic. Add in the salt, black pepper and cayenne pepper.

In a small skillet, toast the sesame seeds for 1 minute or until just fragrant and golden.

To serve, garnish the sautéed carrots with parsley and toasted sesame seeds. Bon appétit!

**Per serving:** Calories: 244; Fat: 16.8g; Carbs: 22.7g; Protein: 3.4g

## 160. Roasted Carrots with Tahini Sauce

(Ready in about 25 minutes | Servings 4)

### Ingredients

2 ½ pounds carrots washed, trimmed and halved lengthwise
4 tablespoons olive oil
Sea salt and ground black pepper, to taste
Sauce:
4 tablespoons tahini

1 teaspoon garlic, pressed
2 tablespoons white vinegar
2 tablespoons soy sauce
1 teaspoon deli mustard
1 teaspoon agave syrup
1/2 teaspoon cumin seed
1/2 teaspoon dried dill weed

### Directions

Begin by preheating your oven to 400 degrees F.

Toss the carrots with the olive oil, salt and black pepper. Arrange them in a single layer on a parchment-lined roasting sheet.

Roast the carrots in the preheated oven for about 20 minutes, until crisp-tender.

Meanwhile, whisk all the sauce ingredients until well combined.

Serve the carrots with the sauce for dipping. Bon appétit!

**Per serving:** Calories: 365; Fat: 23.8g; Carbs: 35.3g; Protein: 6.1g

## 161. Roasted Cauliflower with Herbs

(Ready in about 30 minutes | Servings 4)

### Ingredients

1 ½ pounds cauliflower florets
1/4 cup olive oil
4 cloves garlic, whole
1 tablespoon fresh basil
1 tablespoon fresh coriander
1 tablespoon fresh oregano

1 tablespoon fresh rosemary
1 tablespoon fresh parsley
Sea salt and ground black pepper, to taste
1 teaspoon red pepper flakes

### Directions

Begin by preheating the oven to 425 degrees F. Toss the cauliflower with the olive oil and arrange them on a parchment-lined roasting pan.

Then, roast the cauliflower florets for about 20 minutes; toss them with the garlic and spices and continue cooking an additional 10 minutes.

Serve warm. Bon appétit!

**Per serving:** Calories: 175; Fat: 14g; Carbs: 10.7g; Protein: 3.7g

## 162. Creamy Rosemary Broccoli Mash

(Ready in about 15 minutes | Servings 4)

### Ingredients

1 ½ pounds broccoli florets
3 tablespoons vegan butter
4 cloves garlic, chopped
2 sprigs fresh rosemary, leaves picked and chopped
Sea salt and red pepper, to taste
1/4 cup soy milk, unsweetened

### Directions

Steam the broccoli florets for about 10 minutes; set it aside to cool.

In a saucepan, melt the vegan butter over a moderately high heat; now, sauté the garlic and rosemary for about 1 minute or until they are fragrant.

Add the broccoli florets to your food processor followed by the sautéed garlic/rosemary mixture, salt, pepper and milk. Puree until everything is well incorporated.

Garnish with some extra fresh herbs, if desired and serve hot. Bon appétit!

Per serving: Calories: 155; Fat: 9.8g; Carbs: 14.1g; Protein: 5.7g

## 163. Easy Swiss Chard Skillet

(Ready in about 15 minutes | Servings 4)

### Ingredients

3 tablespoons olive oil
1 shallot, thinly sliced
1 red bell pepper, seeded and diced
4 garlic cloves, chopped
1 cup vegetable broth
2 pounds Swiss chard, tough stalks removed, torn into pieces
Sea salt and ground black pepper, to taste

### Directions

In a saucepan, heat the olive oil over medium-high heat.

Then, sauté the shallot and pepper for about 3 minutes or until tender. Then, sauté the garlic for about 1 minute until aromatic.

Add in the broth and Swiss chard and bring to a boil. Turn the heat to a simmer and continue to cook for 10 minutes longer.

Season with salt and black pepper to taste and serve warm. Bon appétit!

Per serving: Calories: 169; Fat: 11.1g; Carbs: 14.9g; Protein: 6.3g

## 164. Wine-Braised Kale

(Ready in about 10 minutes | Servings 4)

### Ingredients

1/2 cup water
1 ½ pounds kale
3 tablespoons olive oil
4 tablespoons scallions, chopped
4 cloves garlic, minced
1/2 cup dry white wine
1/2 teaspoon mustard seeds
Kosher salt and ground black pepper, to taste

### Directions

In a large saucepan, bring the water to a boil. Add in the kale and let it cook until bright, about 3 minutes. Drain and squeeze dry.

Wipe the saucepan with paper towels and preheat the olive oil over a moderate heat. Once hot, cook the scallions and garlic for approximately 2 minutes, until they are fragrant.

Add in the wine, flowed by the kale, mustard seeds, salt, black pepper; continue to cook, covered, for a further 5 minutes or until heated through.

Ladle into individual bowls and serve hot. Bon appétit!

Per serving: Calories: 205; Fat: 11.8g; Carbs: 17.3g; Protein: 7.6g

## 165. French Haricots Verts

(Ready in about 10 minutes | Servings 4)

### Ingredients

1 ½ cups vegetable broth
1 Roma tomato, pureed
1 ½ pounds Haricots Verts, trimmed
4 tablespoons olive oil
2 garlic cloves, minced
1/2 teaspoon red pepper
1/2 teaspoon cumin seeds
1/2 teaspoon dried oregano
Sea salt and freshly ground black pepper, to taste
1 tablespoon fresh lemon juice

### Directions

Bring the vegetable broth and pureed tomato to a boil. Add in the Haricots Verts and let it cook for about 5 minutes until Haricots Verts are crisp-tender; reserve.

In a saucepan, heat the olive oil over medium-high heat; sauté the garlic for 1 minute or until aromatic.

Add in the spices and reserved green beans; let it cook for about 3 minutes until cooked through.

Serve with a few drizzles of the fresh lemon juice. Bon appétit!

Per serving: Calories: 197; Fat: 14.5g; Carbs: 14.4g; Protein: 5.4g

## 166. Buttery Turnip Mash

(Ready in about 35 minutes | Servings 4)

### Ingredients

2 cups water
1 ½ pounds turnips, peeled and cut into small pieces
4 tablespoons vegan butter
1 cup oat milk
2 fresh rosemary sprigs, chopped
1 tablespoon fresh parsley, chopped
1 teaspoon ginger-garlic paste
Kosher salt and freshly ground black pepper
1 teaspoon red pepper flakes, crushed

### Directions

Bring the water to a boil; turn the heat to a simmer and cook your turnip for about 30 minutes; drain.

Using an immersion blender, puree the turnips with the vegan butter, milk, rosemary, parsley, ginger-garlic paste, salt, black pepper, red pepper flakes, adding the cooking liquid, if necessary.

Bon appétit!

Per serving: Calories: 187; Fat: 13.6g; Carbs: 14g; Protein: 3.6g

# 167. Sautéed Zucchini with Herbs

*(Ready in about 10 minutes | Servings 4)*

## Ingredients

2 tablespoons olive oil
1 onion, sliced
2 garlic cloves, minced
1 ½ pounds zucchini, sliced
Sea salt and fresh ground black pepper, to taste
1 teaspoon cayenne pepper
1/2 teaspoon dried basil
1/2 teaspoon dried oregano
1/2 teaspoon dried rosemary

## Directions

In a saucepan, heat the olive oil over medium-high heat.

Once hot, sauté the onion for about 3 minutes or until tender. Then, sauté the garlic for about 1 minute until aromatic.

Add in the zucchini, along with the spices and continue to sauté for 6 minutes more until tender.

Taste and adjust the seasonings. Bon appétit!

**Per serving:** Calories: 99; Fat: 7.4g; Carbs: 6g; Protein: 4.3g

# 168. Mashed Sweet Potatoes

*(Ready in about 20 minutes | Servings 4)*

## Ingredients

1 ½ pounds sweet potatoes, peeled and diced
2 tablespoons vegan butter, melted
1/2 cup agave syrup
1 teaspoon pumpkin pie spice
A pinch of sea salt
1/2 cup coconut milk

## Directions

Cover the sweet potatoes with an inch or two of cold water. Cook the sweet potatoes in gently boiling water for about 20 minutes; drain well.

Add the sweet potatoes to the bowl of your food processor; add in the vegan butter, agave syrup, pumpkin pie spice and salt.

Continue to puree, gradually adding the milk until everything is well incorporated. Bon appétit!

**Per serving:** Calories: 338; Fat: 6.9g; Carbs: 68g; Protein: 3.7g

# 169. Sherry Roasted King Trumpet

*(Ready in about 20 minutes | Servings 4)*

## Ingredients

1 ½ pounds king trumpet mushrooms, cleaned and sliced in half lengthwise.
2 tablespoons olive oil
4 cloves garlic, minced or chopped
1/2 teaspoon dried rosemary
1/2 teaspoon dried thyme
1/2 teaspoon dried parsley flakes
1 teaspoon Dijon mustard
1/4 cup dry sherry
Sea salt and freshly ground black pepper, to taste

## Directions

Start by preheating your oven to 390 degrees F. Line a large baking pan with parchment paper.

In a mixing bowl, toss the mushrooms with the remaining ingredients until well coated on all sides.

Place the mushrooms in a single layer on the prepared baking pan.

Roast the mushrooms for approximately 20 minutes, tossing them halfway through the cooking. Bon appétit!

**Per serving:** Calories: 138; Fat: 7.8g; Carbs: 11.8g; Protein: 5.7g

# 170. Beetroot and Potato Puree

*(Ready in about 35 minutes | Servings 5)*

## Ingredients

1 ½ pounds potatoes, peeled and diced
1 pound beetroot, peeled and diced
2 tablespoons vegan butter
1/2 teaspoon deli mustard
1/2 cup soy milk
1/2 teaspoon ground cumin
1 teaspoon paprika
Sea salt and ground black pepper, to taste

## Directions

Cook the potatoes and beetroot in boiling salted water until they've softened, about 30 minutes; drain.

Puree the vegetables with the vegan butter, mustard, milk, cumin, paprika, salt and black pepper to your desired consistency.

Bon appétit!

**Per serving:** Calories: 177; Fat: 5.6g; Carbs: 28.2g; Protein: 4g

# 171. Thai Stir-Fried Spinach

*(Ready in about 15 minutes | Servings 4)*

## Ingredients

2 tablespoons sesame oil
1 onion, chopped
1 carrot, trimmed and chopped
1 Bird's eye chili pepper, minced
2 cloves garlic, minced
1 ½ pounds spinach leaves, torn into pieces
1/3 cup vegetable broth
2/3 cup coconut milk, unsweetened

## Directions

In a saucepan, heat the sesame oil over medium-high heat.

Then, sauté the onion and carrot for about 3 minutes or until tender. Then, sauté the garlic and Bird's eye chili for about 1 minute until aromatic.

Add in the broth and spinach and bring to a boil.

Turn the heat to a simmer and continue to cook for 5 minutes longer.

Add in the coconut milk and simmer for a further 5 minutes or until everything is cooked through. Bon appétit!

**Per serving:** Calories: 147; Fat: 8.9g; Carbs: 12.7g; Protein: 7.1g

# 172. Roasted Squash Mash

*(Ready in about 35 minutes | Servings 5)*

## Ingredients

2 tablespoons olive oil
2 pounds butternut squash
1/2 teaspoon garlic powder
Sea salt and ground black pepper, to taste
1/2 teaspoon mustard seeds
1/2 teaspoon celery seeds
A pinch of grated nutmeg
A pinch of kosher salt
2 tablespoons agave nectar

## Directions

Start by preheating your oven to 420 degrees F. Toss the squash with the remaining ingredients.

Roast the butternut squash for about 30 minutes or until tender and caramelized.

Then, in your food processor or blender, puree the roasted squash along with the remaining ingredients until uniform and smooth. Bon appétit!

**Per serving:** Calories: 157; Fat: 5.7g; Carbs: 27g; Protein: 1.7g

# 173. Easy Zucchini Skillet

(Ready in about 10 minutes | Servings 4)

## Ingredients

2 tablespoons vegan butter
1 shallot, thinly sliced
1 teaspoon garlic, minced
1 ½ pounds zucchini, sliced
Flaky sea salt and ground black pepper, to taste

1 teaspoon paprika
1/2 teaspoon cayenne pepper
1/2 teaspoon dried thyme
1/2 teaspoon celery seeds
1/2 teaspoon coriander pepper
2 tablespoons nutritional yeast

## Directions

In a saucepan, melt the vegan butter over medium-high heat.

Once hot, sauté the shallot for about 3 minutes or until tender. Then, sauté the garlic for about 1 minute until aromatic.

Add in the zucchini, along with the spices and continue to sauté for 6 minutes more until tender.

Taste and adjust the seasonings. Top with nutritional yeast and serve. Bon appétit!

**Per serving:** Calories: 137; Fat: 6.7g; Carbs: 13.2g; Protein: 7.7g

# 174. Sweet Potato Puree

(Ready in about 25 minutes | Servings 5)

## Ingredients

2 pounds sweet potatoes, peeled and cubed
2 tablespoons olive oil
1 shallot, chopped
2 garlic cloves, minced
1/4 cup coconut milk, unsweetened

Sea salt and cayenne pepper, to taste
2 tablespoons fresh chives, roughly chopped
2 tablespoons fresh parsley, roughly chopped

## Directions

Cover the sweet potatoes with an inch or two of cold water. Cook the sweet potatoes in gently boiling water for about 20 minutes; drain well.

Meanwhile, heat the olive oil in a cast-iron skillet and sauté the shallot for about 3 minutes until tender; add in the garlic and continue to sauté an additional 30 seconds or until tender.

Then, puree the potatoes, along with the shallot mixture, gradually adding the milk, to your desired consistency.

Season with salt and pepper to taste. Serve garnished with the fresh chives and parsley. Bon appétit!

**Per serving:** Calories: 219; Fat: 5.9g; Carbs: 38.2g; Protein: 3.7g

# 175. Balkan-Style Satarash

(Ready in about 25 minutes | Servings 4)

## Ingredients

4 tablespoons olive oil
1 large onion, chopped
1 pound eggplant, peeled and diced
2 red bell peppers, seeded and diced
1 red chili pepper, seeded and diced

2 garlic cloves, minced
1 teaspoon paprika, slightly heaping
1 bay leaf
Kosher salt and ground black pepper, to taste
1 large tomato, pureed
1/2 cup vegetable broth

## Directions

Heat the oil in a large saucepan over medium-high flame.

Then, sauté the onion for about 3 minutes or until tender and translucent. Add in the eggplant and peppers and continue sautéing an additional 3 minutes.

Add in the garlic and continue to cook for 30 seconds more or until aromatic.

Add in the remaining ingredients, cover and continue to cook for 15 minutes more or until thoroughly cooked. Serve warm.

**Per serving:** Calories: 199; Fat: 14.1g; Carbs: 17.6g; Protein: 2.9g

# 176. Classic Avocado Tartines

(Ready in about 5 minutes | Servings 3)

## Ingredients

2 medium avocados, pitted, peeled and mashed
2 tablespoons fresh lime juice
Sea salt and ground black pepper, to taste
1/2 teaspoon red pepper flakes, crushed

6 slices whole-wheat bread, toasted
1 large tomato, sliced
3 tablespoons sesame seeds, toasted

## Directions

Combine the mashed avocado with the lime juice, salt, black pepper and red pepper.

Spread the mixture onto the toast; top with tomatoes and sesame seeds.

Bon appétit!

**Per serving:** Calories: 384; Fat: 25.9g; Carbs: 34.6g; Protein: 8.3g

# 177. Classic Tomato Bruschetta

(Ready in about 10 minutes | Servings 4)

## Ingredients

4 slices bread
2 tablespoons extra-virgin olive oil
1 clove garlic, halved
2 tomatoes, diced

1 teaspoon dried oregano
1 teaspoon dried basil
Sea salt and ground black pepper, to taste

## Directions

Brush the bread slices with the olive oil and toast them in a skillet.

Now, rub the toasted bread on one side with halved garlic cloves.

Top with the tomatoes; sprinkle oregano, basil, salt and black pepper over everything. Bon appétit!

**Per serving:** Calories: 155; Fat: 7.9g; Carbs: 18.7g; Protein: 3.5g

# 178. Tomato and Hummus Stuffed Avocados

(Ready in about 5 minutes | Servings 4)

## Ingredients

2 avocados, pitted
2 tablespoons fresh lemon juice
2 medium tomatoes, diced
1 chili pepper, seeded and chopped
2 garlic cloves, minced
4 tablespoons hummus
Sea salt and ground black pepper, to taste

## Directions

Drizzle the avocado halves with the lemon juice.

Fill your avocados with tomatoes, chili pepper, garlic and hummus. Season your avocados with salt and black pepper.

Serve immediately. Bon appétit!

**Per serving:** Calories: 211; Fat: 16.5g; Carbs: 17.1g; Protein: 3.8g

# 179. Mediterranean-Style Summer Squash

(Ready in about 35 minutes | Servings 5)

## Ingredients

2 pounds summer yellow squash, peeled, seeded and diced
4 tablespoons olive oil
1 teaspoon garlic, minced
1/2 teaspoon dried oregano
1 teaspoon dried basil
1 teaspoon dried thyme
Sea salt and freshly ground black pepper, to taste
2 ounces Kalamata olives, pitted and sliced

## Directions

Start by preheating your oven to 360 degrees F. Toss the squash with the remaining ingredients, except for the olives.

Roast the squash for about 30 minutes or until fork-tender.

Serve warm, garnished with Kalamata olives. Bon appétit!

**Per serving:** Calories: 145; Fat: 13.1g; Carbs: 6g; Protein: 2.5g

# 180. Braised Wax Beans with Herbs

(Ready in about 10 minutes | Servings 4)

## Ingredients

1 cup water
1 ½ pounds wax beans
4 tablespoons olive oil
4 cloves garlic, minced
1/2 teaspoon ginger, peeled and minced
1/2 teaspoon ground bay leaf
Kosher salt and ground black pepper, to taste
2 tablespoons fresh Italian parsley, chopped
2 tablespoons fresh basil, chopped

## Directions

Bring the water to a boil. Add in the wax beans and let it cook for about 5 minutes until they are crisp-tender; reserve.

In a saucepan, heat the olive oil over medium-high heat; sauté the garlic, ginger and ground bay leaf for 1 minute or until aromatic.

Add in the salt, black pepper and reserved green beans; let it cook for about 3 minutes until cooked through.

Serve with fresh parsley and basil. Bon appétit!

**Per serving:** Calories: 185; Fat: 14g; Carbs: 14.1g; Protein: 3.6g

# 181. Cabbage Braised in Tomato and Wine

(Ready in about 20 minutes | Servings 4)

## Ingredients

4 tablespoons olive oil
1 medium red onion, chopped
1 carrot, trimmed and thinly sliced
1 bell pepper, seeded and diced
1 teaspoon garlic, minced
1 bay leaf
1 chipotle chili pepper, seeded and diced
1/4 cup vegetable broth
1 ½ pounds cabbage, cut into wedges
1 large Roma tomato, pureed
1/4 cup dry white wine
1 teaspoon cayenne pepper
1 teaspoon dried basil
Sea salt and ground black pepper, to season

## Directions

Heat the olive oil in a saucepan over medium flame. Once hot, fry the onion, carrots and peppers for about 4 minutes, stirring periodically to promote even cooking.

Add in the garlic, bay leaf and chili pepper and continue sautéing an additional 1 minute or until fragrant.

Add in the broth, cabbage, Roma tomato, wine, cayenne pepper, dried basil, salt and black pepper.

Then, continue to simmer, covered, for about 13 minutes or until the cabbage has softened and the liquid has thickened slightly. Serve in individual bowls. Bon appétit!

**Per serving:** Calories: 339; Fat: 29g; Carbs: 19.4g; Protein: 5.1g

# 182. Spicy Cauliflower Steaks

(Ready in about 35 minutes | Servings 4)

## Ingredients

2 medium heads cauliflower, sliced lengthwise into "steaks"
1/2 cup olive oil
4 cloves garlic, minced
1 teaspoon red pepper flakes
1/2 teaspoon cumin seeds
1/3 teaspoon ground bay leaf
Kosher salt and ground black pepper, to taste

## Directions

Begin by preheating the oven to 400 degrees F. Brush the cauliflower "steaks" with 1/4 of the olive oil and arrange them on a parchment-lined roasting pan.

Then, in a mixing bowl, mix the remaining 1/4 of the olive oil with the aromatics.

Then, roast the cauliflower steaks for about 20 minutes; brush them with the oil/garlic mixture and continue cooking an additional 10 to 15 minutes.

Bon appétit!

**Per serving:** Calories: 366; Fat: 28.1g; Carbs: 26.2g; Protein: 6.9g

# 183. Mediterranean-Style Sautéed Kale

(Ready in about 10 minutes | Servings 4)

## Ingredients

4 tablespoons olive oil
1 small red onion, chopped
2 cloves garlic, thinly sliced
1 ½ pounds kale, tough stems removed, torn into pieces
2 tomatoes, peeled and pureed
1 teaspoon dried oregano
1 teaspoon dried basil
1/2 teaspoon dried rosemary
1/2 teaspoon dried thyme
Sea salt and freshly ground black pepper, to taste

## Directions

In a saucepan, heat the olive oil over a moderately high heat. Now, sauté the onion and garlic for about 2 minutes or until they are aromatic.

Add in the kale and tomatoes, stirring to promote even cooking.

Turn the heat to a simmer, add in the spices and let it cook for 5 to 6 minutes, until the kale leaves wilt.

Serve warm and enjoy!

**Per serving:** Calories: 222; Fat: 15g; Carbs: 19.1g; Protein: 8.2g

# RICE & GRAINS

## 184. Classic Garlicky Rice

(Ready in about 20 minutes | Servings 4)

### Ingredients

4 tablespoons olive oil
4 cloves garlic, chopped

1 ½ cups white rice
2 ½ cups vegetable broth

### Directions

In a saucepan, heat the olive oil over a moderately high flame. Add in the garlic and sauté for about 1 minute or until aromatic.

Add in the rice and broth. Bring to a boil; immediately turn the heat to a gentle simmer.

Cook for about 15 minutes or until all the liquid has absorbed. Fluff the rice with a fork, season with salt and pepper and serve hot!

**Per serving:** Calories: 422; Fat: 15.1g; Carbs: 61.1g; Protein: 9.3g

## 185. Brown Rice with Vegetables and Tofu

(Ready in about 45 minutes | Servings 4)

### Ingredients

4 teaspoons sesame seeds
2 spring garlic stalks, minced
1 cup spring onions, chopped
1 carrot, trimmed and sliced
1 celery rib, sliced
1/4 cup dry white wine

10 ounces tofu, cubed
1 ½ cups long-grain brown rice, rinsed thoroughly
2 tablespoons soy sauce
2 tablespoons tahini
1 tablespoon lemon juice

### Directions

In a wok or large saucepan, heat 2 teaspoons of the sesame oil over medium-high heat. Now, cook the garlic, onion, carrot and celery for about 3 minutes, stirring periodically to ensure even cooking.

Add the wine to deglaze the pan and push the vegetables to one side of the wok. Add in the remaining sesame oil and fry the tofu for 8 minutes, stirring occasionally.

Bring 2 ½ cups of water to a boil over medium-high heat. Bring to a simmer and cook the rice for about 30 minutes or until it is tender; fluff the rice and stir it with the soy sauce and tahini.

Stir the vegetables and tofu into the hot rice; add a few drizzles of the fresh lemon juice and serve warm. Bon appétit!

**Per serving:** Calories: 410; Fat: 13.2g; Carbs: 60g; Protein: 14.3g

## 186. Basic Amaranth Porridge

(Ready in about 35 minutes | Servings 4)

### Ingredients

3 cups water
1 cup amaranth
1/2 cup coconut milk

4 tablespoons agave syrup
A pinch of kosher salt
A pinch of grated nutmeg

### Directions

Bring the water to a boil over medium-high heat; add in the amaranth and turn the heat to a simmer.

Let it cook for about 30 minutes, stirring periodically to prevent the amaranth from sticking to the bottom of the pan.

Stir in the remaining ingredients and continue to cook for 1 to 2 minutes more until cooked through. Bon appétit!

**Per serving:** Calories: 261; Fat: 4.4g; Carbs: 49g; Protein: 7.3g

## 187. Country Cornbread with Spinach

(Ready in about 50 minutes | Servings 8)

### Ingredients

1 tablespoon flaxseed meal
1 cup all-purpose flour
1 cup yellow cornmeal
1/2 teaspoon baking soda
1/2 teaspoon baking powder
1 teaspoon kosher salt
1 teaspoon brown sugar

A pinch of grated nutmeg
1 ¼ cups oat milk, unsweetened
1 teaspoon white vinegar
1/2 cup olive oil
2 cups spinach, torn into pieces

### Directions

Start by preheating your oven to 420 degrees F. Now, spritz a baking pan with a nonstick cooking spray.

To make the flax eggs, mix flaxseed meal with 3 tablespoons of the water. Stir and let it sit for about 15 minutes.

In a mixing bowl, thoroughly combine the flour, cornmeal, baking soda, baking powder, salt, sugar and grated nutmeg.

Gradually add in the flax egg, oat milk, vinegar and olive oil, whisking constantly to avoid lumps. Afterwards, fold in the spinach.

Scrape the batter into the prepared baking pan. Bake your cornbread for about 25 minutes or until a tester inserted in the middle comes out dry and clean.

Let it stand for about 10 minutes before slicing and serving. Bon appétit!

**Per serving:** Calories: 282; Fat: 15.4g; Carbs: 30g; Protein: 4.6g

## 188. Rice Pudding with Currants

(Ready in about 45 minutes | Servings 4)

### Ingredients

1 ½ cups water
1 cup white rice
2 ½ cups oat milk, divided
1/2 cup white sugar
A pinch of salt

A pinch of grated nutmeg
1 teaspoon ground cinnamon
1/2 teaspoon vanilla extract
1/2 cup dried currants

### Directions

In a saucepan, bring the water to a boil over medium-high heat. Immediately turn the heat to a simmer, add in the rice and let it cook for about 20 minutes.

Add in the milk, sugar and spices and continue to cook for 20 minutes more, stirring constantly to prevent the rice from sticking to the pan.

Top with dried currants and serve at room temperature. Bon appétit!

**Per serving:** Calories: 423; Fat: 5.3g; Carbs: 85g; Protein: 8.8g

## 189. Millet Porridge with Sultanas

(Ready in about 25 minutes | Servings 3)

### Ingredients

1 cup water
1 cup coconut milk
1 cup millet, rinsed
1/4 teaspoon grated nutmeg
1/4 teaspoon ground cinnamon
1 teaspoon vanilla paste
1/4 teaspoon kosher salt
2 tablespoons agave syrup
4 tablespoons sultana raisins

### Directions

Place the water, milk, millet, nutmeg, cinnamon, vanilla and salt in a saucepan; bring to a boil.

Turn the heat to a simmer and let it cook for about 20 minutes; fluff the millet with a fork and spoon into individual bowls.

Serve with agave syrup and sultanas. Bon appétit!

**Per serving:** Calories: 353; Fat: 5.5g; Carbs: 65.2g; Protein: 9.8g

## 190. Quinoa Porridge with Dried Figs

(Ready in about 25 minutes | Servings 3)

### Ingredients

1 cup white quinoa, rinsed
2 cups almond milk
4 tablespoons brown sugar
A pinch of salt
1/4 teaspoon grated nutmeg
1/2 teaspoon ground cinnamon
1/2 teaspoon vanilla extract
1/2 cup dried figs, chopped

### Directions

Place the quinoa, almond milk, sugar, salt, nutmeg, cinnamon and vanilla extract in a saucepan.

Bring it to a boil over medium-high heat. Turn the heat to a simmer and let it cook for about 20 minutes; fluff with a fork.

Divide between three serving bowls and garnish with dried figs. Bon appétit!

**Per serving:** Calories: 414; Fat: 9g; Carbs: 71.2g; Protein: 13.8g

## 191. Bread Pudding with Raisins

(Ready in about 1 hour | Servings 4)

### Ingredients

4 cups day-old bread, cubed
1 cup brown sugar
4 cups coconut milk
1/2 teaspoon vanilla extract
1 teaspoon ground cinnamon
2 tablespoons rum
1/2 cup raisins

### Directions

Start by preheating your oven to 360 degrees F. Lightly oil a casserole dish with a nonstick cooking spray.

Place the cubed bread in the prepared casserole dish.

In a mixing bowl, thoroughly combine the sugar, milk, vanilla, cinnamon, rum and raisins. Pour the custard evenly over the bread cubes.

Let it soak for about 15 minutes.

Bake in the preheated oven for about 45 minutes or until the top is golden and set. Bon appétit!

**Per serving:** Calories: 474; Fat: 12.2g; Carbs: 72g; Protein: 14.4g

## 192. Bulgur Wheat Salad

(Ready in about 25 minutes | Servings 4)

### Ingredients

1 cup bulgur wheat
1 ½ cups vegetable broth
1 teaspoon sea salt
1 teaspoon fresh ginger, minced
4 tablespoons olive oil
1 onion, chopped
8 ounces canned garbanzo beans, drained
2 large roasted peppers, sliced
2 tablespoons fresh parsley, roughly chopped

### Directions

In a deep saucepan, bring the bulgur wheat and vegetable broth to a simmer; let it cook, covered, for 12 to 13 minutes.

Let it stand for about 10 minutes and fluff with a fork.

Add the remaining ingredients to the cooked bulgur wheat; serve at room temperature or well-chilled. Bon appétit!

**Per serving:** Calories: 359; Fat: 15.5g; Carbs: 48.1g; Protein: 10.1g

## 193. Rye Porridge with Blueberry Topping

(Ready in about 15 minutes | Servings 3)

### Ingredients

1 cup rye flakes
1 cup water
1 cup coconut milk
1 cup fresh blueberries
1 tablespoon coconut oil
6 dates, pitted

### Directions

Add the rye flakes, water and coconut milk to a deep saucepan; bring to a boil over medium-high. Turn the heat to a simmer and let it cook for 5 to 6 minutes.

In a blender or food processor, puree the blueberries with the coconut oil and dates.

Ladle into three bowls and garnish with the blueberry topping. Bon appétit!

**Per serving:** Calories: 359; Fat: 11g; Carbs: 56.1g; Protein: 12.1g

## 194. Coconut Sorghum Porridge

(Ready in about 15 minutes | Servings 2)

### Ingredients

1/2 cup sorghum
1 cup water
1/2 cup coconut milk
1/4 teaspoon grated nutmeg
1/4 teaspoon ground cloves
1/2 teaspoon ground cinnamon
Kosher salt, to taste
2 tablespoons agave syrup
2 tablespoons coconut flakes

### Directions

Place the sorghum, water, milk, nutmeg, cloves, cinnamon and kosher salt in a saucepan; simmer gently for about 15 minutes.

Spoon the porridge into serving bowls. Top with agave syrup and coconut flakes. Bon appétit!

**Per serving:** Calories: 289; Fat: 5.1g; Carbs: 57.8g; Protein: 7.3g

## 195. Dad's Aromatic Rice

(Ready in about 20 minutes | Servings 4)

### Ingredients

3 tablespoons olive oil
1 teaspoon garlic, minced
1 teaspoon dried oregano
1 teaspoon dried rosemary
1 bay leaf

1 ½ cups white rice
2 ½ cups vegetable broth
Sea salt and cayenne pepper, to taste

### Directions

In a saucepan, heat the olive oil over a moderately high flame. Add in the garlic, oregano, rosemary and bay leaf; sauté for about 1 minute or until aromatic.

Add in the rice and broth. Bring to a boil; immediately turn the heat to a gentle simmer.

Cook for about 15 minutes or until all the liquid has absorbed. Fluff the rice with a fork, season with salt and pepper and serve immediately.

Bon appétit!

**Per serving:** Calories: 384; Fat: 11.4g; Carbs: 60.4g; Protein: 8.3g

## 196. Everyday Savory Grits

(Ready in about 35 minutes | Servings 4)

### Ingredients

2 tablespoons vegan butter
1 sweet onion, chopped
1 teaspoon garlic, minced
4 cups water

1 cup stone-ground grits
Sea salt and cayenne pepper, to taste

### Directions

In a saucepan, melt the vegan butter over medium-high heat. Once hot, cook the onion for about 3 minutes or until tender.

Add in the garlic and continue to sauté for 30 seconds more or until aromatic; reserve.

Bring the water to a boil over a moderately high heat. Stir in the grits, salt and pepper. Turn the heat to a simmer, cover and continue to cook, for about 30 minutes or until cooked through.

Stir in the sautéed mixture and serve warm. Bon appétit!

**Per serving:** Calories: 238; Fat: 6.5g; Carbs: 38.7g; Protein: 3.7g

## 197. Greek-Style Barley Salad

(Ready in about 35 minutes | Servings 4)

### Ingredients

1 cup pearl barley
2 ¾ cups vegetable broth
2 tablespoons apple cider vinegar
4 tablespoons extra-virgin olive oil
2 bell peppers, seeded and diced

1 shallot, chopped
2 ounces sun-dried tomatoes in oil, chopped
1/2 green olives, pitted and sliced
2 tablespoons fresh cilantro, roughly chopped

### Directions

Bring the barley and broth to a boil over medium-high heat; now, turn the heat to a simmer.

Continue to simmer for about 30 minutes until all the liquid has absorbed; fluff with a fork.

Toss the barley with the vinegar, olive oil, peppers, shallots, sun-dried tomatoes and olives; toss to combine well.

Garnish with fresh cilantro and serve at room temperature or well-chilled. Enjoy!

**Per serving:** Calories: 378; Fat: 15.6g; Carbs: 50g; Protein: 10.7g

## 198. Easy Sweet Maize Meal Porridge

(Ready in about 15 minutes | Servings 2)

### Ingredients

2 cups water
1/2 cup maize meal
1/4 teaspoon ground allspice

1/4 teaspoon salt
2 tablespoons brown sugar
2 tablespoons almond butter

### Directions

In a saucepan, bring the water to a boil; then, gradually add in the maize meal and turn the heat to a simmer.

Add in the ground allspice and salt. Let it cook for 10 minutes.

Add in the brown sugar and almond butter and gently stir to combine. Bon appétit!

**Per serving:** Calories: 278; Fat: 12.7g; Carbs: 37.2g; Protein: 3g

## 199. Mom's Millet Muffins

(Ready in about 20 minutes | Servings 8)

### Ingredients

2 cup whole-wheat flour
1/2 cup millet
2 teaspoons baking powder
1/2 teaspoon salt
1 cup coconut milk
1/2 cup coconut oil, melted
1/2 cup agave nectar

1/2 teaspoon ground cinnamon
1/4 teaspoon ground cloves
A pinch of grated nutmeg
1/2 cup dried apricots, chopped

### Directions

Begin by preheating your oven to 400 degrees F. Lightly oil a muffin tin with a nonstick oil.

In a mixing bowl, mix all dry ingredients. In a separate bowl, mix the wet ingredients. Stir the milk mixture into the flour mixture; mix just until evenly moist and do not overmix your batter.

Fold in the apricots and scrape the batter into the prepared muffin cups.

Bake the muffins in the preheated oven for about 15 minutes, or until a tester inserted in the center of your muffin comes out dry and clean.

Let it stand for 10 minutes on a wire rack before unmolding and serving. Enjoy!

**Per serving:** Calories: 367; Fat: 15.9g; Carbs: 53.7g; Protein: 6.5g

# 200. Ginger Brown Rice

(Ready in about 30 minutes | Servings 4)

## Ingredients

1 ½ cups brown rice, rinsed
2 tablespoons olive oil
1 teaspoon garlic, minced
1 (1-inch) piece ginger, peeled and minced
1/2 teaspoon cumin seeds
Sea salt and ground black pepper, to taste

## Directions

Place the brown rice in a saucepan and cover with cold water by 2 inches. Bring to a boil.

Turn the heat to a simmer and continue to cook for about 30 minutes or until tender.

In a sauté pan, heat the olive oil over medium-high heat. Once hot, cook the garlic, ginger and cumin seeds until aromatic.

Stir the garlic/ginger mixture into the hot rice; season with salt and pepper and serve immediately. Bon appétit!

**Per serving:** Calories: 318; Fat: 8.8g; Carbs: 53.4g; Protein: 5.6g

# 201. Sweet Oatmeal "Grits"

(Ready in about 20 minutes | Servings 4)

## Ingredients

1 ½ cups steel-cut oats, soaked overnight
1 cup almond milk
2 cups water
A pinch of grated nutmeg
A pinch of ground cloves
A pinch of sea salt
4 tablespoons almonds, slivered
6 dates, pitted and chopped
6 prunes, chopped

## Directions

In a deep saucepan, bring the steel cut oats, almond milk and water to a boil.

Add in the nutmeg, cloves and salt. Immediately turn the heat to a simmer, cover and continue to cook for about 15 minutes or until they've softened.

Then, spoon the grits into four serving bowls; top them with the almonds, dates and prunes.

Bon appétit!

**Per serving:** Calories: 380; Fat: 11.1g; Carbs: 59g; Protein: 14.4g

# 202. Freekeh Bowl with Dried Figs

(Ready in about 35 minutes | Servings 2)

## Ingredients

1/2 cup freekeh, soaked for 30 minutes, drained
1 1/3 cups almond milk
1/4 teaspoon sea salt
1/4 teaspoon ground cloves
1/4 teaspoon ground cinnamon
4 tablespoons agave syrup
2 ounces dried figs, chopped

## Directions

Place the freekeh, milk, sea salt, ground cloves and cinnamon in a saucepan. Bring to a boil over medium-high heat.

Immediately turn the heat to a simmer for 30 to 35 minutes, stirring occasionally to promote even cooking.

Stir in the agave syrup and figs. Ladle the porridge into individual bowls and serve. Bon appétit!

**Per serving:** Calories: 458; Fat: 6.8g; Carbs: 90g; Protein: 12.4g

# 203. Cornmeal Porridge with Maple Syrup

(Ready in about 20 minutes | Servings 4)

## Ingredients

2 cups water
2 cups almond milk
1 cinnamon stick
1 vanilla bean
1 cup yellow cornmeal
1/2 cup maple syrup

## Directions

In a saucepan, bring the water and almond milk to a boil. Add in the cinnamon stick and vanilla bean.

Gradually add in the cornmeal, stirring continuously; turn the heat to a simmer. Let it simmer for about 15 minutes.

Drizzle the maple syrup over the porridge and serve warm. Enjoy!

**Per serving:** Calories: 328; Fat: 4.8g; Carbs: 63.4g; Protein: 6.6g

# 204. Mediterranean-Style Rice

(Ready in about 20 minutes | Servings 4)

## Ingredients

3 tablespoons vegan butter, at room temperature
4 tablespoons scallions, chopped
2 cloves garlic, minced
1 bay leaf
1 thyme sprig, chopped
1 rosemary sprig, chopped
1 ½ cups white rice
2 cups vegetable broth
1 large tomato, pureed
Sea salt and ground black pepper, to taste
2 ounces Kalamata olives, pitted and sliced

## Directions

In a saucepan, melt the vegan butter over a moderately high flame. Cook the scallions for about 2 minutes or until tender.

Add in the garlic, bay leaf, thyme and rosemary and continue to sauté for about 1 minute or until aromatic.

Add in the rice, broth and pureed tomato. Bring to a boil; immediately turn the heat to a gentle simmer.

Cook for about 15 minutes or until all the liquid has absorbed. Fluff the rice with a fork, season with salt and pepper and garnish with olives; serve immediately.

Bon appétit!

**Per serving:** Calories: 403; Fat: 12g; Carbs: 64.1g; Protein: 8.3g

# 205. Bulgur Pancakes with a Twist

(Ready in about 50 minutes | Servings 4)

## Ingredients

1/2 cup bulgur wheat flour
1/2 cup almond flour
1 teaspoon baking soda
1/2 teaspoon fine sea salt
1 cup full-fat coconut milk

1/2 teaspoon ground cinnamon
1/4 teaspoon ground cloves
4 tablespoons coconut oil
1/2 cup maple syrup
1 large-sized banana, sliced

## Directions

In a mixing bowl, thoroughly combine the flour, baking soda, salt, coconut milk, cinnamon and ground cloves; let it stand for 30 minutes to soak well.

Heat a small amount of the coconut oil in a frying pan.

Fry the pancakes until the surface is golden brown. Garnish with maple syrup and banana. Bon appétit!

**Per serving:** Calories: 414; Fat: 21.8g; Carbs: 51.8g; Protein: 6.5g

# 206. Chocolate Rye Porridge

(Ready in about 10 minutes | Servings 4)

## Ingredients

2 cups rye flakes
2 ½ cups almond milk
2 ounces dried prunes, chopped

2 ounces dark chocolate chunks

## Directions

Add the rye flakes and almond milk to a deep saucepan; bring to a boil over medium-high. Turn the heat to a simmer and let it cook for 5 to 6 minutes.

Remove from the heat. Fold in the chopped prunes and chocolate chunks, gently stir to combine.

Ladle into serving bowls and serve warm.

Bon appétit!

**Per serving:** Calories: 460; Fat: 13.1g; Carbs: 72.2g; Protein: 15g

# 207. Authentic African Mielie-Meal

(Ready in about 15 minutes | Servings 4)

## Ingredients

3 cups water
1 cup coconut milk
1 cup maize meal
1/3 teaspoon kosher salt

1/4 teaspoon grated nutmeg
1/4 teaspoon ground cloves
4 tablespoons maple syrup

## Directions

In a saucepan, bring the water and milk to a boil; then, gradually add in the maize meal and turn the heat to a simmer.

Add in the salt, nutmeg and cloves. Let it cook for 10 minutes.

Add in the maple syrup and gently stir to combine. Bon appétit!

**Per serving:** Calories: 336; Fat: 15.1g; Carbs: 47.9g; Protein: 4.1g

# 208. Teff Porridge with Dried Figs

(Ready in about 25 minutes | Servings 4)

## Ingredients

1 cup whole-grain teff
1 cup water
2 cups coconut milk
2 tablespoons coconut oil
1/2 teaspoon ground cardamom

1/4 teaspoon ground cinnamon
4 tablespoons agave syrup
7-8 dried figs, chopped

## Directions

Bring the whole-grain teff, water and coconut milk to a boil.

Turn the heat to a simmer and add in the coconut oil, cardamom and cinnamon.

Let it cook for 20 minutes or until the grain has softened and the porridge has thickened. Stir in the agave syrup and stir to combine well.

Top each serving bowl with chopped figs and serve warm. Bon appétit!

**Per serving:** Calories: 356; Fat: 12.1g; Carbs: 56.5g; Protein: 6.8g

# 209. Decadent Bread Pudding with Apricots

(Ready in about 1 hour | Servings 4)

## Ingredients

4 cups day-old ciabatta bread, cubed
4 tablespoons coconut oil, melted
2 cups coconut milk
1/2 cup coconut sugar

4 tablespoons applesauce
1/4 teaspoon ground cloves
1/2 teaspoon ground cinnamon
1 teaspoon vanilla extract
1/3 cup dried apricots, diced

## Directions

Start by preheating your oven to 360 degrees F. Lightly oil a casserole dish with a nonstick cooking spray.

Place the cubed bread in the prepared casserole dish.

In a mixing bowl, thoroughly combine the coconut oil, milk, coconut sugar, applesauce, ground cloves, ground cinnamon and vanilla. Pour the custard evenly over the bread cubes; fold in the apricots.

Press with a wide spatula and let it soak for about 15 minutes.

Bake in the preheated oven for about 45 minutes or until the top is golden and set. Bon appétit!

**Per serving:** Calories: 418; Fat: 18.8g; Carbs: 56.9g; Protein: 7.3g

## 210. Chipotle Cilantro Rice

(Ready in about 25 minutes | Servings 4)

### Ingredients

4 tablespoons olive oil
1 chipotle pepper, seeded and chopped
1 cup jasmine rice

1 ½ cups vegetable broth
1/4 cup fresh cilantro, chopped
Sea salt and cayenne pepper, to taste

### Directions

In a saucepan, heat the olive oil over a moderately high flame. Add in the pepper and rice and cook for about 3 minutes or until aromatic.

Pour the vegetable broth into the saucepan and bring to a boil; immediately turn the heat to a gentle simmer.

Cook for about 18 minutes or until all the liquid has absorbed. Fluff the rice with a fork, add in the cilantro, salt and cayenne pepper; stir to combine well. Bon appétit!

**Per serving:** Calories: 313; Fat: 15g; Carbs: 37.1g; Protein: 5.7g

## 211. Oat Porridge with Almonds

(Ready in about 20 minutes | Servings 2)

### Ingredients

1 cup water
2 cups almond milk, divided
1 cup rolled oats
2 tablespoons coconut sugar

1/2 vanilla essence
1/4 teaspoon cardamom
1/2 cup almonds, chopped
1 banana, sliced

### Directions

In a deep saucepan, bring the water and milk to a rapid boil. Add in the oats, cover the saucepan and turn the heat to medium.

Add in the coconut sugar, vanilla and cardamom. Continue to cook for about 12 minutes, stirring periodically.

Spoon the mixture into serving bowls; top with almonds and banana. Bon appétit!

**Per serving:** Calories: 533; Fat: 13.7g; Carbs: 85g; Protein: 21.6g

## 212. Aromatic Millet Bowl

(Ready in about 20 minutes | Servings 3)

### Ingredients

1 cup water
1 ½ cups coconut milk
1 cup millet, rinsed and drained
1/4 teaspoon crystallized ginger

1/4 teaspoon ground cinnamon
A pinch of grated nutmeg
A pinch of Himalayan salt
2 tablespoons maple syrup

### Directions

Place the water, milk, millet, crystallized ginger cinnamon, nutmeg and salt in a saucepan; bring to a boil.

Turn the heat to a simmer and let it cook for about 20 minutes; fluff the millet with a fork and spoon into individual bowls.

Serve with maple syrup. Bon appétit!

**Per serving:** Calories: 363; Fat: 6.7g; Carbs: 63.5g; Protein: 11.6g

## 213. Harissa Bulgur Bowl

(Ready in about 25 minutes | Servings 4)

### Ingredients

1 cup bulgur wheat
1 ½ cups vegetable broth
2 cups sweet corn kernels, thawed
1 cup canned kidney beans, drained
1 red onion, thinly sliced
1 garlic clove, minced

Sea salt and ground black pepper, to taste
1/4 cup harissa paste
1 tablespoon lemon juice
1 tablespoon white vinegar
1/4 cup extra-virgin olive oil
1/4 cup fresh parsley leaves, roughly chopped

### Directions

In a deep saucepan, bring the bulgur wheat and vegetable broth to a simmer; let it cook, covered, for 12 to 13 minutes.

Let it stand for 5 to 10 minutes and fluff your bulgur with a fork.

Add the remaining ingredients to the cooked bulgur wheat; serve warm or at room temperature. Bon appétit!

**Per serving:** Calories: 353; Fat: 15.5g; Carbs: 48.5g; Protein: 8.4g

## 214. Coconut Quinoa Pudding

(Ready in about 20 minutes | Servings 3)

### Ingredients

1 cup water
1 cup coconut milk
1 cup quinoa
A pinch of kosher salt
A pinch of ground allspice

1/2 teaspoon cinnamon
1/2 teaspoon vanilla extract
4 tablespoons agave syrup
1/2 cup coconut flakes

### Directions

Place the water, coconut milk, quinoa, salt, ground allspice, cinnamon and vanilla extract in a saucepan.

Bring it to a boil over medium-high heat. Turn the heat to a simmer and let it cook for about 20 minutes; fluff with a fork and add in the agave syrup.

Divide between three serving bowls and garnish with coconut flakes. Bon appétit!

**Per serving:** Calories: 391; Fat: 10.6g; Carbs: 65.2g; Protein: 11.1g

# 215. Cremini Mushroom Risotto

(Ready in about 20 minutes | Servings 3)

## Ingredients

3 tablespoons vegan butter

1 teaspoon garlic, minced

1 teaspoon thyme

1 pound Cremini mushrooms, sliced

1 ½ cups white rice

2 ½ cups vegetable broth

1/4 cup dry sherry wine

Kosher salt and ground black pepper, to taste

3 tablespoons fresh scallions, thinly sliced

## Directions

In a saucepan, melt the vegan butter over a moderately high flame. Cook the garlic and thyme for about 1 minute or until aromatic.

Add in the mushrooms and continue to sauté until they release the liquid or about 3 minutes.

Add in the rice, vegetable broth and sherry wine. Bring to a boil; immediately turn the heat to a gentle simmer.

Cook for about 15 minutes or until all the liquid has absorbed. Fluff the rice with a fork, season with salt and pepper and garnish with fresh scallions.

Bon appétit!

Per serving: Calories: 513; Fat: 12.5g; Carbs: 88g; Protein: 11.7g

# 216. Colorful Risotto with Vegetables

(Ready in about 35 minutes | Servings 5)

## Ingredients

2 tablespoons sesame oil

1 onion, chopped

2 bell peppers, chopped

1 parsnip, trimmed and chopped

1 carrot, trimmed and chopped

1 cup broccoli florets

2 garlic cloves, finely chopped

1/2 teaspoon ground cumin

2 cups brown rice

Sea salt and black pepper, to taste

1/2 teaspoon ground turmeric

2 tablespoons fresh cilantro, finely chopped

## Directions

Heat the sesame oil in a saucepan over medium-high heat.

Once hot, cook the onion, peppers, parsnip, carrot and broccoli for about 3 minutes until aromatic.

Add in the garlic and ground cumin; continue to cook for 30 seconds more until aromatic.

Place the brown rice in a saucepan and cover with cold water by 2 inches. Bring to a boil. Turn the heat to a simmer and continue to cook for about 30 minutes or until tender.

Stir the rice into the vegetable mixture; season with salt, black pepper and ground turmeric; garnish with fresh cilantro and serve immediately. Bon appétit!

Per serving: Calories: 363; Fat: 7.5g; Carbs: 66.3g; Protein: 7.7g

# 217. Amarant Grits with Walnuts

(Ready in about 35 minutes | Servings 4)

## Ingredients

2 cups water

2 cups coconut milk

1 cup amaranth

1 cinnamon stick

1 vanilla bean

4 tablespoons maple syrup

4 tablespoons walnuts, chopped

## Directions

Bring the water and coconut milk to a boil over medium-high heat; add in the amaranth, cinnamon and vanilla and turn the heat to a simmer.

Let it cook for about 30 minutes, stirring periodically to prevent the amaranth from sticking to the bottom of the pan.

Top with maple syrup and walnuts. Bon appétit!

Per serving: Calories: 356; Fat: 12g; Carbs: 51.3g; Protein: 12.2g

# 218. Barley Pilaf with Wild Mushrooms

(Ready in about 45 minutes | Servings 4)

## Ingredients

2 tablespoons vegan butter

1 small onion, chopped

1 teaspoon garlic, minced

1 jalapeno pepper, seeded and minced

1 pound wild mushrooms, sliced

1 cup medium pearl barley, rinsed

2 ¾ cups vegetable broth

## Directions

Melt the vegan butter in a saucepan over medium-high heat.

Once hot, cook the onion for about 3 minutes until just tender.

Add in the garlic, jalapeno pepper, mushrooms; continue to sauté for 2 minutes or until aromatic.

Add in the barley and broth, cover and continue to simmer for about 30 minutes. Once all the liquid has absorbed, allow the barley to rest for about 10 minutes fluff with a fork.

Taste and adjust the seasonings. Bon appétit!

Per serving: Calories: 288; Fat: 7.7g; Carbs: 45.3g; Protein: 12.1g

# 219. Sweet Cornbread Muffins

(Ready in about 30 minutes | Servings 8)

## Ingredients

1 cup all-purpose flour
1 cup yellow cornmeal
1 teaspoon baking powder
1 teaspoon baking soda
1 teaspoon kosher salt
1/2 cup sugar
1/2 teaspoon ground cinnamon
1 1/2 cups almond milk
1/2 cup vegan butter, melted
2 tablespoons applesauce

## Directions

Start by preheating your oven to 420 degrees F. Now, spritz a muffin tin with a nonstick cooking spray.

In a mixing bowl, thoroughly combine the flour, cornmeal, baking soda, baking powder, salt, sugar and cinnamon.

Gradually add in the milk, butter and applesauce, whisking constantly to avoid lumps.

Scrape the batter into the prepared muffin tin. Bake your muffins for about 25 minutes or until a tester inserted in the middle comes out dry and clean.

Transfer them to a wire rack to rest for 5 minutes before unmolding and serving. Bon appétit!

**Per serving:** Calories: 311; Fat: 13.7g; Carbs: 42.3g; Protein: 4.5g

# 220. Aromatic Rice Pudding with Dried Figs

(Ready in about 45 minutes | Servings 4)

## Ingredients

2 cups water
1 cup medium-grain white rice
3 ½ cups coconut milk
1/2 cup coconut sugar
1 cinnamon stick
1 vanilla bean
1/2 cup dried figs, chopped
4 tablespoons coconut, shredded

## Directions

In a saucepan, bring the water to a boil over medium-high heat. Immediately turn the heat to a simmer, add in the rice and let it cook for about 20 minutes.

Add in the milk, sugar and spices and continue to cook for 20 minutes more, stirring constantly to prevent the rice from sticking to the pan.

Top with dried figs and coconut; serve your pudding warm or at room temperature. Bon appétit!

**Per serving:** Calories: 407; Fat: 7.5g; Carbs: 74.3g; Protein: 10.7g

# 221. Potage au Quinoa

(Ready in about 25 minutes | Servings 4)

## Ingredients

2 tablespoons olive oil
1 onion, chopped
4 medium potatoes, peeled and diced
1 carrot, trimmed and diced
1 parsnip, trimmed and diced
1 jalapeno pepper, seeded and chopped
4 cups vegetable broth
1 cup quinoa
Sea salt and ground white pepper, to taste

## Directions

In a heavy-bottomed pot, heat the olive oil over medium-high heat. Sauté the onion, potatoes, carrots, parsnip and pepper for about 5 minutes or until they've softened.

Add in the vegetable broth and quinoa; bring to a boil.

Immediately turn the heat to a simmer for about 15 minutes or until the quinoa is tender.

Season with salt and pepper to taste. Puree your potage with an immersion blender. Reheat the potage just before serving and enjoy!

**Per serving:** Calories: 466; Fat: 11.1g; Carbs: 76g; Protein: 16.1g

# 222. Sorghum Bowl with Almonds

(Ready in about 15 minutes | Servings 4)

## Ingredients

1 cup sorghum
3 cups almond milk
A pinch of sea salt
A pinch of grated nutmeg
1/2 teaspoon ground cinnamon
1/4 teaspoon ground cardamom
1 teaspoon crystallized ginger
4 tablespoons brown sugar
4 tablespoons almonds, slivered

## Directions

Place the sorghum, almond milk, salt, nutmeg, cinnamon, cardamom and crystallized ginger in a saucepan; simmer gently for about 15 minutes.

Add in the brown sugar, stir and spoon the porridge into serving bowls.

Top with almonds and serve immediately. Bon appétit!

**Per serving:** Calories: 384; Fat: 14.7g; Carbs: 54.6g; Protein: 13.9g

# 223. Bulgur Muffins with Raisins

(Ready in about 20 minutes | Servings 6)

## Ingredients

1 cup bulgur, cooked
4 tablespoons coconut oil, melted
1 teaspoon baking powder
1 teaspoon baking soda
2 tablespoons flax egg
1 ¼ cups all-purpose flour
1/2 cup coconut flour
1 cup coconut milk
4 tablespoons brown sugar
1/2 cup raisins, packed

## Directions

Start by preheating your oven to 420 degrees F. Spritz a muffin tin with a nonstick cooking oil.

Thoroughly combine all the dry ingredients. Add in the cooked bulgur.

In another bowl, whisk all the wet ingredients; add the wet mixture to the bulgur mixture; fold in the raisins.

Mix until everything is well combined, but not overmixed; spoon the batter into the prepared muffin.

Now, bake your muffins for about 16 minutes or until a tester comes out dry and clean. Bon appétit!

**Per serving:** Calories: 306; Fat: 12.1g; Carbs: 44.6g; Protein: 6.1g

# 224. Old-Fashioned Pilaf

(Ready in about 45 minutes | Servings 4)

## Ingredients

2 tablespoons sesame oil
1 shallot, sliced
2 bell peppers, seeded and sliced
3 cloves garlic, minced
10 ounces oyster mushrooms, cleaned and sliced
2 cups brown rice
2 tomatoes, pureed
2 cups vegetable broth
Salt and black pepper, to taste
1 cup sweet corn kernels
1 cup green peas

## Directions

Heat the sesame oil in a saucepan over medium-high heat.

Once hot, cook the shallot and peppers for about 3 minutes until just tender.

Add in the garlic and oyster mushrooms; continue to sauté for 1 minute or so until aromatic.

In a lightly oiled casserole dish, place the rice, flowed by the mushroom mixture, tomatoes, broth, salt, black pepper, corn and green peas.

Bake, covered, at 375 degrees F for about 40 minutes, stirring after 20 minutes. Bon appétit!

**Per serving:** Calories: 532; Fat: 11.4g; Carbs: 93g; Protein: 16.3g

# 225. Freekeh Salad with Za'atar

(Ready in about 35 minutes | Servings 4)

## Ingredients

1 cup freekeh
2 ½ cups water
1 cup grape tomatoes, halved
2 bell peppers, seeded and sliced
1 habanero pepper, seeded and sliced
1 onion, thinly sliced
2 tablespoons fresh cilantro, chopped
2 tablespoons fresh parsley, chopped
2 ounces green olives, pitted and sliced
1/4 cup extra-virgin olive oil
2 tablespoons lemon juice
1 teaspoon deli mustard
1 teaspoon za'atar
Sea salt and ground black pepper, to taste

## Directions

Place the freekeh and water in a saucepan. Bring to a boil over medium-high heat.

Immediately turn the heat to a simmer for 30 to 35 minutes, stirring occasionally to promote even cooking. Let it cool completely.

Toss the cooked freekeh with the remaining ingredients. Toss to combine well.

Bon appétit!

**Per serving:** Calories: 352; Fat: 17.1g; Carbs: 46.3g; Protein: 8g

# 226. Vegetable Amaranth Soup

(Ready in about 30 minutes | Servings 4)

## Ingredients

2 tablespoons olive oil
1 small shallot, chopped
1 carrot, trimmed and chopped
1 parsnip, trimmed and chopped
1 cup yellow squash, peeled and chopped
1 teaspoon fennel seeds
1 teaspoon celery seeds
1 teaspoon turmeric powder
1 bay laurel
1/2 cup amaranth
2 cups cream of celery soup
2 cups water
2 cups collard greens, torn into pieces
Sea salt and ground black pepper, to taste

## Directions

In a heavy-bottomed pot, heat the olive oil until sizzling. Once hot, sauté the shallot, carrot, parsnip and squash for 5 minutes or until just tender.

Then, sauté the fennel seeds, celery seeds, turmeric powder and bay laurel for about 30 seconds, until aromatic.

Add in the amaranth, soup and water. Turn the heat to a simmer. Cover and let it simmer for 15 to 18 minutes.

Afterwards, add in the collard greens, season with salt and black pepper and continue to simmer for 5 minutes longer. Enjoy!

**Per serving:** Calories: 196; Fat: 8.7g; Carbs: 26.1g; Protein: 4.7g

# 227. Polenta with Mushrooms and Chickpeas

(Ready in about 25 minutes | Servings 4)

## Ingredients

3 cups vegetable broth
1 cup yellow cornmeal
2 tablespoons olive oil
1 onion, chopped
1 bell pepper, seeded and sliced
1 pound Cremini mushrooms, sliced
2 garlic cloves, minced
1/2 cup dry white wine
1/2 cup vegetable broth
Kosher salt and freshly ground black pepper, to taste
1 teaspoon paprika
1 cup canned chickpeas, drained

## Directions

In a medium saucepan, bring the vegetable broth to a boil over medium-high heat. Now, add in the cornmeal, whisking continuously to prevent lumps.

Reduce the heat to a simmer. Continue to simmer, whisking periodically, for about 18 minutes, until the mixture has thickened.

Meanwhile, heat the olive oil in a saucepan over a moderately high heat. Cook the onion and pepper for about 3 minutes or until just tender and fragrant.

Add in the mushrooms and garlic; continue to sauté, gradually adding the wine and broth, for 4 more minutes or until cooked through. Season with salt, black pepper and paprika. Stir in the chickpeas.

Spoon the mushroom mixture over your polenta and serve warm. Bon appétit!

**Per serving:** Calories: 488; Fat: 12.2g; Carbs: 71g; Protein: 21.4g

## 228. Teff Salad with Avocado and Beans

(Ready in about 20 minutes + chilling time | Servings 2)

### Ingredients

2 cups water
1/2 cup teff grain
1 teaspoon fresh lemon juice
3 tablespoons vegan mayonnaise
1 teaspoon deli mustard
1 small avocado, pitted, peeled and sliced
1 small red onion, thinly sliced
1 small Persian cucumber, sliced
1/2 cup canned kidney beans, drained
2 cups baby spinach

### Directions

In a deep saucepan, bring the water to a boil over high heat. Add in the teff grain and turn the heat to a simmer.

Continue to cook, covered, for about 20 minutes or until tender. Let it cool completely.

Add in the remaining ingredients and toss to combine. Serve at room temperature. Bon appétit!

Per serving: Calories: 463; Fat: 21.2g; Carbs: 58.9g; Protein: 13.1g

## 229. Overnight Oatmeal with Walnuts

(Ready in about 5 minutes + chilling time | Servings 3)

### Ingredients

1 cup old-fashioned oats
3 tablespoons chia seeds
1 ½ cups coconut milk
3 teaspoons agave syrup
1 teaspoon vanilla extract
1/2 teaspoon ground cinnamon
3 tablespoons walnuts, chopped
A pinch of salt
A pinch of grated nutmeg

### Directions

Divide the ingredients between three mason jars.

Cover and shake to combine well. Let them sit overnight in your refrigerator.

You can add some extra milk before serving. Enjoy!

Per serving: Calories: 423; Fat: 16.8g; Carbs: 53.1g; Protein: 17.3g

## 230. Colorful Spelt Salad

(Ready in about 50 minutes + chilling time | Servings 4)

### Ingredients

3 ½ cups water
1 cup dry spelt
1 cup canned kidney beans, drained
1 bell pepper, seeded and diced
2 medium tomatoes, diced
2 tablespoons basil, chopped
2 tablespoons parsley, chopped
2 tablespoons mint, chopped
1/4 cup extra-virgin olive oil
1 teaspoon deli mustard
1 tablespoon fresh lime juice
1 tablespoon white vinegar
Sea salt and cayenne pepper, to taste

### Directions

Bring the water to a boil over medium-high heat. Now, add in the spelt, turn the heat to a simmer and continue to cook for approximately 50 minutes, until the spelt is tender. Drain and allow it to cool completely.

Toss the spelt with the remaining ingredients; toss to combine well and place the salad in your refrigerator until ready to serve.

Bon appétit!

Per serving: Calories: 373; Fat: 15.6g; Carbs: 49.9g; Protein: 12.8g

## 231. Powerful Teff Bowl with Tahini Sauce

(Ready in about 20 minutes + chilling time | Servings 4)

### Ingredients

3 cups water
1 cup teff
2 garlic cloves, pressed
4 tablespoons tahini
2 tablespoons tamari sauce
2 tablespoons white vinegar
1 teaspoon agave nectar
1 teaspoon deli mustard
1 teaspoon Italian herb mix
1 cup canned chickpeas, drained
2 cups mixed greens
1 cup grape tomatoes, halved
1 Italian peppers, seeded and diced

### Directions

In a deep saucepan, bring the water to a boil over high heat. Add in the teff grain and turn the heat to a simmer.

Continue to cook, covered, for about 20 minutes or until tender. Let it cool completely and transfer to a salad bowl.

In the meantime, mix the garlic, tahini, tamari sauce, vinegar, agave nectar, mustard and Italian herb mix; whisk until everything is well incorporated.

Add the canned chickpeas, mixed greens, tomatoes and peppers to the salad bowl; toss to combine. Dress the salad and toss again. Serve at room temperature. Bon appétit!

Per serving: Calories: 366; Fat: 10.4g; Carbs: 54.2g; Protein: 13.5g

# 232. Polenta Toasts with Balsamic Onions

(Ready in about 25 minutes + chilling time | Servings 5)

## Ingredients

3 cups vegetable broth
1 cup yellow cornmeal
4 tablespoons vegan butter, divided
2 tablespoons olive oil
2 large onions, sliced
Sea salt and ground black pepper, to taste
1 thyme sprig, chopped
1 tablespoon balsamic vinegar

## Directions

In a medium saucepan, bring the vegetable broth to a boil over medium-high heat. Now, add in the cornmeal, whisking continuously to prevent lumps.

Reduce the heat to a simmer. Continue to simmer, whisking periodically, for about 18 minutes, until the mixture has thickened. Stir the vegan butter into the cooked polenta.

Spoon the cooked polenta into a lightly greased square baking dish. Cover with the plastic wrap and chill for about 2 hours or until firm.

Meanwhile, heat the olive oil in a nonstick skillet over a moderately high heat. Cook the onions for about 3 minutes or until just tender and fragrant.

Stir in the salt, black pepper, thyme and balsamic vinegar and continue to sauté for 1 minute or so; remove from the heat.

Cut your polenta into squares. Spritz a nonstick skillet with a cooking spray. Fry the polenta squares for about 5 minutes per side or until golden brown.

Top each polenta toast with the balsamic onion and serve. Bon appétit!

**Per serving:** Calories: 299; Fat: 16.2g; Carbs: 32.5g; Protein: 6.4g

# 233. Freekeh Pilaf with Chickpeas

(Ready in about 40 minutes | Servings 4)

## Ingredients

4 tablespoons olive oil
1 cup shallots, chopped
1 celery stalks, chopped
1 carrot, chopped
1 teaspoon garlic, minced
Sea salt and ground black pepper, to taste
1 teaspoon cayenne pepper
1 teaspoon dried basil
1 teaspoon dried oregano
1 cup freekeh
2 ½ cups water
1 cup boiled chickpeas, drained
2 tablespoons roasted peanuts, roughly chopped
2 tablespoons fresh mint, roughly chopped

## Directions

Heat the olive oil in a heavy-bottomed pot over medium-high heat. Once hot, sauté the shallot, celery and carrot for about 3 minutes until just tender.

Then, add in the garlic and continue to sauté for 30 seconds more or until aromatic. Add in the spices, freekeh and water.

Turn the heat to a simmer for 30 to 35 minutes, stirring occasionally to promote even cooking. Fold in the boiled chickpeas.

To serve, spoon into individual bowls and garnish with roasted peanuts and fresh mint. Bon appétit!

**Per serving:** Calories: 392; Fat: 18.1g; Carbs: 49.9g; Protein: 12.1g

# 234. Grandma's Pilau with Garden Vegetables

(Ready in about 45 minutes | Servings 4)

## Ingredients

2 tablespoons olive oil
1 onion, chopped
1 carrot, trimmed and grated
1 parsnip, trimmed and grated
1 celery with leaves, chopped
1 teaspoon garlic, chopped
1 cup brown rice
2 cups vegetable broth
2 tablespoons fresh parsley, chopped
2 tablespoons finely basil, chopped

## Directions

Heat the olive oil in a saucepan over medium-high heat.

Once hot, cook the onion, carrot, parsnip and celery for about 3 minutes until just tender. Add in the garlic and continue to sauté for 1 minute or so until aromatic.

In a lightly oiled casserole dish, place the rice, flowed by the sautéed vegetables and broth.

Bake, covered, at 375 degrees F for about 40 minutes, stirring after 20 minutes.

Garnish with fresh parsley and basil and serve warm. Bon appétit!

**Per serving:** Calories: 292; Fat: 8.4g; Carbs: 45g; Protein: 7g

# 235. Easy Barley Risotto

(Ready in about 35 minutes | Servings 4)

## Ingredients

2 tablespoons vegan butter
1 medium onion, chopped
1 bell pepper, seeded and chopped
2 garlic cloves, minced
1 teaspoon ginger, minced
2 cups vegetable broth
2 cups water
1 cup medium pearl barley
1/2 cup white wine
2 tablespoons fresh chives, chopped

## Directions

Melt the vegan butter in a saucepan over medium-high heat.

Once hot, cook the onion and pepper for about 3 minutes until just tender.

Add in the garlic and ginger and continue to sauté for 2 minutes or until aromatic.

Add in the vegetable broth, water, barley and wine; cover and continue to simmer for about 30 minutes. Once all the liquid has been absorbed; fluff the barley with a fork.

Garnish with fresh chives and serve warm. Bon appétit!

**Per serving:** Calories: 269; Fat: 7.1g; Carbs: 43.9g; Protein: 8g

## 236. Traditional Portuguese Papas

(Ready in about 35 minutes | Servings 4)

### Ingredients

4 cups water
2 cups rice milk
1 cup grits
1/4 teaspoon grated nutmeg
1/4 teaspoon kosher salt
4 tablespoon vegan butter
1/4 cup maple syrup

### Directions

Bring the water and milk to a boil over a moderately high heat.

Stir in the grits, nutmeg and salt. Turn the heat to a simmer, cover and continue to cook, for about 30 minutes or until cooked through.

Stir in the vegan butter and maple syrup. Bon appétit!

**Per serving:** Calories: 373; Fat: 16.1g; Carbs: 50.3g; Protein: 6.7g

## 237. The Best Millet Patties Ever

(Ready in about 40 minutes | Servings 4)

### Ingredients

1 cup millet
3 cups water
2 tablespoons olive oil
1 onion, finely chopped
2 cloves garlic, crushed
1 teaspoon smoked paprika
1/2 teaspoon ground cumin
Sea salt and ground black pepper, to taste

### Directions

Bring the millet and water to a boil; turn the heat to a simmer and continue to cook for 30 minutes.

Fluff your millet with a fork and combine it with the remaining ingredients, except for the oil. Shape the mixture into patties.

Heat the olive oil in a nonstick skillet over medium-high heat. Fry the patties for 5 minutes per side or until golden-brown and cooked through. Enjoy!

**Per serving:** Calories: 285; Fat: 9.1g; Carbs: 44.5g; Protein: 6.6g

## 238. One-Pot Italian Rice with Broccoli

(Ready in about 30 minutes | Servings 4)

### Ingredients

2 tablespoons olive oil
1 shallot, chopped
1 teaspoon ginger, minced
1 teaspoon garlic, minced
1/2 pound broccoli florets
1 cup Arborio rice
4 cups roasted vegetable broth

### Directions

In a medium-sized pot, heat the olive oil over a moderately high flame. Add in the shallot and cook for about 3 minutes or until tender and translucent.

Then, add in the ginger and garlic and continue to cook for 30 seconds more. Add in the broccoli and rice and continue to cook for 4 minutes more.

Pour the vegetable broth into the saucepan and bring to a boil; immediately turn the heat to a gentle simmer.

Cook for about 20 minutes or until all the liquid has absorbed. Taste and adjust the seasonings. Bon appétit!

**Per serving:** Calories: 292; Fat: 8.6g; Carbs: 43.2g; Protein: 9.7g

## 239. Overnight Oatmeal with Prunes

(Ready in about 5 minutes + chilling time | Servings 2)

### Ingredients

1 cup hemp milk
1 tablespoon flax seed, ground
2/3 cup rolled oats
2 ounces prunes, sliced
2 tablespoons agave syrup
A pinch of salt
1/2 teaspoon ground cinnamon

### Directions

Divide the ingredients, except for the prunes, between two mason jars.

Cover and shake to combine well. Let them sit overnight in your refrigerator.

Garnish with sliced prunes just before serving. Enjoy!

**Per serving:** Calories: 398; Fat: 9.9g; Carbs: 66.2g; Protein: 13.7g

## 240. Holiday Mini Cornbread Puddings

(Ready in about 30 minutes | Servings 8)

### Ingredients

1 cup all-purpose flour
1 cup yellow cornmeal
1 teaspoon baking powder
1 teaspoon baking soda
1 teaspoon sea salt
2 tablespoons brown sugar
1/2 teaspoon ground allspice
1 cup soy yogurt
1/4 cup vegan butter, melted
1 teaspoon apple cider vinegar
1 red bell pepper, seeded and chopped
1 green bell pepper, seeded and chopped
1 cup marinated mushrooms, chopped
2 small pickled cucumbers, chopped
1 tablespoon fresh basil, chopped
1 tablespoon fresh cilantro, chopped
1 tablespoon fresh chives, chopped

### Directions

Start by preheating your oven to 420 degrees F. Now, spritz a muffin tin with a nonstick cooking spray.

In a mixing bowl, thoroughly combine the flour, cornmeal, baking soda, baking powder, salt, sugar and ground allspice.

Gradually add in the yogurt, vegan butter and apple cider vinegar, whisking constantly to avoid lumps. Fold in the vegetables and herbs.

Scrape the batter into the prepared muffin tin. Bake your muffins for about 25 minutes or until a toothpick inserted in the middle comes out dry and clean.

Transfer them to a wire rack to rest for 5 minutes before unmolding and serving. Bon appétit!

**Per serving:** Calories: 233; Fat: 8.1g; Carbs: 33.1g; Protein: 5.7g

## 241. Last-Minute Baked Rice

(Ready in about 35 minutes | Servings 4)

### Ingredients

2 cups boiling vegetable broth
2 tablespoons olive oil
1 cup white rice
3 cups vegetable broth
4 scallion stalks, chopped
1 celery stalk, chopped
2 garlic cloves, minced

### Directions

Start by preheating your oven to 350 degrees F.

In a lightly oiled baking dish, thoroughly combine all ingredients until well combined.

Bake in the preheated oven for about 35 minutes or until all the liquid has been absorbed. Serve hot!

**Per serving:** Calories: 309; Fat: 8.4g; Carbs: 47g; Protein: 10.3g

## 242. Millet Salad with Pine Nuts

(Ready in about 20 minutes + chilling time | Servings 4)

### Ingredients

2 ½ cups vegetable broth
1 cup millet
1 carrot, grated
1 tomato, diced
1 cucumber, diced
1 onion, sliced thinly
1/4 cup extra-virgin olive oil
Sea salt and ground black pepper, to taste
1/2 cup pine nuts, chopped
2 tablespoons fresh cilantro, chopped

### Directions

Place the vegetable broth and millet in a saucepan; bring to a boil over medium-high heat.

Turn the heat to a simmer and let it cook for about 20 minutes; fluff the millet with a fork and let it cool completely.

Toss the millet with the other ingredients; toss to combine well. Bon appétit!

**Per serving:** Calories: 469; Fat: 28.4g; Carbs: 44.3g; Protein: 11.8g

## 243. Barley with Portobello Mushrooms and Chard

(Ready in about 35 minutes | Servings 4)

### Ingredients

4 tablespoons olive oil
1 onion, chopped
3 cloves garlic, minced
12 ounces Portobello mushrooms, sliced
4 cups vegetable broth
1 cup pearl barley
1/2 cup dry white wine
Sea salt and ground black pepper, to taste
1 teaspoon dried oregano
1 teaspoon dried thyme
4 cups Swiss chard, torn into pieces

### Directions

Heat the olive oil in a saucepan over medium-high heat. Once hot, cook the onion for about 3 minutes until just tender.

Add in the garlic and mushrooms and continue to sauté for 2 minutes or until aromatic.

Add in the vegetable broth, barley, wine, salt, black pepper, oregano and thyme; cover and continue to simmer for about 25 minutes.

Add in the Swiss chard and continue to cook for 5 to 6 minutes more until it wilts. Bon appétit!

**Per serving:** Calories: 389; Fat: 15.9g; Carbs: 49.3g; Protein: 13.3g

## 244. Red Rice and Vegetable Stir-Fry

(Ready in about 55 minutes | Servings 4)

### Ingredients

1 cup cream of celery soup
1/2 cup water
1 cup red rice
2 tablespoons vegan butter
1 small leek, chopped
1 cup green cabbage, chopped
2 bell peppers, sliced
3 cloves garlic, minced
4 tablespoons rice wine
Sea salt and ground black pepper, to season
2 tablespoons soy sauce

### Directions

Bring the soup and water to a boil over medium-high heat. Turn the heat to a simmer.

Cook the brown rice for about 45 minutes or until all the liquid has been absorbed.

In a saucepan, melt the vegan butter over a moderately high heat. Once hot, cook the leek, cabbage and peppers for about 3 minutes until they've softened.

Add in the garlic and continue to sauté an additional 30 seconds. Add a splash of wine to deglaze the pan.

Add in the salt, black pepper and the reserved rice. Stir fry for about 5 minutes or until cooked through; add in the soy sauce and stir again to combine. Serve immediately.

**Per serving:** Calories: 299; Fat: 9.4g; Carbs: 46.8g; Protein: 7g

# LEGUMES

# 245. Traditional Indian Rajma Dal

(Ready in about 20 minutes | Servings 4)

## Ingredients

3 tablespoons sesame oil

1 teaspoon ginger, minced

1 teaspoon cumin seeds

1 teaspoon coriander seeds

1 large onion, chopped

1 celery stalk, chopped

1 teaspoon garlic, minced

1 cup tomato sauce

1 teaspoon garam masala

1/2 teaspoon curry powder

1 small cinnamon stick

1 green chili, seeded and minced

2 cups canned red kidney beans, drained

2 cups vegetable broth

Kosher salt and ground black pepper, to taste

## Directions

In a saucepan, heat the sesame oil over medium-high heat; now, sauté the ginger, cumin seeds and coriander seeds until fragrant or about 30 seconds or so.

Add in the onion and celery and continue to sauté for 3 minutes more until they've softened.

Add in the garlic and continue to sauté for 1 minute longer.

Stir the remaining ingredients into the saucepan and turn the heat to a simmer. Continue to cook for 10 to 12 minutes or until thoroughly cooked. Serve warm and enjoy!

**Per serving:** Calories: 269; Fat: 15.2g; Carbs: 22.9g; Protein: 7.2g

# 246. Red Kidney Bean Salad

(Ready in about 1 hour + chilling time | Servings 6)

## Ingredients

3/4 pound red kidney beans, soaked overnight

2 bell peppers, chopped

1 carrot, trimmed and grated

3 ounces frozen or canned corn kernels, drained

3 heaping tablespoons scallions, chopped

2 cloves garlic, minced

1 red chile pepper, sliced

1/2 cup extra-virgin olive oil

2 tablespoons apple cider vinegar

2 tablespoons fresh lemon juice

Sea salt and ground black pepper, to taste

2 tablespoons fresh cilantro, chopped

2 tablespoons fresh parsley, chopped

2 tablespoons fresh basil, chopped

## Directions

Cover the soaked beans with a fresh change of cold water and bring to a boil. Let it boil for about 10 minutes. Turn the heat to a simmer and continue to cook for 50 to 55 minutes or until tender.

Allow your beans to cool completely, then, transfer them to a salad bowl.

Add in the remaining ingredients and toss to combine well. Bon appétit!

**Per serving:** Calories: 443; Fat: 19.2g; Carbs: 52.2g; Protein: 18.1g

# 247. Anasazi Bean and Vegetable Stew

(Ready in about 1 hour | Servings 3)

## Ingredients

1 cup Anasazi beans, soaked overnight and drained

3 cups roasted vegetable broth

1 bay laurel

1 thyme sprig, chopped

1 rosemary sprig, chopped

3 tablespoons olive oil

1 large onion, chopped

2 celery stalks, chopped

2 carrots, chopped

2 bell peppers, seeded and chopped

1 green chili pepper, seeded and chopped

2 garlic cloves, minced

Sea salt and ground black pepper, to taste

1 teaspoon cayenne pepper

1 teaspoon paprika

## Directions

In a saucepan, bring the Anasazi beans and broth to a boil. Once boiling, turn the heat to a simmer. Add in the bay laurel, thyme and rosemary; let it cook for about 50 minutes or until tender.

Meanwhile, in a heavy-bottomed pot, heat the olive oil over medium-high heat. Now, sauté the onion, celery, carrots and peppers for about 4 minutes until tender.

Add in the garlic and continue to sauté for 30 seconds more or until aromatic.

Add the sautéed mixture to the cooked beans. Season with salt, black pepper, cayenne pepper and paprika.

Continue to simmer, stirring periodically, for 10 minutes more or until everything is cooked through. Bon appétit!

**Per serving:** Calories: 444; Fat: 15.8g; Carbs: 58.2g; Protein: 20.2g

# 248. Easy and Hearty Shakshuka

(Ready in about 50 minutes | Servings 4)

## Ingredients

2 tablespoons olive oil

1 onion, chopped

2 bell peppers, chopped

1 poblano pepper, chopped

2 cloves garlic, minced

2 tomatoes, pureed

Sea salt and black pepper, to taste

1 teaspoon dried basil

1 teaspoon red pepper flakes

1 teaspoon paprika

2 bay leaves

1 cup chickpeas, soaked overnight, rinsed and drained

3 cups vegetable broth

2 tablespoons fresh cilantro, roughly chopped

## Directions

Heat the olive oil in a saucepan over medium heat. Once hot, cook the onion, peppers and garlic for about 4 minutes, until tender and aromatic.

Add in the pureed tomato tomatoes, sea salt, black pepper, basil, red pepper, paprika and bay leaves.

Turn the heat to a simmer and add in the chickpeas and vegetable broth. Cook for 45 minutes or until tender.

Taste and adjust seasonings. Spoon your shakshuka into individual bowls and serve garnished with the fresh cilantro. Bon appétit!

**Per serving:** Calories: 324; Fat: 11.2g; Carbs: 42.2g; Protein: 15.8g

## 249. Old-Fashioned Chili

(Ready in about 1 hour 30 minutes | Servings 4)

### Ingredients

3/4 pound red kidney beans, soaked overnight
2 tablespoons olive oil
1 onion, chopped
2 bell peppers, chopped
1 red chili pepper, chopped
2 ribs celery, chopped
2 cloves garlic, minced
2 bay leaves
1 teaspoon ground cumin

1 teaspoon thyme, chopped
1 teaspoon black peppercorns
20 ounces tomatoes, crushed
2 cups vegetable broth
1 teaspoon smoked paprika
Sea salt, to taste
2 tablespoons fresh cilantro, chopped
1 avocado, pitted, peeled and sliced

### Directions

Cover the soaked beans with a fresh change of cold water and bring to a boil. Let it boil for about 10 minutes. Turn the heat to a simmer and continue to cook for 50 to 55 minutes or until tender.

In a heavy-bottomed pot, heat the olive oil over medium heat. Once hot, sauté the onion, bell pepper and celery.

Sauté the garlic, bay leaves, ground cumin, thyme and black peppercorns for about 1 minute or so.

Add in the diced tomatoes, vegetable broth, paprika, salt and cooked beans. Let it simmer, stirring periodically, for 25 to 30 minutes or until cooked through.

Serve garnished with fresh cilantro and avocado. Bon appétit!

**Per serving:** Calories: 514; Fat: 16.4g; Carbs: 72g; Protein: 25.8g

## 250. Easy Red Lentil Salad

(Ready in about 20 minutes + chilling time | Servings 3)

### Ingredients

1/2 cup red lentils, soaked overnight and drained
1 ½ cups water
1 sprig rosemary
1 bay leaf
1 cup grape tomatoes, halved
1 cucumber, thinly sliced

1 bell pepper, thinly sliced
1 clove garlic, minced
1 onion, thinly sliced
2 tablespoons fresh lime juice
4 tablespoons olive oil
Sea salt and ground black pepper, to taste

### Directions

Add the red lentils, water, rosemary and bay leaf to a saucepan and bring to a boil over high heat. Then, turn the heat to a simmer and continue to cook for 20 minutes or until tender.

Place the lentils in a salad bowl and let them cool completely.

Add in the remaining ingredients and toss to combine well. Serve at room temperature or well-chilled.

Bon appétit!

**Per serving:** Calories: 295; Fat: 18.8g; Carbs: 25.2g; Protein: 8.5g

## 251. Mediterranean-Style Chickpea Salad

(Ready in about 40 minutes + chilling time | Servings 4)

### Ingredients

2 cups chickpeas, soaked overnight and drained
1 Persian cucumber, sliced
1 cup cherry tomatoes, halved
1 red bell peppers, seeded and sliced
1 green bell pepper, seeded and sliced
1 teaspoon deli mustard
1 teaspoon coriander seeds

1 teaspoon jalapeno pepper, minced
1 tablespoon fresh lemon juice
1 tablespoon balsamic vinegar
1/4 cup extra-virgin olive oil
Sea salt and ground black pepper, to taste
2 tablespoons fresh cilantro, chopped
2 tablespoons Kalamata olives, pitted and sliced

### Directions

Place the chickpeas in a stockpot; cover the chickpeas with water by 2 inches. Bring it to a boil.

Immediately turn the heat to a simmer and continue to cook for about 40 minutes or until tender.

Transfer your chickpeas to a salad bowl. Add in the remaining ingredients and toss to combine well. Bon appétit!

**Per serving:** Calories: 468; Fat: 12.5g; Carbs: 73g; Protein: 21.8g

## 252. Traditional Tuscan Bean Stew (Ribollita)

(Ready in about 25 minutes | Servings 5)

### Ingredients

3 tablespoons olive oil
1 medium leek, chopped
1 celery with leaves, chopped
1 zucchini, diced
1 Italian pepper, sliced
3 garlic cloves, crushed
2 bay leaves
Kosher salt and ground black pepper, to taste

1 teaspoon cayenne pepper
1 (28-ounce) can tomatoes, crushed
2 cups vegetable broth
2 (15-ounce) cans Great Northern beans, drained
2 cups Lacinato kale, torn into pieces
1 cup crostini

### Directions

In a heavy-bottomed pot, heat the olive oil over medium heat. Once hot, sauté the leek, celery, zucchini and pepper for about 4 minutes.

Sauté the garlic and bay leaves for about 1 minute or so.

Add in the spices, tomatoes, broth and canned beans. Let it simmer, stirring occasionally, for about 15 minutes or until cooked through.

Add in the Lacinato kale and continue simmering, stirring occasionally, for 4 minutes.

Serve garnished with crostini. Bon appétit!

**Per serving:** Calories: 388; Fat: 10.3g; Carbs: 57.3g; Protein: 19.5g

# 253. Beluga Lentil and Vegetable Mélange

(Ready in about 25 minutes | Servings 5)

## Ingredients

3 tablespoons olive oil
1 onion, minced
2 bell peppers, seeded and chopped
1 carrot, trimmed and chopped
1 parsnip, trimmed and chopped
1 teaspoon ginger, minced
2 cloves garlic, minced
Sea salt and ground black pepper, to taste
1 large-sized zucchini, diced
1 cup tomato sauce
1 cup vegetable broth
1 ½ cups beluga lentils, soaked overnight and drained
2 cups Swiss chard

## Directions

In a Dutch oven, heat the olive oil until sizzling. Now, sauté the onion, bell pepper, carrot and parsnip, until they've softened.

Add in the ginger and garlic and continue sautéing an additional 30 seconds.

Now, add in the salt, black pepper, zucchini, tomato sauce, vegetable broth and lentils; let it simmer for about 20 minutes until everything is thoroughly cooked.

Add in the Swiss chard; cover and let it simmer for 5 minutes more. Bon appétit!

**Per serving:** Calories: 382; Fat: 9.3g; Carbs: 59g; Protein: 17.2g

# 254. Mexican Chickpea Taco Bowls

(Ready in about 15 minutes | Servings 4)

## Ingredients

2 tablespoons sesame oil
1 red onion, chopped
1 habanero pepper, minced
2 garlic cloves, crushed
2 bell peppers, seeded and diced
Sea salt and ground black pepper
1/2 teaspoon Mexican oregano
1 teaspoon ground cumin
2 ripe tomatoes, pureed
1 teaspoon brown sugar
16 ounces canned chickpeas, drained
4 (8-inch) flour tortillas
2 tablespoons fresh coriander, roughly chopped

## Directions

In a large skillet, heat the sesame oil over a moderately high heat. Then, sauté the onions for 2 to 3 minutes or until tender.

Add in the peppers and garlic and continue to sauté for 1 minute or until fragrant.

Add in the spices, tomatoes and brown sugar and bring to a boil. Immediately turn the heat to a simmer, add in the canned chickpeas and let it cook for 8 minutes longer or until heated through.

Toast your tortillas and arrange them with the prepared chickpea mixture.

Top with fresh coriander and serve immediately. Bon appétit!

**Per serving:** Calories: 409; Fat: 13.5g; Carbs: 61.3g; Protein: 13.8g

# 255. Indian Dal Makhani

(Ready in about 20 minutes | Servings 6)

## Ingredients

3 tablespoons sesame oil
1 large onion, chopped
1 bell pepper, seeded and chopped
2 garlic cloves, minced
1 tablespoon ginger, grated
2 green chilies, seeded and chopped
1 teaspoon cumin seeds
1 bay laurel
1 teaspoon turmeric powder
1/4 teaspoon red peppers
1/4 teaspoon ground allspice
1/2 teaspoon garam masala
1 cup tomato sauce
4 cups vegetable broth
1 ½ cups black lentils, soaked overnight and drained
4-5 curry leaves, for garnish

## Directions

In a saucepan, heat the sesame oil over medium-high heat; now, sauté the onion and bell pepper for 3 minutes more until they've softened.

Add in the garlic, ginger, green chilies, cumin seeds and bay laurel; continue to sauté, stirring frequently, for 1 minute or until fragrant.

Stir in the remaining ingredients, except for the curry leaves. Now, turn the heat to a simmer. Continue to cook for 15 minutes more or until thoroughly cooked.

Garnish with curry leaves and serve hot!

**Per serving:** Calories: 329; Fat: 8.5g; Carbs: 44.1g; Protein: 16.8g

# 256. Mexican-Style Bean Bowl

(Ready in about 1 hour + chilling time | Servings 6)

## Ingredients

1 pound red beans, soaked overnight and drained
1 cup canned corn kernels, drained
2 roasted bell peppers, sliced
1 chili pepper, finely chopped
1 cup cherry tomatoes, halved
1 red onion, chopped
1/4 cup fresh cilantro, chopped
1/4 cup fresh parsley, chopped
1 teaspoon Mexican oregano
1/4 cup red wine vinegar
2 tablespoons fresh lemon juice
1/3 cup extra-virgin olive oil
Sea salt and ground black, to taste
1 avocado, peeled, pitted and sliced

## Directions

Cover the soaked beans with a fresh change of cold water and bring to a boil. Let it boil for about 10 minutes. Turn the heat to a simmer and continue to cook for 50 to 55 minutes or until tender.

Allow your beans to cool completely, then, transfer them to a salad bowl.

Add in the remaining ingredients and toss to combine well. Serve at room temperature.

Bon appétit!

**Per serving:** Calories: 465; Fat: 17.9g; Carbs: 60.4g; Protein: 20.2g

## 257. Classic Italian Minestrone

(Ready in about 30 minutes | Servings 5)

### Ingredients

2 tablespoons olive oil
1 large onion, diced
2 carrots, sliced
4 cloves garlic, minced
1 cup elbow pasta
5 cups vegetable broth
1 (15-ounce) can white beans, drained
1 large zucchini, diced
1 (28-ounce) can tomatoes, crushed
1 tablespoon fresh oregano leaves, chopped
1 tablespoon fresh basil leaves, chopped
1 tablespoon fresh Italian parsley, chopped

### Directions

In a Dutch oven, heat the olive oil until sizzling. Now, sauté the onion and carrots until they've softened.

Add in the garlic, uncooked pasta and broth; let it simmer for about 15 minutes.

Stir in the beans, zucchini, tomatoes and herbs. Continue to cook, covered, for about 10 minutes until everything is thoroughly cooked.

Garnish with some extra herbs, if desired. Bon appétit!

**Per serving:** Calories: 305; Fat: 8.6g; Carbs: 45.1g; Protein: 14.2g

## 258. Green Lentil Stew with Collard Greens

(Ready in about 30 minutes | Servings 5)

### Ingredients

2 tablespoons olive oil
1 onion, chopped
2 sweet potatoes, peeled and diced
1 bell pepper, chopped
2 carrots, chopped
1 parsnip, chopped
1 celery, chopped
2 cloves garlic
1 ½ cups green lentils
1 tablespoon Italian herb mix
1 cup tomato sauce
5 cups vegetable broth
1 cup frozen corn
1 cup collard greens, torn into pieces

### Directions

In a Dutch oven, heat the olive oil until sizzling. Now, sauté the onion, sweet potatoes, bell pepper, carrots, parsnip and celery until they've softened.

Add in the garlic and continue sautéing an additional 30 seconds.

Now, add in the green lentils, Italian herb mix, tomato sauce and vegetable broth; let it simmer for about 20 minutes until everything is thoroughly cooked.

Add in the frozen corn and collard greens; cover and let it simmer for 5 minutes more. Bon appétit!

**Per serving:** Calories: 415; Fat: 6.6g; Carbs: 71g; Protein: 18.4g

## 259. Chickpea Garden Vegetable Medley

(Ready in about 30 minutes | Servings 4)

### Ingredients

2 tablespoons olive oil
1 onion, finely chopped
1 bell pepper, chopped
1 fennel bulb, chopped
3 cloves garlic, minced
2 ripe tomatoes, pureed
2 tablespoons fresh parsley, roughly chopped
2 tablespoons fresh basil, roughly chopped
2 tablespoons fresh coriander, roughly chopped
2 cups vegetable broth
14 ounces canned chickpeas, drained
Kosher salt and ground black pepper, to taste
1/2 teaspoon cayenne pepper
1 teaspoon paprika
1 avocado, peeled and sliced

### Directions

In a heavy-bottomed pot, heat the olive oil over medium heat. Once hot, sauté the onion, bell pepper and fennel bulb for about 4 minutes.

Sauté the garlic for about 1 minute or until aromatic.

Add in the tomatoes, fresh herbs, broth, chickpeas, salt, black pepper, cayenne pepper and paprika. Let it simmer, stirring occasionally, for about 20 minutes or until cooked through.

Taste and adjust the seasonings. Serve garnished with the slices of the fresh avocado. Bon appétit!

**Per serving:** Calories: 369; Fat: 18.1g; Carbs: 43.5g; Protein: 13.2g

## 260. Hot Bean Dipping Sauce

(Ready in about 30 minutes | Servings 10)

### Ingredients

2 (15-ounce) cans Great Northern beans, drained
2 tablespoons olive oil
2 tablespoons Sriracha sauce
2 tablespoons nutritional yeast
4 ounces vegan cream cheese
1/2 teaspoon paprika
1/2 teaspoon cayenne pepper
1/2 teaspoon ground cumin
Sea salt and ground black pepper, to taste
4 ounces tortilla chips

### Directions

Start by preheating your oven to 360 degrees F.

Pulse all the ingredients, except for the tortilla chips, in your food processor until your desired consistency is reached.

Bake your dip in the preheated oven for about 25 minutes or until hot.

Serve with tortilla chips and enjoy!

**Per serving:** Calories: 175; Fat: 4.7g; Carbs: 24.9g; Protein: 8.8g

# 261. Chinese-Style Soybean Salad

(Ready in about 10 minutes | Servings 4)

## Ingredients

1 (15-ounce) can soybeans, drained
1 cup arugula
1 cup baby spinach
1 cup green cabbage, shredded
1 onion, thinly sliced
1/2 teaspoon garlic, minced
1 teaspoon ginger, minced
1/2 teaspoon deli mustard
2 tablespoons soy sauce
1 tablespoon rice vinegar
1 tablespoon lime juice
2 tablespoons tahini
1 teaspoon agave syrup

## Directions

In a salad bowl, place the soybeans, arugula, spinach, cabbage and onion; toss to combine.

In a small mixing dish, whisk the remaining ingredients for the dressing.

Dress your salad and serve immediately. Bon appétit!

Per serving: Calories: 265; Fat: 13.7g; Carbs: 21g; Protein: 18g

# 262. Old-Fashioned Lentil and Vegetable Stew

(Ready in about 25 minutes | Servings 5)

## Ingredients

3 tablespoons olive oil
1 large onion, chopped
1 carrot, chopped
1 bell pepper, diced
1 habanero pepper, chopped
3 cloves garlic, minced
Kosher salt and black pepper, to taste
1 teaspoon ground cumin
1 teaspoon smoked paprika
1 (28-ounce) can tomatoes, crushed
2 tablespoons tomato ketchup
4 cups vegetable broth
3/4 pound dry red lentils, soaked overnight and drained
1 avocado, sliced

## Directions

In a heavy-bottomed pot, heat the olive oil over medium heat. Once hot, sauté the onion, carrot and peppers for about 4 minutes.

Sauté the garlic for about 1 minute or so.

Add in the spices, tomatoes, ketchup, broth and canned lentils. Let it simmer, stirring occasionally, for about 20 minutes or until cooked through.

Serve garnished with the slices of avocado. Bon appétit!

Per serving: Calories: 475; Fat: 17.3g; Carbs: 61.4g; Protein: 23.7g

# 263. Indian Chana Masala

(Ready in about 15 minutes | Servings 4)

## Ingredients

1 cup tomatoes, pureed
1 Kashmiri chile pepper, chopped
1 large shallot, chopped
1 teaspoon fresh ginger, peeled and grated
4 tablespoons olive oil
2 cloves garlic, minced
1 teaspoon coriander seeds
1 teaspoon garam masala
1/2 teaspoon turmeric powder
Sea salt and ground black pepper, to taste
1/2 cup vegetable broth
16 ounces canned chickpeas
1 tablespoon fresh lime juice

## Directions

In your blender or food processor, blend the tomatoes, Kashmiri chile pepper, shallot and ginger into a paste.

In a saucepan, heat the olive oil over medium heat. Once hot, cook the prepared paste and garlic for about 2 minutes.

Add in the remaining spices, broth and chickpeas. Turn the heat to a simmer. Continue to simmer for 8 minutes more or until cooked through.

Remove from the heat. Drizzle fresh lime juice over the top of each serving. Bon appétit!

Per serving: Calories: 305; Fat: 17.1g; Carbs: 30.1g; Protein: 9.4g

# 264. Red Kidney Bean Pâté

(Ready in about 10 minutes | Servings 8)

## Ingredients

2 tablespoons olive oil
1 onion, chopped
1 bell pepper, chopped
2 cloves garlic, minced
2 cups red kidney beans, boiled and drained
1/4 cup olive oil
1 teaspoon stone-ground mustard
2 tablespoons fresh parsley, chopped
2 tablespoons fresh basil, chopped
Sea salt and ground black pepper, to taste

## Directions

In a saucepan, heat the olive oil over medium-high heat. Now, cook the onion, pepper and garlic until just tender or about 3 minutes.

Add the sautéed mixture to your blender; add in the remaining ingredients. Puree the ingredients in your blender or food processor until smooth and creamy. Bon appétit!

Per serving: Calories: 135; Fat: 12.1g; Carbs: 4.4g; Protein: 1.6g

# 265. Brown Lentil Bowl

(Ready in about 20 minutes + chilling time | Servings 4)

## Ingredients

1 cup brown lentils, soaked overnight and drained
3 cups water
2 cups brown rice, cooked
1 zucchini, diced
1 red onion, chopped
1 teaspoon garlic, minced
1 cucumber, sliced
1 bell pepper, sliced
4 tablespoons olive oil
1 tablespoon rice vinegar
2 tablespoons lemon juice
2 tablespoons soy sauce
1/2 teaspoon dried oregano
1/2 teaspoon ground cumin
Sea salt and ground black pepper, to taste
2 cups arugula
2 cups Romaine lettuce, torn into pieces

## Directions

Add the brown lentils and water to a saucepan and bring to a boil over high heat. Then, turn the heat to a simmer and continue to cook for 20 minutes or until tender.

Place the lentils in a salad bowl and let them cool completely.

Add in the remaining ingredients and toss to combine well. Serve at room temperature or well-chilled. Bon appétit!

Per serving: Calories: 452; Fat: 16.6g; Carbs: 61.7g; Protein: 16.4g

## 266. Hot and Spicy Anasazi Bean Soup

(Ready in about 1 hour 10 minutes | Servings 5)

### Ingredients

2 cups Anasazi beans, soaked overnight, drained and rinsed
8 cups water
2 bay leaves
3 tablespoons olive oil
2 medium onions, chopped
2 bell peppers, chopped
1 habanero pepper, chopped
3 cloves garlic, pressed or minced
Sea salt and ground black pepper, to taste

### Directions

In a soup pot, bring the Anasazi beans and water to a boil. Once boiling, turn the heat to a simmer. Add in the bay leaves and let it cook for about 1 hour or until tender.

Meanwhile, in a heavy-bottomed pot, heat the olive oil over medium-high heat. Now, sauté the onion, peppers and garlic for about 4 minutes until tender.

Add the sautéed mixture to the cooked beans. Season with salt and black pepper.

Continue to simmer, stirring periodically, for 10 minutes more or until everything is cooked through. Bon appétit!

**Per serving:** Calories: 352; Fat: 8.5g; Carbs: 50.1g; Protein: 19.7g

## 267. Black-Eyed Pea Salad (Ñebbe)

(Ready in about 1 hour | Servings 5)

### Ingredients

2 cups dried black-eyed peas, soaked overnight and drained
2 tablespoons basil leaves, chopped
2 tablespoons parsley leaves, chopped
1 shallot, chopped
1 cucumber, sliced
2 bell peppers, seeded and diced
1 Scotch bonnet chili pepper, seeded and finely chopped
1 cup cherry tomatoes, quartered
Sea salt and ground black pepper, to taste
2 tablespoons fresh lime juice
1 tablespoon apple cider vinegar
1/4 cup extra-virgin olive oil
1 avocado, peeled, pitted and sliced

### Directions

Cover the black-eyed peas with water by 2 inches and bring to a gentle boil. Let it boil for about 15 minutes.

Then, turn the heat to a simmer for about 45 minutes. Let it cool completely.

Place the black-eyed peas in a salad bowl. Add in the basil, parsley, shallot, cucumber, bell peppers, cherry tomatoes, salt and black pepper.

In a mixing bowl, whisk the lime juice, vinegar and olive oil.

Dress the salad, garnish with fresh avocado and serve immediately. Bon appétit!

**Per serving:** Calories: 471; Fat: 17.5g; Carbs: 61.5g; Protein: 20.6g

## 268. Mom's Famous Chili

(Ready in about 1 hour 30 minutes | Servings 5)

### Ingredients

1 pound red black beans, soaked overnight and drained
3 tablespoons olive oil
1 large red onion, diced
2 bell peppers, diced
1 poblano pepper, minced
1 large carrot, trimmed and diced
2 cloves garlic, minced
2 bay leaves
1 teaspoon mixed peppercorns
Kosher salt and cayenne pepper, to taste
1 tablespoon paprika
2 ripe tomatoes, pureed
2 tablespoons tomato ketchup
3 cups vegetable broth

### Directions

Cover the soaked beans with a fresh change of cold water and bring to a boil. Let it boil for about 10 minutes. Turn the heat to a simmer and continue to cook for 50 to 55 minutes or until tender.

In a heavy-bottomed pot, heat the olive oil over medium heat. Once hot, sauté the onion, peppers and carrot.

Sauté the garlic for about 30 seconds or until aromatic.

Add in the remaining ingredients along with the cooked beans. Let it simmer, stirring periodically, for 25 to 30 minutes or until cooked through.

Discard the bay leaves, ladle into individual bowls and serve hot!

**Per serving:** Calories: 455; Fat: 10.5g; Carbs: 68.6g; Protein: 24.7g

## 269. Creamed Chickpea Salad with Pine Nuts

(Ready in about 10 minutes | Servings 4)

### Ingredients

16 ounces canned chickpeas, drained
1 teaspoon garlic, minced
1 shallot, chopped
1 cup cherry tomatoes, halved
1 bell pepper, seeded and sliced
1/4 cup fresh basil, chopped
1/4 cup fresh parsley, chopped
1/2 cup vegan mayonnaise
1 tablespoon lemon juice
1 teaspoon capers, drained
Sea salt and ground black pepper, to taste
2 ounces pine nuts

### Directions

Place the chickpeas, vegetables and herbs in a salad bowl.

Add in the mayonnaise, lemon juice, capers, salt and black pepper. Stir to combine.

Top with pine nuts and serve immediately. Bon appétit!

**Per serving:** Calories: 386; Fat: 22.5g; Carbs: 37.2g; Protein: 12.9g

## 270. Black Bean Buda Bowl

(Ready in about 1 hour | Servings 4)

### Ingredients

1/2 pound black beans, soaked overnight and drained

2 cups brown rice, cooked

1 medium-sized onion, thinly sliced

1 cup bell pepper, seeded and sliced

1 jalapeno pepper, seeded and sliced

2 cloves garlic, minced

1 cup arugula

1 cup baby spinach

1 teaspoon lime zest

1 tablespoon Dijon mustard

1/4 cup red wine vinegar

1/4 cup extra-virgin olive oil

2 tablespoons agave syrup

Flaky sea salt and ground black pepper, to taste

1/4 cup fresh Italian parsley, roughly chopped

### Directions

Cover the soaked beans with a fresh change of cold water and bring to a boil. Let it boil for about 10 minutes. Turn the heat to a simmer and continue to cook for 50 to 55 minutes or until tender.

To serve, divide the beans and rice between serving bowls; top with the vegetables.

In a small mixing dish, thoroughly combine the lime zest, mustard, vinegar, olive oil, agave syrup, salt and pepper. Drizzle the vinaigrette over the salad.

Garnish with fresh Italian parsley. Bon appétit!

**Per serving:** Calories: 365; Fat: 14.1g; Carbs: 45.6g; Protein: 15.5g

## 271. Middle Eastern Chickpea Stew

(Ready in about 20 minutes | Servings 4)

### Ingredients

1 onion, chopped

1 chili pepper, chopped

2 garlic cloves, chopped

1 teaspoon mustard seeds

1 teaspoon coriander seeds

1 bay leaf

1/2 cup tomato puree

2 tablespoons olive oil

1 celery with leaves, chopped

2 medium carrots, trimmed and chopped

2 cups vegetable broth

1 teaspoon ground cumin

1 small-sized cinnamon stick

16 ounces canned chickpeas, drained

2 cups Swiss chard, torn into pieces

### Directions

In your blender or food processor, blend the onion, chili pepper, garlic, mustard seeds, coriander seeds, bay leaf and tomato puree into a paste.

In a stockpot, heat the olive oil until sizzling. Now, cook the celery and carrots for about 3 minutes or until they've softened. Add in the paste and continue to cook for a further 2 minutes.

Then, add in the vegetable broth, cumin, cinnamon and chickpeas; bring to a gentle boil.

Turn the heat to simmer and let it cook for 6 minutes; fold in Swiss chard and continue to cook for 4 to 5 minutes more or until the leaves wilt. Serve hot and enjoy!

**Per serving:** Calories: 305; Fat: 11.2g; Carbs: 38.6g; Protein: 12.7g

## 272. Lentil and Tomato Dip

(Ready in about 10 minutes | Servings 8)

### Ingredients

16 ounces lentils, boiled and drained

4 tablespoons sun-dried tomatoes, chopped

1 cup tomato paste

4 tablespoons tahini

1 teaspoon stone-ground mustard

1 teaspoon ground cumin

1/4 teaspoon ground bay leaf

1 teaspoon red pepper flakes

Sea salt and ground black pepper, to taste

### Directions

Blitz all the ingredients in your blender or food processor until your desired consistency is reached.

Place in your refrigerator until ready to serve.

Serve with toasted pita wedges or vegetable sticks. Enjoy!

**Per serving:** Calories: 144; Fat: 4.5g; Carbs: 20.2g; Protein: 8.1g

## 273. Creamed Green Pea Salad

(Ready in about 10 minutes + chilling time | Servings 6)

### Ingredients

2 (14.5 ounce) cans green peas, drained

1/2 cup vegan mayonnaise

1 teaspoon Dijon mustard

2 tablespoons scallions, chopped

2 pickles, chopped

1/2 cup marinated mushrooms, chopped and drained

1/2 teaspoon garlic, minced

Sea salt and ground black pepper, to taste

### Directions

Place all the ingredients in a salad bowl. Gently stir to combine.

Place the salad in your refrigerator until ready to serve.

Bon appétit!

**Per serving:** Calories: 154; Fat: 6.7g; Carbs: 17.3g; Protein: 6.9g

## 274. Middle Eastern Za'atar Hummus

(Ready in about 10 minutes | Servings 8)

### Ingredients

10 ounces chickpeas, boiled and drained

1/4 cup tahini

2 tablespoons extra-virgin olive oil

2 tablespoons sun-dried tomatoes, chopped

1 lemon, freshly squeezed

2 garlic cloves, minced

Kosher salt and ground black pepper, to taste

1/2 teaspoon smoked paprika

1 teaspoon Za'atar

### Directions

Blitz all the ingredients in your food processor until creamy and uniform.

Place in your refrigerator until ready to serve.

Bon appétit!

**Per serving:** Calories: 140; Fat: 8.5g; Carbs: 12.4g; Protein: 4.6g

## 275. Lentil Salad with Pine Nuts

(Ready in about 20 minutes + chilling time | Servings 3)

### Ingredients

1/2 cup brown lentils
1 ½ cups vegetable broth
1 carrot, cut into matchsticks
1 small onion, chopped
1 cucumber, sliced
2 cloves garlic, minced
3 tablespoons extra-virgin olive oil
1 tablespoon red wine vinegar
2 tablespoons lemon juice
2 tablespoons basil, chopped
2 tablespoons parsley, chopped
2 tablespoons chives, chopped
Sea salt and ground black pepper, to taste
2 tablespoons pine nuts, roughly chopped

### Directions

Add the brown lentils and vegetable broth to a saucepan and bring to a boil over high heat. Then, turn the heat to a simmer and continue to cook for 20 minutes or until tender.

Place the lentils in a salad bowl.

Add in the vegetables and toss to combine well. In a mixing bowl, whisk the oil, vinegar, lemon juice, basil, parsley, chives, salt and black pepper.

Dress your salad, garnish with pine nuts and serve at room temperature. Bon appétit!

**Per serving:** Calories: 332; Fat: 19.7g; Carbs: 28.2g; Protein: 12.2g

## 276. Hot Anasazi Bean Salad

(Ready in about 1 hour | Servings 5)

### Ingredients

2 cups Anasazi beans, soaked overnight, drained and rinsed
6 cups water
1 poblano pepper, chopped
1 onion, chopped
1 cup cherry tomatoes, halved
2 cups mixed greens, ton into pieces
Dressing:
1 teaspoon garlic, chopped
1/2 cup extra-virgin olive oil
1 tablespoon lemon juice
2 tablespoons red wine vinegar
1 tablespoon stone-ground mustard
1 tablespoon soy sauce
1/2 teaspoon dried oregano
1/2 teaspoon dried basil
Sea salt and ground black pepper, to taste

### Directions

In a saucepan, bring the Anasazi beans and water to a boil. Once boiling, turn the heat to a simmer and let it cook for about 1 hour or until tender.

Drain the cooked beans and place them in a salad bowl; add in the other salad ingredients.

Then, in a small mixing bowl, whisk all the dressing ingredients until well blended. Dress your salad and toss to combine. Serve at room temperature and enjoy!

**Per serving:** Calories: 482; Fat: 23.1g; Carbs: 54.2g; Protein: 17.2g

## 277. Traditional Mnazaleh Stew

(Ready in about 25 minutes | Servings 4)

### Ingredients

4 tablespoons olive oil
1 onion, chopped
1 large-sized eggplant, peeled and diced
1 cup carrots, chopped
2 garlic cloves, minced
2 large-sized tomatoes, pureed
1 teaspoon Baharat seasoning
2 cups vegetable broth
14 ounces canned chickpeas, drained
Kosher salt and ground black pepper, to taste
1 medium-sized avocado, pitted, peeled and sliced

### Directions

In a heavy-bottomed pot, heat the olive oil over medium heat. Once hot, sauté the onion, eggplant and carrots for about 4 minutes.

Sauté the garlic for about 1 minute or until aromatic.

Add in the tomatoes, Baharat seasoning, broth and canned chickpeas. Let it simmer, stirring occasionally, for about 20 minutes or until cooked through.

Season with salt and pepper. Serve garnished with slices of the fresh avocado. Bon appétit!

**Per serving:** Calories: 439; Fat: 24g; Carbs: 44.9g; Protein: 13.5g

## 278. Peppery Red Lentil Spread

(Ready in about 25 minutes | Servings 9)

### Ingredients

1 ½ cups red lentils, soaked overnight and drained
4 ½ cups water
1 sprig rosemary
2 bay leaves
2 roasted peppers, seeded and diced
1 shallot, chopped
2 cloves garlic, minced
1/4 cup olive oil
2 tablespoons tahini
Sea salt and ground black pepper, to taste

### Directions

Add the red lentils, water, rosemary and bay leaves to a saucepan and bring to a boil over high heat. Then, turn the heat to a simmer and continue to cook for 20 minutes or until tender.

Place the lentils in a food processor.

Add in the remaining ingredients and process until everything is well incorporated.

Bon appétit!

**Per serving:** Calories: 193; Fat: 8.5g; Carbs: 22.3g; Protein: 8.5g

## 279. Wok-Fried Spiced Snow Pea

(Ready in about 10 minutes | Servings 4)

### Ingredients

2 tablespoons sesame oil
1 onion, chopped
1 carrot, trimmed and chopped
1 teaspoon ginger-garlic paste

1 pound snow peas
Szechuan pepper, to taste
1 teaspoon Sriracha sauce
2 tablespoons soy sauce
1 tablespoon rice vinegar

### Directions

Heat the sesame oil in a wok until sizzling. Now, stir-fry the onion and carrot for 2 minutes or until crisp-tender.

Add in the ginger-garlic paste and continue to cook for 30 seconds more.

Add in the snow peas and stir-fry over high heat for about 3 minutes until lightly charred.

Then, stir in the pepper, Sriracha, soy sauce and rice vinegar and stir-fry for 1 minute more. Serve immediately and enjoy!

**Per serving:** Calories: 196; Fat: 8.7g; Carbs: 23g; Protein: 7.3g

## 280. Quick Everyday Chili

(Ready in about 35 minutes | Servings 5)

### Ingredients

2 tablespoons olive oil
1 large onion, chopped
1 celery with leaves, trimmed and diced
1 carrot, trimmed and diced
1 sweet potato, peeled and diced
3 cloves garlic, minced
1 jalapeno pepper, minced
1 teaspoon cayenne pepper
1 teaspoon coriander seeds
1 teaspoon fennel seeds

1 teaspoon paprika
2 cups stewed tomatoes, crushed
2 tablespoons tomato ketchup
2 teaspoons vegan bouillon granules
1 cup water
1 cup cream of onion soup
2 pounds canned pinto beans, drained
1 lime, sliced

### Directions

In a heavy-bottomed pot, heat the olive oil over medium heat. Once hot, sauté the onion, celery, carrot and sweet potato for about 4 minutes.

Sauté the garlic and jalapeno pepper for about 1 minute or so.

Add in the spices, tomatoes, ketchup, vegan bouillon granules, water, cream of onion soup and canned beans. Let it simmer, stirring occasionally, for about 30 minutes or until cooked through.

Serve garnished with the slices of lime. Bon appétit!

**Per serving:** Calories: 345; Fat: 8.7g; Carbs: 54.5g; Protein: 15.2g

## 281. Creamed Black-Eyed Pea Salad

(Ready in about 1 hour | Servings 5)

### Ingredients

1 ½ cups black-eyed peas, soaked overnight and drained
4 scallion stalks, sliced
1 carrot, julienned
1 cup green cabbage, shredded
2 bell peppers, seeded and chopped
2 medium tomatoes, diced

1 tablespoon sun-dried tomatoes, chopped
1 teaspoon garlic, minced
1/2 cup vegan mayonnaise
1 tablespoon lime juice
1/4 cup white wine vinegar
Sea salt and ground black pepper, to taste

### Directions

Cover the black-eyed peas with water by 2 inches and bring to a gentle boil. Let it boil for about 15 minutes.

Then, turn the heat to a simmer for about 45 minutes. Let it cool completely.

Place the black-eyed peas in a salad bowl. Add in the remaining ingredients and stir to combine well. Bon appétit!

**Per serving:** Calories: 325; Fat: 8.6g; Carbs: 48.2g; Protein: 17.2g

## 282. Chickpea Stuffed Avocados

(Ready in about 10 minutes | Servings 4)

### Ingredients

2 avocados, pitted and sliced in half
1/2 lemon, freshly squeezed
4 tablespoons scallions, chopped
1 garlic clove, minced
1 medium tomato, chopped

1 bell pepper, seeded and chopped
1 red chili pepper, seeded and chopped
2 ounces chickpeas, boiled or cabbed, drained
Kosher salt and ground black pepper, to taste

### Directions

Place your avocados on a serving platter. Drizzle the lemon juice over each avocado.

In a mixing bowl, gently stir the remaining ingredients for the stuffing until well incorporated.

Fill the avocados with the prepared mixture and serve immediately. Bon appétit!

**Per serving:** Calories: 205; Fat: 15.2g; Carbs: 16.8g; Protein: 4.1g

## 283. Black Bean Soup

(Ready in about 1 hour 50 minutes | Servings 4)

### Ingredients

2 cups black beans, soaked overnight and drained
1 thyme sprig
2 tablespoons coconut oil
2 onions, chopped
1 celery rib, chopped
1 carrot, peeled and chopped
1 Italian pepper, seeded and chopped
1 chili pepper, seeded and chopped
4 garlic cloves, pressed or minced
Sea salt and freshly ground black pepper, to taste
1/2 teaspoon ground cumin
1/4 teaspoon ground bay leaf
1/4 teaspoon ground allspice
1/2 teaspoon dried basil
4 cups vegetable broth
1/4 cup fresh cilantro, chopped
2 ounces tortilla chips

### Directions

In a soup pot, bring the beans and 6 cups of water to a boil. Once boiling, turn the heat to a simmer. Add in the thyme sprig and let it cook for about 1 hour 30 minutes or until tender.

Meanwhile, in a heavy-bottomed pot, heat the oil over medium-high heat. Now, sauté the onion, celery, carrot and peppers for about 4 minutes until tender.

Then, sauté the garlic for about 1 minute or until fragrant.

Add the sautéed mixture to the cooked beans. Then, add in the salt, black pepper, cumin, ground bay leaf, ground allspice, dried basil and vegetable broth.

Continue to simmer, stirring periodically, for 15 minutes longer or until everything is cooked through.

Garnish with fresh cilantro and tortilla chips. Bon appétit!

**Per serving:** Calories: 505; Fat: 11.6g; Carbs: 80.3g; Protein: 23.2g

## 284. Beluga Lentil Salad with Herbs

(Ready in about 20 minutes + chilling time | Servings 4)

### Ingredients

1 cup red lentils
3 cups water
1 cup grape tomatoes, halved
1 green bell pepper, seeded and diced
1 red bell pepper, seeded and diced
1 red chili pepper, seeded and diced
1 cucumber, sliced
4 tablespoons shallots, chopped
2 tablespoons fresh parsley, roughly chopped
2 tablespoons fresh cilantro, roughly chopped
2 tablespoons fresh chives, roughly chopped
2 tablespoons fresh basil, roughly chopped
1/4 cup olive oil
1/2 teaspoon cumin seeds
1/2 teaspoon ginger, minced
1/2 teaspoon garlic, minced
1 teaspoon agave syrup
2 tablespoons fresh lemon juice
1 teaspoon lemon zest
Sea salt and ground black pepper, to taste
2 ounces black olives, pitted and halved

### Directions

Add the brown lentils and water to a saucepan and bring to a boil over high heat. Then, turn the heat to a simmer and continue to cook for 20 minutes or until tender.

Place the lentils in a salad bowl.

Add in the vegetables and herbs and toss to combine well. In a mixing bowl, whisk the oil, cumin seeds, ginger, garlic, agave syrup, lemon juice, lemon zest, salt and black pepper.

Dress your salad, garnish with olives and serve at room temperature. Bon appétit!

**Per serving:** Calories: 364; Fat: 17g; Carbs: 40.2g; Protein: 13.3g

## 285. Italian Bean Salad

(Ready in about 1 hour + chilling time | Servings 4)

### Ingredients

3/4 pound cannellini beans, soaked overnight and drained
2 cups cauliflower florets
1 red onion, thinly sliced
1 teaspoon garlic, minced
1/2 teaspoon ginger, minced
1 jalapeno pepper, minced
1 cup grape tomatoes, quartered
1/3 cup extra-virgin olive oil
1 tablespoon lime juice
1 teaspoon Dijon mustard
1/4 cup white vinegar
2 cloves garlic, pressed
1 teaspoon Italian herb mix
Kosher salt and ground black pepper, to season
2 ounces green olives, pitted and sliced

### Directions

Cover the soaked beans with a fresh change of cold water and bring to a boil. Let it boil for about 10 minutes. Turn the heat to a simmer and continue to cook for 60 minutes or until tender.

Meanwhile, boil the cauliflower florets for about 6 minutes or until just tender.

Allow your beans and cauliflower to cool completely; then, transfer them to a salad bowl.

Add in the remaining ingredients and toss to combine well. Taste and adjust the seasonings.

Bon appétit!

**Per serving:** Calories: 495; Fat: 21.1g; Carbs: 58.4g; Protein: 22.1g

## 286. White Bean Stuffed Tomatoes

(Ready in about 10 minutes | Servings 3)

### Ingredients

3 medium tomatoes, cut a thin slice off the top and remove pulp
1 carrot, grated
1 red onion, chopped
1 garlic clove, peeled
1/2 teaspoon dried basil
1/2 teaspoon dried oregano
1 teaspoon dried rosemary
3 tablespoons olive oil
3 ounces canned white beans, drained
3 ounces sweet corn kernels, thawed
1/2 cup tortilla chips, crushed

### Directions

Place your tomatoes on a serving platter.

In a mixing bowl, stir the remaining ingredients for the stuffing until everything is well combined.

Fill the avocados and serve immediately. Bon appétit!

**Per serving:** Calories: 245; Fat: 14.9g; Carbs: 24.4g; Protein: 5.1g

## 287. Winter Black-Eyed Pea Soup

(Ready in about 1 hour 5 minutes | Servings 5)

### Ingredients

2 tablespoons olive oil
1 onion, chopped
1 carrot, chopped
1 parsnip, chopped
1 cup fennel bulbs, chopped
2 cloves garlic, minced

2 cups dried black-eyed peas, soaked overnight
5 cups vegetable broth
Kosher salt and freshly ground black pepper, to season

### Directions

In a Dutch oven, heat the olive oil over medium-high heat. Once hot, sauté the onion, carrot, parsnip and fennel for 3 minutes or until just tender.

Add in the garlic and continue to sauté for 30 seconds or until aromatic.

Add in the peas, vegetable broth, salt and black pepper. Continue to cook, partially covered, for 1 hour more or until cooked through.

Bon appétit!

**Per serving:** Calories: 147; Fat: 6g; Carbs: 13.5g; Protein: 7.5g

## 288. Red Kidney Bean Patties

(Ready in about 15 minutes | Servings 4)

### Ingredients

12 ounces canned or boiled red kidney beans, drained
1/3 cup old-fashioned oats
1/4 cup all-purpose flour
1 teaspoon baking powder
1 small shallot, chopped
2 cloves garlic, minced

Sea salt and ground black pepper, to taste
1 teaspoon paprika
1/2 teaspoon chili powder
1/2 teaspoon ground bay leaf
1/2 teaspoon ground cumin
1 chia egg
4 tablespoon olive oil

### Directions

Place the beans in a mixing bowl and mash them with a fork.

Thoroughly combine the beans, oats, flour, baking powder, shallot, garlic, salt, black pepper, paprika, chili powder, ground bay leaf, cumin and chia egg.

Shape the mixture into four patties.

Then, heat the olive oil in a frying pan over a moderately high heat. Fry the patties for about 8 minutes, turning them over once or twice.

Serve with your favorite toppings. Bon appétit!

**Per serving:** Calories: 318; Fat: 15.1g; Carbs: 36.5g; Protein: 10.9g

## 289. Homemade Pea Burgers

(Ready in about 15 minutes | Servings 4)

### Ingredients

1 pound green peas, frozen and thawed
1/2 cup chickpea flour
1/2 cup plain flour
1/2 cup breadcrumbs
1 teaspoon baking powder
2 flax eggs

1 teaspoon paprika
1/2 teaspoon dried basil
1/2 teaspoon dried oregano
Sea salt and ground black pepper, to taste
4 tablespoons olive oil
4 hamburger buns

### Directions

In a mixing bowl, thoroughly combine the green peas, flour, breadcrumbs, baking powder, flax eggs, paprika, basil, oregano, salt and black pepper.

Shape the mixture into four patties.

Then, heat the olive oil in a frying pan over a moderately high heat. Fry the patties for about 8 minutes, turning them over once or twice. Serve on burger buns and enjoy!

**Per serving:** Calories: 467; Fat: 19.1g; Carbs: 58.5g; Protein: 15.8g

## 290. Black Bean and Spinach Stew

(Ready in about 1 hour 35 minutes | Servings 4)

### Ingredients

2 cups black beans, soaked overnight and drained
2 tablespoons olive oil
1 onion, peeled, halved
1 jalapeno pepper, sliced
2 peppers, seeded and sliced
1 cup button mushrooms, sliced

2 garlic cloves, chopped
2 cups vegetable broth
1 teaspoon paprika
Kosher salt and ground black pepper, to taste
1 bay leaf
2 cups spinach, torn into pieces

### Directions

Cover the soaked beans with a fresh change of cold water and bring to a boil. Let it boil for about 10 minutes. Turn the heat to a simmer and continue to cook for 50 to 55 minutes or until tender.

In a heavy-bottomed pot, heat the olive oil over medium heat. Once hot, sauté the onion and peppers for about 3 minutes.

Sauté the garlic and mushrooms for approximately 3 minutes or until the mushrooms release the liquid and the garlic is fragrant.

Add in the vegetable broth, paprika, salt, black pepper, bay leaf and cooked beans. Let it simmer, stirring periodically, for about 25 minutes or until cooked through.

Afterwards, add in the spinach and let it simmer, covered, for about 5 minutes. Bon appétit!

**Per serving:** Calories: 459; Fat: 9.1g; Carbs: 72g; Protein: 25.4g

## 291. Basic Homemade Hummus

(Ready in about 10 minutes | Servings 8)

### Ingredients

1/4 cup good-quality tahini
2 tablespoons extra-virgin olive oil
1/2 teaspoon ground cumin
1/4 teaspoon ground bay laurel
1/2 teaspoon red pepper flakes
Sea salt and ground black pepper, to taste

1 teaspoon dried onion powder
1 teaspoon parsley flakes
2 cloves garlic, crushed
2 tablespoons lemon juice
16 ounces chickpeas, boiled and drained

### Directions

Blitz all the ingredients in your blender or food processor until your desired consistency is reached.

Place in your refrigerator until ready to serve.

Serve with toasted pita wedges or chips. Bon appétit!

**Per serving:** Calories: 174; Fat: 9.1g; Carbs: 18.5g; Protein: 6.4g

## 292. Asian Green Peas Stir-Fry

(Ready in about 10 minutes | Servings 4)

### Ingredients

2 tablespoons peanut oil
4 garlic cloves, pressed
4 tablespoons scallions
1/2 teaspoon dried dill
1 pound green peas, fresh or thawed
1/4 teaspoon red pepper, flakes
1/2 teaspoon Five-spice powder
2 tablespoons soy sauce
2 tablespoons pine nuts, chopped

### Directions

Heat the peanut oil in a wok until sizzling. Now, stir-fry the garlic and scallions for 2 minutes or until crisp-tender.

Add in the dried dill and continue to cook for 30 seconds more or until fragrant.

Add in the green peas and stir-fry over high heat for about 3 minutes until lightly charred. Then, stir in the red pepper, Five-spice powder and soy sauce; stir-fry for 1 minute more.

Garnish with chopped pine nuts and enjoy.

**Per serving:** Calories: 184; Fat: 8.7g; Carbs: 20.2g; Protein: 7.1g

## 293. Sweet Pea Salad with Tofu

(Ready in about 10 minutes | Servings 4)

### Ingredients

16 ounces sweet peas
4 tablespoons shallots, chopped
1 Persian cucumber, diced
4 tablespoons extra-virgin olive oil
1 tablespoon fresh lemon juice
1 teaspoon Dijon mustard
1 teaspoon garlic, minced
1 teaspoon fresh dill, chopped
2 tablespoons fresh parsley, chopped
6 ounces tofu, pressed and cubed

### Directions

Cook the green peas in a pot of a lightly salted water for 5 to 6 minutes. Let it cool completely.

Add the peas to a salad bowl; add in the shallot, cucumber, olive oil, lemon juice, mustard, garlic, dill and parsley.

Gently toss to combine and top with the cubed tofu. Serve at room temperature or place in your refrigerator until ready to serve. Bon appétit!

**Per serving:** Calories: 344; Fat: 22.7g; Carbs: 24.5g; Protein: 14.2g

## 294. Black Bean Stuffed Avocado

(Ready in about 10 minutes | Servings 6)

### Ingredients

3 avocados, seeded and cut into halves
1 lemon, freshly squeezed
1 cup cherry tomatoes, quartered
3 tablespoons tahini
1 garlic clove, minced
6 tablespoons black beans, mashed
Sea salt and ground black pepper, to taste
1 teaspoon red pepper flakes
2 tablespoons fresh mint, roughly chopped
2 tablespoons balsamic glaze reduction to drizzle

### Directions

Place your avocados on a serving platter. Drizzle the lemon juice over each avocado.

In a mixing bowl, stir the remaining ingredients for the stuffing until well incorporated.

Fill the avocados with the prepared mixture and serve immediately. Bon appétit!

**Per serving:** Calories: 247; Fat: 18.9g; Carbs: 19.3g; Protein: 5.2g

## 295. Split Pea and Potato Soup

(Ready in about 1 hour 5 minutes | Servings 5)

### Ingredients

2 tablespoons olive oil
1 large onion, chopped
2 medium carrots, chopped
2 medium potatoes, diced
1 teaspoon garlic, minced
2 cups split peas, soaked overnight and drained
5 cups vegetable broth
2 tablespoons fresh cilantro, chopped

### Directions

In a Dutch oven, heat the olive oil over medium-high heat. Once hot, sauté the onion, carrot and potatoes for 4 minutes, stirring periodically to ensure even cooking.

Add in the garlic and continue to sauté for 30 seconds or until aromatic.

Add in the peas and vegetable broth. Continue to cook, partially covered, for 1 hour more or until cooked through.

Bon appétit!

**Per serving:** Calories: 501; Fat: 8.1g; Carbs: 82.3g; Protein: 27.2g

## 296. Spiced Roasted Chickpeas

(Ready in about 25 minutes | Servings 6)

### Ingredients

2 cups canned chickpeas, drained
2 tablespoons olive oil
Sea salt and red pepper, to taste
1 teaspoon chili powder
1/2 teaspoon curry powder
1/2 teaspoon garlic powder

### Directions

Pat the chickpeas dry using paper towels. Drizzle olive oil over the chickpeas.

Roast the chickpeas in the preheated oven at 400 degrees F for about 25 minutes, tossing them once or twice.

Toss your chickpeas with the spices and enjoy!

**Per serving:** Calories: 163; Fat: 6.9g; Carbs: 20.2g; Protein: 6.2g

## 297. Easy Homemade Falafel

(Ready in about 20 minutes | Servings 6)

### Ingredients

1 ½ cups dried chickpeas, soaked overnight and drained
1 medium onion
3 garlic cloves
2 tablespoons fresh parsley leaves
2 tablespoons fresh basil leaves
1 teaspoon fresh mint leaves
Sea salt and ground black pepper, to taste
1/2 teaspoon paprika
1/2 teaspoon ground bay leaf
1 teaspoon cumin
6 tablespoons all-purpose flour
1 teaspoon baking powder
4 tablespoons olive oil

### Directions

Place the chickpeas, onion, garlic, parsley, basil, mint and spices in the bowl of your food processor.

Pulse until well blended. Add in the flour and baking powder and stir to combine well. Roll the mixture into equal balls.

Heat the olive oil in a frying pan over medium-high heat.

Fry your falafel until golden brown. Serve with flatbread and vegetables, if desired. Enjoy!

Per serving: Calories: 313; Fat: 12.3g; Carbs: 40.5g; Protein: 11.6g

## 298. Pea Dip with Herbs

(Ready in about 1 hour 5 minutes | Servings 8)

### Ingredients

2 cups black-eyed peas, soaked overnight and drained
1 lemon, freshly squeezed
2 cloves garlic, minced
1 teaspoon fresh dill
2 tablespoons fresh basil, chopped
2 tablespoons fresh parsley, chopped
3 tablespoons olive oil
Sea salt and red pepper, to taste

### Directions

Cover the black-eyed peas with water by 2 inches and bring to a gentle boil. Let it boil for about 15 minutes.

Then, turn the heat to a simmer for about 45 minutes. Let it cool completely.

Add the peas to the bowl of your food processor. Add in the remaining ingredients and process until well combined.

Garnish with some extra herbs and serve with your favorite dippers. Bon appétit!

Per serving: Calories: 201; Fat: 5.5g; Carbs: 30g; Protein: 9.9g

## 299. Classic Snow Pea Salad

(Ready in about 10 minutes | Servings 4)

### Ingredients

14 ounce frozen snow peas
1 red onion, thinly sliced
1 garlic clove, minced
1 red bell pepper, seeded and sliced
1 green bell pepper, seeded and sliced
4 tablespoons olive oil
2 tablespoons rice vinegar
1/4 teaspoon dried dill weed
1/4 teaspoon dried oregano
1 teaspoon dried basil
1 teaspoon red pepper flakes
Sea salt and ground black pepper, to taste

### Directions

Place the snow peas in steamer; place it in a saucepan over boiling water; steam the snow peas for about 5 minutes or until crisp-tender.

Transfer the peas to a salad bowl.

Toss them with the remaining ingredients and serve at room temperature or well-chilled. Bon appétit!

Per serving: Calories: 209; Fat: 13.9g; Carbs: 16.1g; Protein: 5.7g

## 300. Sunday Three-Bean Soup

(Ready in about 20 minutes | Servings 6)

### Ingredients

2 tablespoons olive oil
1 large shallot, chopped
2 carrots, diced
2 celery stalks, diced
1 red bell pepper, seeded and diced
2 sweet potatoes, peeled and diced
1 tablespoon ginger-garlic paste
1 bay laurel
1 cup tomatoes, pureed
5 cups vegetable broth
1/2 teaspoon red pepper flakes, crushed
Sea salt and ground black pepper, to taste
1 (15-ounces) canned white beans, drained
1 (15-ounces) canned red kidney beans, drained
1 (15-ounces) canned garbanzo beans, drained

### Directions

In a heavy-bottomed pot, heat the olive oil over medium-high heat. Now, sauté the shallot, carrots, celery, peppers and sweet potatoes for about 4 minutes until your vegetables have softened.

Add in the ginger-garlic paste and bay laurel and continue sautéing an additional 30 seconds or until fragrant.

Add in the tomatoes, broth, red pepper, salt and black pepper. Afterwards, add in the canned beans and turn the heat to a simmer.

Let it cook, partially covered, for 10 minutes more or until everything is thoroughly cooked. Bon appétit!

Per serving: Calories: 329; Fat: 6.9g; Carbs: 50.6g; Protein: 17.7g

# 301. Classic Chickpea Curry

(Ready in about 15 minutes | Servings 4)

## Ingredients

1 onion, diced
1 Thai chili pepper
2 ripe tomatoes, diced
1 teaspoon fresh ginger, minced
2 garlic cloves, peeled
1 teaspoon cumin seeds
1/2 teaspoon mustard seeds
1 bay leaf
3 tablespoons coconut oil

Sea salt and ground black pepper, to taste
1 tablespoon garam masala
1 teaspoon curry powder
14 ounces canned chickpeas, drained
1/2 cup vegetable broth
1 (13.5-ounce) can coconut milk, unsweetened
1 lime, freshly squeezed

## Directions

In your blender or food processor, blend the onion, chili pepper, tomatoes, ginger, garlic, cumin, mustard and bay leaf into a paste.

In a saucepan, heat the coconut oil over medium heat. Once hot, cook the prepared paste for about 2 minutes or until aromatic.

Add in the salt, pepper, garam masala, curry powder canned, chickpeas, vegetable broth and coconut milk. Turn the heat to a simmer.

Continue to simmer for 8 minutes more or until cooked through.

Remove from the heat. Drizzle fresh lime juice over the top of each serving. Bon appétit!

**Per serving:** Calories: 505; Fat: 37.7g; Carbs: 37.2g; Protein: 11.7g

# 302. Pinto Bean Soup with Herbs

(Ready in about 1 hour 35 minutes | Servings 5)

## Ingredients

2 cups pinto beans, soaked overnight and drained
3 tablespoons olive oil
1 large onion, chopped
1 celery with leaves, chopped
1 bell pepper, seeded and chopped
1 red chili pepper, seeded and chopped

1 teaspoon garlic, minced
1 teaspoon dried thyme
1 teaspoon dried marjoram
1 teaspoon dried oregano
1 cup tomato, pureed
4 cups vegetable broth
Sea salt and ground black pepper, to taste
1 bay leaf

## Directions

Cover the soaked beans with a fresh change of cold water and bring to a boil. Let it boil for about 10 minutes. Turn the heat to a simmer and continue to cook for 50 to 55 minutes or until tender.

In a heavy-bottomed pot, heat the olive oil over medium heat. Once hot, sauté the onion, celery and peppers for about 3 minutes.

Sauté the garlic and herbs for approximately 3 minutes or until fragrant.

Add in the vegetable broth, salt, black pepper, bay leaf and cooked beans. Let it simmer, stirring periodically, for about 25 minutes or until cooked through. Bon appétit!

**Per serving:** Calories: 409; Fat: 10.3g; Carbs: 56g; Protein: 21.6g

# 303. Greek-Style Chickpea Bowl

(Ready in about 45 minutes | Servings 4)

## Ingredients

2 cups dry chickpeas, soaked overnight and drained
1 bay leaf
1 thyme sprig
1/2 teaspoon ground cumin
Sea salt and cayenne pepper, to taste
2 cups baby spinach
1 cucumber, sliced
1 bell pepper, sliced

1 cup cherry tomatoes, halved
1/2 cup green olives, pitted and sliced
6 tablespoons olive oil
2 tablespoons lemon juice
1 teaspoon deli mustard
1 teaspoon dried basil
1 teaspoon dried oregano
4 pita bread, cut into wedges

## Directions

Place the chickpeas, bay leaf and thyme sprig in a stockpot; cover the chickpeas with water by 2 inches. Bring it to a boil.

Immediately turn the heat to a simmer and continue to cook for about 40 minutes or until tender.

Transfer your chickpeas to a salad bowl. Add in the cumin, salt, cayenne pepper, spinach, cucumber, pepper, tomatoes and olives; toss to combine well.

Then, in a mixing bowl, whisk 4 tablespoons of the olive oil, lemon juice and mustard. Dress the salad and place it in your refrigerator until ready to serve.

Heat the remaining 2 tablespoons of the olive oil in a nonstick skillet. Toast the pita bread with the basil and oregano. Top the chickpea salad with the toasted pita wedges and serve. Bon appétit!

**Per serving:** Calories: 675; Fat: 26.9g; Carbs: 87.1g; Protein: 24.5g

# 304. One-Pot Winter Chili with Tofu

(Ready in about 1 hour 30 minutes | Servings 4)

## Ingredients

3/4 pound cannellini beans, soaked overnight and drained
3 tablespoons olive oil
1 large onion, diced
1 cup turnip, chopped
1 carrot, chopped
1 bell pepper, sliced
1 sweet potato, chopped
3 cloves garlic, minced

2 ripe tomatoes, pureed
3 tablespoons tomato paste
2 cups vegetable broth
2 bay leaves
1 tablespoon red chili powder
1 tablespoon brown sugar
Sea salt and cayenne pepper, to taste
12 ounces silken tofu, cubed

## Directions

Cover the soaked beans with a fresh change of cold water and bring to a boil. Let it boil for about 10 minutes. Turn the heat to a simmer and continue to cook for 50 to 55 minutes or until tender.

In a heavy-bottomed pot, heat the olive oil over medium heat. Once hot, sauté the onion, turnip, carrot, bell pepper and sweet potato.

Sauté the garlic for about 1 minute or so.

Add in the tomatoes, tomato paste, vegetable broth, bay leaves, red chili powder, brown sugar, salt, cayenne pepper and cooked beans. Let it simmer, stirring periodically, for 25 to 30 minutes or until cooked through.

Serve garnished with the silken tofu. Bon appétit!

**Per serving:** Calories: 605; Fat: 20.1g; Carbs: 74g; Protein: 38.3g

# 305. Indian Chaat Bean Salad

(Ready in about 1 hour + chilling time | Servings 3)

## Ingredients

1/2 pound chawli (black-eyed) beans, soaked overnight and drained

2 tablespoons shallots, chopped

1 clove garlic, minced

1 bell pepper, seeded and chopped

1 green chili pepper, seeded and chopped

1 teaspoon turmeric powder

1/2 teaspoon turmeric powder

Dressing:

1/4 cup olive oil

1/4 cup wine vinegar

1 tablespoon agave syrup

1 teaspoon chaat masala

1 teaspoon coriander seeds

Kosher salt and ground black pepper, to season

## Directions

Cover the soaked beans with a fresh change of cold water and bring to a boil. Turn the heat to a simmer and continue to cook for 50 to 55 minutes or until tender.

Allow your beans to cool completely; then, transfer them to a salad bowl.

Add in the remaining ingredients for the salad and toss to combine well.

Mix all the dressing ingredients. Dress your salad and serve well-chilled. Bon appétit!

**Per serving:** Calories: 495; Fat: 21.1g; Carbs: 58.4g; Protein: 22.1g

# SNACKS & APPETIZERS

# 306. Carrot Energy Balls

(Ready in about 10 minutes + chilling time | Servings 8)

## Ingredients

1 large carrot, grated carrot
1 ½ cups old-fashioned oats
1 cup raisins
1 cup dates, pitted

1 cup coconut flakes
1/4 teaspoon ground cloves
1/2 teaspoon ground cinnamon

## Directions

In your food processor, pulse all ingredients until it forms a sticky and uniform mixture.

Shape the batter into equal balls.

Place in your refrigerator until ready to serve. Bon appétit!

**Per serving:** Calories: 495; Fat: 21.1g; Carbs: 58.4g; Protein: 22.1g

# 307. Crunchy Sweet Potato Bites

(Ready in about 25 minutes + chilling time | Servings 4)

## Ingredients

4 sweet potatoes, peeled and grated
2 chia eggs
1/4 cup nutritional yeast
2 tablespoons tahini
2 tablespoons chickpea flour

1 teaspoon shallot powder
1 teaspoon garlic powder
1 teaspoon paprika
Sea salt and ground black pepper, to taste

## Directions

Start by preheating your oven to 395 degrees F. Line a baking pan with parchment paper or Silpat mat.

Thoroughly combine all the ingredients until everything is well incorporated.

Roll the batter into equal balls and place them in your refrigerator for about 1 hour.

Bake these balls for approximately 25 minutes, turning them over halfway through the cooking time. Bon appétit!

**Per serving:** Calories: 215; Fat: 4.5g; Carbs: 35g; Protein: 8.7g

# 308. Roasted Glazed Baby Carrots

(Ready in about 30 minutes | Servings 6)

## Ingredients

2 pounds baby carrots
1/4 cup olive oil
1/4 cup apple cider vinegar
1/2 teaspoon red pepper flakes

Sea salt and freshly ground black pepper, to taste
1 tablespoon agave syrup
2 tablespoons soy sauce
1 tablespoon fresh cilantro, minced

## Directions

Start by preheating your oven 395 degrees F.

Then, toss the carrots with the olive oil, vinegar, red pepper, salt, black pepper, agave syrup and soy sauce.

Roast the carrots for about 30 minutes, rotating the pan once or twice. Garnish with fresh cilantro and serve. Bon appétit!

**Per serving:** Calories: 165; Fat: 10.1g; Carbs: 16.5g; Protein: 1.4g

# 309. Oven-Baked Kale Chips

(Ready in about 20 minutes | Servings 8)

## Ingredients

2 bunches kale, leaves separated
2 tablespoons olive oil
1/2 teaspoon mustard seeds
1/2 teaspoon celery seeds

1/2 teaspoon dried oregano
1/4 teaspoon ground cumin
1 teaspoon garlic powder
Coarse sea salt and ground black pepper, to taste

## Directions

Start by preheating your oven to 340 degrees F. Line a baking sheet with parchment paper or Silpat mar.

Toss the kale leaves with the remaining ingredients until well coated.

Bake in the preheated oven for about 13 minutes, rotating the pan once or twice. Bon appétit!

**Per serving:** Calories: 65; Fat: 3.9g; Carbs: 5.3g; Protein: 2.4g

# 310. Cheesy Cashew Dip

(Ready in about 10 minutes | Servings 8)

## Ingredients

1 cup raw cashews
1 lemon, freshly squeezed
2 tablespoons tahini
2 tablespoons nutritional yeast
1/2 teaspoon turmeric powder

1/2 teaspoon red pepper flakes, crushed
Sea salt and ground black pepper, to taste

## Directions

Place all the ingredients in the bowl of your food processor. Blend until uniform, creamy and smooth. You can add a splash of water to thin it out, as needed.

Spoon your dip into a serving bowl; serve with veggie sticks, chips, or crackers.

Bon appétit!

**Per serving:** Calories: 115; Fat: 8.6g; Carbs: 6.6g; Protein: 4.4g

# 311. Peppery Hummus Dip

(Ready in about 10 minutes | Servings 10)

## Ingredients

20 ounces canned or boiled chickpeas, drained
1/4 cup tahini
2 garlic cloves, minced
2 tablespoons lemon juice, freshly squeezed
1/2 cup chickpea liquid

2 red roasted peppers, seeded and sliced
1/2 teaspoon paprika
1 teaspoon dried basil
Sea salt and ground black pepper, to taste
2 tablespoons olive oil

## Directions

Blitz all the ingredients, except for the oil, in your blender or food processor until your desired consistency is reached.

Place in your refrigerator until ready to serve.

Serve with toasted pita wedges or chips, if desired. Bon appétit!

**Per serving:** Calories: 155; Fat: 7.9g; Carbs: 17.4g; Protein: 5.9g

## 312. Traditional Lebanese Mutabal

(Ready in about 10 minutes | Servings 6)

### Ingredients

1 pound eggplant
1 onion, chopped
1 tablespoon garlic paste
4 tablespoons tahini
1 tablespoon coconut oil
2 tablespoons lemon juice

1/2 teaspoon ground coriander
1/4 cup ground cloves
1 teaspoon red pepper flakes
1 teaspoon smoked peppers
Sea salt and ground black pepper, to taste

### Directions

Roast the eggplant until the skin turns black; peel the eggplant and transfer it to the bowl of your food processor.

Add in the remaining ingredients. Blend until everything is well incorporated.

Serve with crostini or pita bread, if desired. Bon appétit!

**Per serving:** Calories: 115; Fat: 7.8g; Carbs: 9.8g; Protein: 2.9g

## 313. Indian-Style Roasted Chickpeas

(Ready in about 10 minutes | Servings 8)

### Ingredients

2 cups canned chickpeas, drained
2 tablespoons olive oil
1/2 teaspoon garlic powder
1/2 teaspoon paprika

1 teaspoon curry powder
1 teaspoon garam masala
Sea salt and red pepper, to taste

### Directions

Pat the chickpeas dry using paper towels. Drizzle olive oil over the chickpeas.

Roast the chickpeas in the preheated oven at 400 degrees F for about 25 minutes, tossing them once or twice.

Toss your chickpeas with the spices and enjoy!

**Per serving:** Calories: 223; Fat: 6.4g; Carbs: 32.2g; Protein: 10.4g

## 314. Avocado with Tahini Sauce

(Ready in about 10 minutes | Servings 4)

### Ingredients

2 large-sized avocados, pitted and halved
4 tablespoons tahini
4 tablespoons soy sauce
1 tablespoon lemon juice

1/2 teaspoon red pepper flakes
Sea salt and ground black pepper, to taste
1 teaspoon garlic powder

### Directions

Place the avocado halves on a serving platter.

Mix the tahini, soy sauce, lemon juice, red pepper, salt, black pepper and garlic powder in a small bowl. Divide the sauce between the avocado halves.

Bon appétit!

**Per serving:** Calories: 304; Fat: 25.7g; Carbs: 17.6g; Protein: 6g

## 315. Sweet Potato Tater Tots

(Ready in about 25 minutes + chilling time | Servings 4)

### Ingredients

1 ½ pounds sweet potatoes, grated
2 chia eggs
1/2 cup plain flour
1/2 cup breadcrumbs

3 tablespoons hummus
Sea salt and black pepper, to taste
1 tablespoon olive oil
1/2 cup salsa sauce

### Directions

Start by preheating your oven to 395 degrees F. Line a baking pan with parchment paper or Silpat mat.

Thoroughly combine all the ingredients, except for the salsa, until everything is well incorporated.

Roll the batter into equal balls and place them in your refrigerator for about 1 hour.

Bake these balls for approximately 25 minutes, turning them over halfway through the cooking time. Bon appétit!

**Per serving:** Calories: 232; Fat: 7.1g; Carbs: 37g; Protein: 8.4g

## 316. Roasted Pepper and Tomato Dip

(Ready in about 35 minutes | Servings 10)

### Ingredients

4 red bell peppers
4 tomatoes
4 tablespoons olive oil
1 red onion, chopped
4 garlic cloves

4 ounces canned garbanzo beans, drained
Sea salt and ground black pepper, to taste

### Directions

Start by preheating your oven to 400 degrees F.

Place the peppers and tomatoes on a parchment-lined baking pan. Bake for about 30 minutes; peel the peppers and transfer them to your food processor along with the roasted tomatoes.

Meanwhile, heat 2 tablespoons of the olive oil in a frying pan over medium-high heat. Sauté the onion and garlic for about 5 minutes or until they've softened.

Add the sautéed vegetables to your food processor. Add in the garbanzo beans, salt, pepper and the remaining olive oil; process until creamy and smooth.

Bon appétit!

**Per serving:** Calories: 90; Fat: 5.7g; Carbs: 8.5g; Protein: 1.9g

## 317. Classic Party Mix

(Ready in about 1 hour 5 minutes | Servings 15)

### Ingredients

5 cups vegan corn cereal
3 cups vegan mini pretzels
1 cup almonds, roasted
1/2 cup pepitas, toasted
1 tablespoon nutritional yeast
1 tablespoon balsamic vinegar
1 tablespoon soy sauce
1 teaspoon garlic powder
1/3 cup vegan butter

### Directions

Start by preheating your oven to 250 degrees F. Line a large baking pan with parchment paper or Silpat mat.

Mix the cereal, pretzels, almonds and pepitas in a serving bowl.

In a small saucepan, melt the remaining ingredients over a moderate heat. Pour the sauce over the cereal/nut mixture.

Bake for about 1 hour, stirring every 15 minutes, until golden and fragrant. Transfer it to a wire rack to cool completely. Bon appétit!

**Per serving:** Calories: 290; Fat: 12.2g; Carbs: 39g; Protein: 7.5g

## 318. Olive Oil Garlic Crostini

(Ready in about 10 minutes | Servings 4)

### Ingredients

1 whole-grain baguette, sliced
4 tablespoons extra-virgin olive oil
1/2 teaspoon sea salt
3 cloves garlic, halved

### Directions

Preheat your broiler.

Brush each slice of bread with the olive oil and sprinkle with sea salt. Place under the preheated broiler for about 2 minutes or until lightly toasted.

Rub each slice of bread with the garlic and serve. Bon appétit!

**Per serving:** Calories: 289; Fat: 8.2g; Carbs: 44.9g; Protein: 9.5g

## 319. Classic Vegan Meatballs

(Ready in about 15 minutes | Servings 4)

### Ingredients

1 cup brown rice, cooked and cooled
1 cup canned or boiled red kidney beans, drained
1 teaspoon fresh garlic, minced
1 small onion, chopped
Sea salt and ground black pepper, to taste
1/2 teaspoon cayenne pepper
1/2 teaspoon smoked paprika
1/2 teaspoon coriander seeds
1/2 teaspoon coriander mustard seeds
2 tablespoons olive oil

### Directions

In a mixing bowl, thoroughly combine all the ingredients, except for the olive oil. Mix to combine well and then, shape the mixture into equal balls using oiled hands.

Then, heat the olive oil in a nonstick skillet over medium heat. Once hot, fry the meatballs for about 10 minutes until golden brown on all sides.

Serve with cocktail sticks and enjoy!

**Per serving:** Calories: 159; Fat: 9.2g; Carbs: 16.3g; Protein: 2.9g

## 320. Balsamic Roasted Parsnip

(Ready in about 30 minutes | Servings 6)

### Ingredients

1 ½ pounds parsnips, cut into sticks
1/4 cup olive oil
1/4 cup balsamic vinegar
1 teaspoon Dijon mustard
1 teaspoon fennel seeds
Sea salt and ground black pepper, to taste
1 teaspoon Mediterranean spice mix

### Directions

Toss all ingredients in a mixing bowl until the parsnips are well coated.

Roast the parsnip in the preheated oven at 400 degrees F for about 30 minutes, stirring halfway through the cooking time.

Serve at room temperature and enjoy!

**Per serving:** Calories: 174; Fat: 9.3g; Carbs: 22.2g; Protein: 1.4g

## 321. Traditional Baba Ganoush

(Ready in about 25 minutes | Servings 8)

### Ingredients

1 pound eggplant, cut into rounds
1 teaspoon coarse sea salt
3 tablespoons olive oil
3 tablespoons fresh lime juice
2 cloves garlic, minced
3 tablespoons tahini
1/4 teaspoon ground cloves
1/2 teaspoon ground cumin
2 tablespoons fresh parsley, roughly chopped

### Directions

Rub the sea salt all over the eggplant rounds. Then, place them in a colander and let it sit for about 15 minutes; drain, rinse and pat dry with kitchen towels.

Roast the eggplant until the skin turns black; peel the eggplant and transfer it to the bowl of your food processor.

Add in the olive oil, lime juice, garlic, tahini, cloves and cumin. Blend until everything is well incorporated.

Garnish with fresh parsley leaves and enjoy!

**Per serving:** Calories: 104; Fat: 8.2g; Carbs: 5.3g; Protein: 1.6g

## 322. Peanut Butter Date Bites

(Ready in about 5 minutes | Servings 2)

### Ingredients

8 fresh dates, pitted and cut into halves
8 teaspoons peanut butter
1/4 teaspoon ground cinnamon

### Directions

Divide the peanut butter between the date halves.

Dust with cinnamon and serve immediately. Bon appétit!

**Per serving:** Calories: 143; Fat: 3.9g; Carbs: 26.3g; Protein: 2.6g

## 323. Roasted Cauliflower Dip

(Ready in about 30 minutes | Servings 7)

### Ingredients

1 pound cauliflower florets
1/4 cup olive oil
4 tablespoons tahini
1/2 teaspoon paprika

Sea salt and ground black pepper, to taste
2 tablespoons fresh lime juice
2 cloves garlic, minced

### Directions

Start by preheating your oven to 420 degrees F. Toss the cauliflower florets with the olive oil and arrange them on a parchment-lined baking pan.

Bake for about 25 minutes or until tender.

Then, puree the cauliflower along with the remaining ingredients, adding cooking liquid, as needed.

Drizzle with some extra olive oil, if desired. Bon appétit!

**Per serving:** Calories: 142; Fat: 12.5g; Carbs: 6.3g; Protein: 2.9g

## 324. Easy Zucchini Roll-Ups

(Ready in about 10 minutes | Servings 5)

### Ingredients

1 cup hummus, preferably homemade
1 medium tomato, chopped
1 teaspoon mustard
1/4 teaspoon oregano
1/2 teaspoon cayenne pepper

Sea salt and ground black pepper, to taste
1 large zucchini, cut into strips
2 tablespoons fresh basil, chopped
2 tablespoons fresh parsley, chopped

### Directions

In a mixing bowl, thoroughly combine the hummus, tomato, mustard, oregano, cayenne pepper, salt and black pepper.

Divide the filling between the zucchini strips and spread it out evenly. Roll the zucchini up and garnish with fresh basil and parsley.

Bon appétit!

**Per serving:** Calories: 99; Fat: 4.4g; Carbs: 12.1g; Protein: 3.1g

## 325. Chipotle Sweet Potato Fries

(Ready in about 45 minutes | Servings 4)

### Ingredients

4 medium sweet potatoes, peeled and cut into sticks
2 tablespoons peanut oil
Sea salt and ground black pepper, to taste

1 teaspoon chipotle pepper powder
1/4 teaspoon ground allspice
1 teaspoon brown sugar
1 teaspoon dried rosemary

### Directions

Toss the sweet potato fries with the remaining ingredients.

Bake your fries at 375 degrees F for about 45 minutes or until browned; make sure to stir the fries once or twice.

Serve with your favorite dipping sauce, if desired. Bon appétit!

**Per serving:** Calories: 186; Fat: 7.1g; Carbs: 29.6g; Protein: 2.5g

## 326. Cannellini Bean Dipping Sauce

(Ready in about 10 minutes | Servings 6)

### Ingredients

10 ounces canned cannellini beans, drained
1 clove garlic, minced
2 roasted peppers, sliced
Sea freshly ground black pepper, to taste
1/2 teaspoon ground cumin

1/2 teaspoon mustard seeds
1/2 teaspoon ground bay leaves
3 tablespoons tahini
2 tablespoons fresh Italian parsley, chopped

### Directions

Place all the ingredients, except for the parsley, in the bowl of your blender or food processor. Blitz until well blended.

Transfer the sauce to a serving bowl and garnish with fresh parsley.

Serve with pita wedges, tortilla chips, or veggie sticks, if desired. Enjoy!

**Per serving:** Calories: 123; Fat: 4.5g; Carbs: 15.6g; Protein: 5.6g

## 327. Spiced Roasted Cauliflower

(Ready in about 25 minutes | Servings 6)

### Ingredients

1 ½ pounds cauliflower florets
1/4 cup olive oil
4 tablespoons apple cider vinegar
2 cloves garlic, pressed

1 teaspoon dried basil
1 teaspoon dried oregano
Sea salt and ground black pepper, to taste

### Directions

Begin by preheating your oven to 420 degrees F.

Toss the cauliflower florets with the remaining ingredients.

Arrange the cauliflower florets on a parchment-lined baking sheet. Bake the cauliflower florets in the preheated oven for about 25 minutes or until they are slightly charred.

Bon appétit!

**Per serving:** Calories: 115; Fat: 9.3g; Carbs: 6.9g; Protein: 5.6g

## 328. Easy Lebanese Toum

(Ready in about 10 minutes | Servings 6)

### Ingredients

2 heads garlic
1 teaspoon coarse sea salt
1 ½ cups olive oil

1 lemon, freshly squeezed
2 cups carrots, cut into matchsticks

### Directions

Puree the garlic cloves and salt in your food processor of a high-speed blender until creamy and smooth, scraping down the sides of the bowl.

Gradually and slowly, add in the olive oil and lemon juice, alternating between these two ingredients to create a fluffy sauce.

Blend until the sauce has thickened. Serve with carrot sticks and enjoy!

**Per serving:** Calories: 252; Fat: 27g; Carbs: 3.1g; Protein: 0.4g

## 329. Avocado with Tangy Ginger Dressing

(Ready in about 10 minutes | Servings 4)

### Ingredients

2 avocados, pitted and halved
1 clove garlic, pressed
1 teaspoon fresh ginger, peeled and minced
2 tablespoons balsamic vinegar
4 tablespoons extra-virgin olive oil
Kosher salt and ground black pepper, to taste

### Directions

Place the avocado halves on a serving platter.

Mix the garlic, ginger, vinegar, olive oil, salt and black pepper in a small bowl. Divide the sauce between the avocado halves.

Bon appétit!

**Per serving:** Calories: 295; Fat: 28.2g; Carbs: 11.3g; Protein: 2.3g

## 330. Chickpea Snack Mix

(Ready in about 30 minutes | Servings 8)

### Ingredients

1 cup roasted chickpeas, drained
2 tablespoons coconut oil, melted
1/4 cup raw pumpkin seeds
1/4 cup raw pecan halves
1/3 cup dried cherries

### Directions

Pat the chickpeas dry using paper towels. Drizzle coconut oil over the chickpeas.

Roast the chickpeas in the preheated oven at 380 degrees F for about 20 minutes, tossing them once or twice.

Toss your chickpeas with the pumpkin seeds and pecan halves. Continue baking until the nuts are fragrant about 8 minutes; let cool completely.

Add in the dried cherries and stir to combine. Bon appétit!

**Per serving:** Calories: 109; Fat: 7.9g; Carbs: 7.4g; Protein: 3.4g

## 331. Muhammara Dip with a Twist

(Ready in about 35 minutes | Servings 9)

### Ingredients

3 red bell peppers
5 tablespoons olive oil
2 garlic cloves, chopped
1 tomato, chopped
3/4 cup bread crumbs
2 tablespoons molasses
1 teaspoon ground cumin
1/4 sunflower seeds, toasted
1 Maras pepper, minced
2 tablespoons tahini
Sea salt and red pepper, to taste

### Directions

Start by preheating your oven to 400 degrees F.

Place the peppers on a parchment-lined baking pan. Bake for about 30 minutes; peel the peppers and transfer them to your food processor.

Meanwhile, heat 2 tablespoons of the olive oil in a frying pan over medium-high heat. Sauté the garlic and tomatoes for about 5 minutes or until they've softened.

Add the sautéed vegetables to your food processor. Add in the remaining ingredients and process until creamy and smooth. Bon appétit!

**Per serving:** Calories: 149; Fat: 11.5g; Carbs: 8.9g; Protein: 2.4g

## 332. Spinach, Chickpea and Garlic Crostini

(Ready in about 10 minutes | Servings 6)

### Ingredients

1 baguette, cut into slices
4 tablespoons extra-virgin olive oil
Sea salt and red pepper, to season
3 garlic cloves, minced
1 cup boiled chickpeas, drained
2 cups spinach
1 tablespoon fresh lemon juice

### Directions

Preheat your broiler.

Brush the slices of bread with 2 tablespoons of the olive oil and sprinkle with sea salt and red pepper. Place under the preheated broiler for about 2 minutes or until lightly toasted.

In a mixing bowl, thoroughly combine the garlic, chickpeas, spinach, lemon juice and the remaining 2 tablespoons of the olive oil.

Spoon the chickpea mixture onto each toast. Bon appétit!

**Per serving:** Calories: 242; Fat: 6.1g; Carbs: 38.5g; Protein: 8.9g

## 333. Mushroom and Cannellini Bean "Meatballs"

(Ready in about 15 minutes | Servings 4)

### Ingredients

4 tablespoons olive oil
1 cup button mushrooms, chopped
1 shallot, chopped
2 garlic cloves, crushed
1 cup canned or boiled cannellini beans, drained
1 cup quinoa, cooked
Sea salt and ground black pepper, to taste
1 teaspoon smoked paprika
1/2 teaspoon red pepper flakes
1 teaspoon mustard seeds
1/2 teaspoon dried dill

### Directions

Heat 2 tablespoons of the olive oil in a nonstick skillet. Once hot, cook the mushrooms and shallot for 3 minutes or until just tender.

Add in the garlic, beans, quinoa and spices. Mix to combine well and then, shape the mixture into equal balls using oiled hands.

Then, heat the remaining 2 tablespoons of the olive oil in a nonstick skillet over medium heat. Once hot, fry the meatballs for about 10 minutes until golden brown on all sides.

Serve with cocktail sticks. Bon appétit!

**Per serving:** Calories: 195; Fat: 14.1g; Carbs: 13.2g; Protein: 3.9g

## 334. Cucumber Rounds with Hummus

(Ready in about 10 minutes | Servings 6)

### Ingredients

1 cup hummus, preferably homemade
2 large tomatoes, diced
1/2 teaspoon red pepper flakes

Sea salt and ground black pepper, to taste
2 English cucumbers, sliced into rounds

### Directions

Divide the hummus dip between the cucumber rounds.

Top them with tomatoes; sprinkle red pepper flakes, salt and black pepper over each cucumber.

Serve well chilled and enjoy!

**Per serving:** Calories: 88; Fat: 3.6g; Carbs: 11.3g; Protein: 2.6g

## 335. Stuffed Jalapeño Bites

(Ready in about 15 minutes | Servings 6)

### Ingredients

1/2 cup raw sunflower seeds, soaked overnight and drained
4 tablespoons scallions, chopped
1 teaspoon garlic, minced
3 tablespoons nutritional yeast

1/2 cup cream of onion soup
1/2 teaspoon cayenne pepper
1/2 teaspoon mustard seeds
12 jalapeños, halved and seeded
1/2 cup breadcrumbs

### Directions

In your food processor or high-speed blender, blitz raw sunflower seeds, scallions, garlic, nutritional yeast, soup, cayenne pepper and mustard seeds until well combined.

Spoon the mixture into the jalapeños and top them with the breadcrumbs.

Bake in the preheated oven at 400 degrees F for about 13 minutes or until the peppers have softened. Serve warm.

Bon appétit!

**Per serving:** Calories: 108; Fat: 6.6g; Carbs: 7.3g; Protein: 5.3g

## 336. Mexican-Style Onion Rings

(Ready in about 35 minutes | Servings 6)

### Ingredients

2 medium onions, cut into rings
1/4 cup all-purpose flour
1/4 cup spelt flour
1/3 cup rice milk, unsweetened
1/3 cup ale beer

Sea salt and ground black pepper, to season
1/2 teaspoon cayenne pepper
1/2 teaspoon mustard seeds
1 cup tortilla chips, crushed
1 tablespoon olive oil

### Directions

Start by preheating your oven to 420 degrees F.

In a shallow bowl, mix the flour, milk and beer.

In another shallow bowl, mix the spices with the crushed tortilla chips. Dredge the onion rings in the flour mixture.

Then, roll them over the spiced mixture, pressing down to coat well.

Arrange the onion rings on a parchment-lined baking pan. Brush them with olive oil and bake for approximately 30 minutes. Bon appétit!

**Per serving:** Calories: 213; Fat: 10.6g; Carbs: 26.2g; Protein: 4.3g

## 337. Roasted Root Vegetables

(Ready in about 35 minutes | Servings 6)

### Ingredients

1/4 cup olive oil
2 carrots, peeled and cut into 1 ½-inch pieces
2 parsnips, peeled and cut into 1 ½-inch pieces
1 celery stalk, peeled and cut into 1 ½-inch pieces
1 pound sweet potatoes, peeled and cut into 1 ½-inch pieces

1/4 cup olive oil
1 teaspoon mustard seeds
1/2 teaspoon basil
1/2 teaspoon oregano
1 teaspoon red pepper flakes
1 teaspoon dried thyme
Sea salt and ground black pepper, to taste

### Directions

Toss the vegetables with the remaining ingredients until well coated.

Roast the vegetables in the preheated oven at 400 degrees F for about 35 minutes, stirring halfway through the cooking time.

Taste, adjust the seasonings and serve warm. Bon appétit!

**Per serving:** Calories: 261; Fat: 18.2g; Carbs: 23.3g; Protein: 2.3g

## 338. Indian-Style Hummus Dip

(Ready in about 10 minutes | Servings 10)

### Ingredients

20 ounces canned or boiled chickpeas, drained
1 teaspoon garlic, sliced
1/4 cup tahini
1/4 cup olive oil
1 lime, freshly squeezed
1/4 teaspoon turmeric

1/2 teaspoon cumin powder
1 teaspoon curry powder
1 teaspoon coriander seeds
1/4 cup chickpea liquid, or more, as needed
2 tablespoons fresh cilantro, roughly chopped

### Directions

Blitz the chickpeas, garlic, tahini, olive oil, lime, turmeric, cumin, curry powder and coriander seeds in your blender or food processor.

Blend until your desired consistency is reached, gradually adding the chickpea liquid.

Place in your refrigerator until ready to serve. Garnish with fresh cilantro.

Serve with naan bread or veggie sticks, if desired. Bon appétit!

**Per serving:** Calories: 171; Fat: 10.4g; Carbs: 15.3g; Protein: 5.4g

# 339. Roasted Carrot and Bean Dip

(Ready in about 55 minutes | Servings 10)

## Ingredients

1 ½ pounds carrots, trimmed
2 tablespoons olive oil
4 tablespoons tahini
8 ounces canned cannellini beans, drained
1 teaspoon garlic, chopped
2 tablespoons lemon juice
2 tablespoons soy sauce
Sea salt and ground black pepper, to taste
1/2 teaspoon paprika
1/2 teaspoon dried dill
1/4 cup pepitas, toasted

## Directions

Begin by preheating your oven to 390 degrees F. Line a roasting pan with parchment paper.

Now, toss the carrots with the olive oil and arrange them on the prepared roasting pan.

Roast the carrots for about 50 minutes or until tender. Transfer the roasted carrots to the bowl of your food processor.

Add in the tahini, beans, garlic, lemon juice, soy sauce, salt, black pepper, paprika and dill. Process until your dip is creamy and uniform.

Garnish with toasted pepitas and serve with dippers of choice. Bon appétit!

**Per serving:** Calories: 121; Fat: 8.3g; Carbs: 11.2g; Protein: 2.8g

# 340. Quick and Easy Zucchini Sushi

(Ready in about 10 minutes | Servings 5)

## Ingredients

1 cup rice, cooked
1 carrot, grated
1 small onion, grated
1 avocado, chopped
1 garlic clove, minced
Sea salt and ground black pepper, to taste
1 medium zucchini, cut into strips
Wasabi sauce, to serve

## Directions

In a mixing bowl, thoroughly combine the rice, carrot, onion, avocado, garlic, salt and black pepper.

Divide the filling between the zucchini strips and spread it out evenly. Roll the zucchini up and serve with Wasabi sauce. Bon appétit!

**Per serving:** Calories: 129; Fat: 6.3g; Carbs: 15.9g; Protein: 2.5g

# 341. Cherry Tomatoes with Hummus

(Ready in about 10 minutes | Servings 8)

## Ingredients

1/2 cup hummus, preferably homemade
2 tablespoons vegan mayonnaise
1/4 cup scallions, chopped
16 cherry tomatoes, scoop out pulp
2 tablespoons fresh cilantro, chopped

## Directions

In a mixing bowl, thoroughly combine the hummus, mayonnaise and scallions.

Divide the hummus mixture between the tomatoes. Garnish with fresh cilantro and serve. Bon appétit!

**Per serving:** Calories: 49; Fat: 2.5g; Carbs: 4.7g; Protein: 1.3g

# 342. Oven-Roasted Button Mushrooms

(Ready in about 20 minutes | Servings 4)

## Ingredients

1 ½ pounds button mushrooms, cleaned
3 tablespoons olive oil
3 garlic cloves, minced
1 teaspoon dried oregano
1 teaspoon dried basil
1/2 teaspoon dried rosemary
Kosher salt and ground black pepper, to taste

## Directions

Toss the mushrooms with the remaining ingredients.

Arrange the mushrooms on a parchment-lined roasting pan.

Bake the mushrooms in the preheated oven at 420 degrees F for about 20 minutes or until tender and fragrant.

Arrange the mushrooms on a serving platter and serve with cocktail sticks. Bon appétit!

**Per serving:** Calories: 136; Fat: 10.5g; Carbs: 7.6g; Protein: 5.6g

# 343. Cheesy Kale Chips

(Ready in about 1 hour 30 minutes | Servings 6)

## Ingredients

1/2 cup sunflower seeds, soaked overnight and drained
1/2 cup cashews, soaked overnight and drained
1/3 cup nutritional yeast
2 tablespoons lemon juice
1 teaspoon onion powder
1 teaspoon garlic powder
1 teaspoon paprika
Sea salt and ground black pepper, to taste
1/2 cup water
4 cups kale, torn into pieces

## Directions

In your food processor or high-speed blender, blitz the raw sunflower seeds, cashews, nutritional yeast, lemon juice, onion powder, garlic powder, paprika, salt, ground black pepper and water until well combined.

Pour the mixture over the kale leaves and mix until they are well coated.

Bake in the preheated oven at 220 degrees F for about 1 hour 30 minutes or until crispy. Bon appétit!

**Per serving:** Calories: 121; Fat: 7.5g; Carbs: 8.4g; Protein: 6.5g

# 344. Hummus Avocado Boats

(Ready in about 10 minutes | Servings 4)

## Ingredients

1 tablespoon fresh lemon juice
2 ripe avocados, halved and pitted
8 ounces hummus
1 garlic clove, minced
1 medium tomato, chopped
Sea salt and ground black pepper, to taste
1/2 teaspoon turmeric powder
1/2 teaspoon cayenne pepper
1 tablespoon tahini

## Directions

Drizzle the fresh lemon juice over the avocado halves.

Mix the hummus, garlic, tomato, salt, black pepper, turmeric powder, cayenne pepper and tahini. Spoon the filling into your avocados. Serve immediately.

**Per serving:** Calories: 297; Fat: 21.2g; Carbs: 23.9g; Protein: 6g

## 345. Nacho Stuffed Button Mushrooms

(Ready in about 25 minutes | Servings 5)

### Ingredients

1 cup tortilla chips, crushed
1 cup canned or cooked black beans, drained
4 tablespoons vegan butter
2 tablespoons tahini
4 tablespoons scallions, chopped
1 teaspoon garlic, minced

1 jalapeno, chopped
1 teaspoon Mexican oregano
1 teaspoon cayenne pepper
Sea salt and ground black pepper, to taste
15 medium button mushrooms, cleaned, stalks removed

### Directions

Thoroughly combine all the ingredients, except for the mushrooms, in a mixing bowl.

Divide the nacho mixture between your mushrooms.

Bake in the preheated oven at 350 degrees F for about 20 minutes or until tender and cooked through. Bon appétit!

**Per serving:** Calories: 210; Fat: 13.4g; Carbs: 17.7g; Protein: 6.9g

## 346. Lettuce Wraps with Hummus and Avocado

(Ready in about 10 minutes | Servings 6)

### Ingredients

1/2 cup hummus
1 tomato, chopped
1 carrot, shredded
1 medium avocado, pitted and diced
1 teaspoon white vinegar
1 teaspoon soy sauce
1 teaspoon agave syrup

1 tablespoon Sriracha sauce
1 teaspoon garlic, minced
1 teaspoon ginger, freshly grated
Kosher salt and ground black pepper, to taste
1 head butter lettuce, separated into leaves

### Directions

Thoroughly combine the hummus, tomato, carrot and avocado. Combine the white vinegar, soy sauce, agave syrup, Sriracha sauce, garlic, ginger, salt and black pepper.

Divide the filling between lettuce leaves, roll them up and serve with sauce on the side.

Bon appétit!

**Per serving:** Calories: 115; Fat: 6.9g; Carbs: 11.6g; Protein: 2.6g

## 347. Roasted Brussels Sprouts

(Ready in about 35 minutes | Servings 6)

### Ingredients

2 pounds Brussels sprouts
1/4 cup olive oil
Coarse sea salt and ground black pepper, to taste

1 teaspoon red pepper flakes
1 teaspoon dried oregano
1 teaspoon dried parsley
1 teaspoon mustard seeds

### Directions

Toss the Brussels sprouts with the remaining ingredients until well coated.

Roast the vegetables in the preheated oven at 400 degrees F for about 35 minutes, stirring halfway through the cooking time.

Taste, adjust the seasonings and serve warm. Bon appétit!

**Per serving:** Calories: 151; Fat: 9.6g; Carbs: 14.5g; Protein: 5.3g

## 348. Sweet Potato Poblano Poppers

(Ready in about 25 minutes | Servings 7)

### Ingredients

1/2 pound cauliflower, trimmed and diced
1 pound sweet potatoes, peeled and diced
1/2 cup cashew milk, unsweetened
1/4 cup vegan mayonnaise
1/2 teaspoon curry powder

1/2 teaspoon cayenne pepper
1/4 teaspoon dried dill
Sea and ground black pepper, to taste
1/2 cup fresh breadcrumbs
14 fresh poblano chiles, cut into halves, seeds removed

### Directions

Steam the cauliflower and sweet potatoes for about 10 minutes or until they've softened. Now, mash them with the cashew milk.

Add in the vegan mayo, curry powder, cayenne pepper, dill, salt and black pepper.

Spoon the mixture into the peppers and top them with the breadcrumbs.

Bake in the preheated oven at 400 degrees F for about 13 minutes or until the peppers have softened.

Bon appétit!

**Per serving:** Calories: 145; Fat: 3.6g; Carbs: 24.9g; Protein: 5.3g

## 349. Baked Zucchini Chips

(Ready in about 1 hour 30 minutes | Servings 7)

### Ingredients

1 pound zucchini, cut into 1/8-inch thick slices
2 tablespoons olive oil
1/2 teaspoon dried oregano
1/2 teaspoon dried basil

1/2 teaspoon red pepper flakes
Sea salt and ground black pepper, to taste

### Directions

Toss the zucchini with the remaining ingredients.

Lay the zucchini slices in a single layer on a parchment-lined baking pan.

Bake at 235 degrees F for about 90 minutes until crisp and golden. Zucchini chips will crisp up as it cools.

Bon appétit!

**Per serving:** Calories: 48; Fat: 4.2g; Carbs: 2g; Protein: 1.7g

## 350. Authentic Lebanese Dip

(Ready in about 10 minutes | Servings 12)

### Ingredients

2 (15-ounce) can chickpeas/ garbanzo beans
4 tablespoons lemon juice
4 tablespoons tahini
2 tablespoons olive oil
1 teaspoon ginger-garlic paste

1 teaspoon Lebanese 7 spice blend
Sea salt and ground black pepper, to taste
1/3 cup chickpea liquid

### Directions

Blitz the chickpeas, lemon juice, tahini, olive oil, ginger-garlic paste and spices in your blender or food processor.

Blend until your desired consistency is reached, gradually adding the chickpea liquid.

Place in your refrigerator until ready to serve. Serve with veggie sticks, if desired. Bon appétit!

**Per serving:** Calories: 117; Fat: 6.6g; Carbs: 12.2g; Protein: 4.3g

## 351. Oat Vegan Meatballs

(Ready in about 15 minutes | Servings 4)

### Ingredients

1 cup rolled oats
1 cup boiled or canned chickpeas
2 cloves garlic, minced
1 teaspoon onion powder
1/2 teaspoon cumin powder
1 teaspoon dried parsley flakes
1 teaspoon dried marjoram

1 tablespoon chia seeds, soaked with 2 tablespoons of water
A few drizzles liquid smoke
Sea salt and freshly ground black pepper, to taste
2 tablespoons olive oil

### Directions

Thoroughly combine the ingredients, except for the olive oil. Mix to combine well and then, shape the mixture into equal balls using oiled hands.

Then, heat the olive oil in a nonstick skillet over medium heat. Once hot, fry the meatballs for about 10 minutes until golden brown on all sides.

Arrange your meatballs on a serving platter and serve with cocktail sticks. Bon appétit!

**Per serving:** Calories: 284; Fat: 10.5g; Carbs: 38.2g; Protein: 10.4g

## 352. Bell Pepper Boats with Mango Salsa

(Ready in about 5 minutes | Servings 4)

### Ingredients

1 mango, peeled, pitted, cubed
1 small shallot, chopped
2 tablespoons fresh cilantro, minced

1 red chile pepper, seeded and chopped
1 tablespoon fresh lime juice
4 bell peppers, seeded and halved

### Directions

Thoroughly combine the mango, shallot, cilantro, red chile pepper and lime juice.

Spoon the mixture into the pepper halves and serve immediately. Bon appétit!

**Per serving:** Calories: 74; Fat: 0.5g; Carbs: 17.6g; Protein: 1.6g

## 353. Tangy Rosemary Broccoli Florets

(Ready in about 35 minutes | Servings 6)

### Ingredients

2 pounds broccoli florets
1/4 cup extra-virgin olive oil
Sea salt and ground black pepper, to taste

1 teaspoon ginger-garlic paste
1 tablespoon fresh rosemary, chopped
1/2 teaspoon lemon zest

### Directions

Toss the broccoli with the remaining ingredients until well coated.

Roast the vegetables in the preheated oven at 400 degrees F for about 35 minutes, stirring halfway through the cooking time.

Taste, adjust the seasonings and serve warm. Bon appétit!

**Per serving:** Calories: 135; Fat: 9.5g; Carbs: 10.9g; Protein: 4.4g

## 354. Crispy Baked Beetroot Chips

(Ready in about 35 minutes | Servings 6)

### Ingredients

2 red beetroots, peeled and cut into 1/8-inch-thick slices
1/4 cup olive oil

Sea salt and ground black pepper, to taste
1/2 teaspoon red pepper flakes

### Directions

Toss the beetroot slices with the remaining ingredients.

Arrange the beetroot slices in a single layer on a parchment-lined baking pan.

Bake at 400 degrees F for about 30 minutes until crisp. Bon appétit!

**Per serving:** Calories: 92; Fat: 9.1g; Carbs: 2.6g; Protein: 0.5g

## 355. Collard Wraps with Beans and Broccoli Spread

(Ready in about 10 minutes | Servings 6)

### Ingredients

2 cups broccoli florets
1 small onion, chopped
2 tablespoons fresh lemon juice
1 sprig thyme, leaves removed
1 sprig rosemary, leaves removed
1 tablespoon fresh parsley
Sea salt and ground black pepper, to taste

1 teaspoon garlic powder
1 teaspoon paprika
4 tablespoons olive oil
6 collard leaves
1 cup canned sweet corn kernels, drained
1 cup canned pinto beans, drained

### Directions

Steam the broccoli for about 4 minutes until crisp-tender. Transfer the broccoli florets to your food processor and blitz them along with the onion, lemon juice, herbs and spices until well combined.

With the machine running, gradually add olive oil and blend until creamy and smooth.

Then, spoon the mixture onto collard leaves; top with corn and beans, wrap the leaves and serve immediately. Enjoy!

**Per serving:** Calories: 164; Fat: 9.7g; Carbs: 16.8g; Protein: 4.4g

## 356. Stuffed Portobellos with Rice and Herbs

(Ready in about 25 minutes | Servings 6)

### Ingredients

1 cup cooked brown rice
1 garlic clove, minced
3 tablespoons scallions, chopped
1 red bell pepper, seeded and chopped
1/4 cup raw walnuts, crushed
1 tablespoon parsley, minced
1 tablespoon basil, minced

1 tablespoon cilantro, minced
1 teaspoon cayenne pepper
1/2 teaspoon smoked paprika
Sea salt and ground black pepper, to taste
2 tablespoons olive oil
6 portobello mushrooms, stems removed

### Directions

Thoroughly combine the rice, garlic, scallions, pepper, walnuts, herbs and spices.

Divide the mixture between your mushrooms.

Drizzle olive oil over the mushrooms.

Bake in the preheated oven at 350 degrees F for about 20 minutes or until tender and cooked through. Bon appétit!

**Per serving:** Calories: 125; Fat: 7g; Carbs: 13.2g; Protein: 3.6g

## 357. The Best Homemade Raisins Ever

(Ready in about 6 hours | Servings 6)

### Ingredients

2 bunches seedless grapes, seeded

A pinch of salt

### Directions

Arrange your grapes on a parchment-lined baking pan. Sprinkle a pinch of salt over them.

Bake in a preheated oven at 220 degrees F for about 6 hours or until they are shriveled.

Let them cool completely. Store in your refrigerator in a sealed container for about 3 weeks.

Bon appétit!

**Per serving:** Calories: 83; Fat: 0.1g; Carbs: 21.7g; Protein: 0.8g

## 358. Easy Za'atar Popcorn

(Ready in about 10 minutes | Servings 2)

### Ingredients

2 tablespoons coconut oil
1/4 cup of popcorn kernels

1 tablespoon za'atar spice blend
Sea salt, to taste

### Directions

Heat the oil in a thick-bottomed saucepan over medium-high heat.

Once hot, add the popcorn kernels in an even layer.

Cover the saucepan, remove from the heat and wait for 30 seconds.

Return the saucepan to the heat, shaking it occasionally. Toss the prepared popcorn with the spices. Bon appétit!

**Per serving:** Calories: 295; Fat: 23.5g; Carbs: 20g; Protein: 2.8g

## 359. Greek-Style Yam Chips

(Ready in about 25 minutes | Servings 6)

### Ingredients

1 pound yam, peeled and cut into 1/8-inch-thick slices
1/4 cup extra-virgin olive oil
1 teaspoon dried basil

1 teaspoon dried oregano
1/2 teaspoon cayenne pepper
Sea salt and ground black pepper, to taste

### Directions

Toss the yam slices with the remaining ingredients.

Arrange the yam slices in a single layer on a parchment-lined baking pan.

Bake at 400 degrees F for about 20 minutes or until golden and crisp. Bon appétit!

**Per serving:** Calories: 169; Fat: 9.1g; Carbs: 21g; Protein: 1.1g

## 360. Za'atar Roasted Zucchini Sticks

(Ready in about 1 hour 35 minutes | Servings 5)

### Ingredients

1 ½ pounds zucchini, cut into sticks lengthwise
2 garlic cloves, crushed
2 tablespoons extra-virgin olive oil

1 teaspoon za'atar spice
Kosher salt and ground black pepper, to taste

### Directions

Toss the zucchini with the remaining ingredients.

Lay the zucchini sticks in a single layer on a parchment-lined baking pan.

Bake at 235 degrees F for about 90 minutes until crisp and golden. Zucchini sticks will crisp up as they cool.

Bon appétit!

**Per serving:** Calories: 85; Fat: 6.1g; Carbs: 5.7g; Protein: 4.1g

## 361. Lettuce Boats with Avocado Salsa

(Ready in about 10 minutes | Servings 5)

### Ingredients

1 large avocado, pitted, peeled and diced
1 large tomato, peeled and chopped
1 small onion, chopped
1/4 cup fresh cilantro, chopped
1 poblano pepper, minced

1/2 teaspoon Mexican oregano
Sea salt and red pepper, to taste
1 head Romaine lettuce, leaves separated
1 tablespoon fresh lime juice

### Directions

Thoroughly combine the avocado, tomato, onion, cilantro, poblano pepper, Mexican oregano, salt and black pepper.

Divide the filling between lettuce leaves, drizzle lime juice over them and serve immediately.

Bon appétit!

**Per serving:** Calories: 104; Fat: 6.3g; Carbs: 11.4g; Protein: 3.1g

## 362. Buffalo Cauliflower "Wings"

(Ready in about 40 minutes | Servings 5)

### Ingredients

1/2 cup all-purpose flour
2 tablespoons tahini
1/2 cup cornstarch
1/2 teaspoon baking powder
Kosher salt and ground black pepper, to taste
1/2 cup vodka

2 tablespoons soy sauce
1 teaspoon onion powder
1 teaspoon garlic powder
1 teaspoon cayenne pepper
1 teaspoon red pepper flakes
1 pound cauliflower florets
2 tablespoons sesame oil

### Directions

Start by preheating your oven to 420 degrees F. Line a baking pan with parchment pepper.

In a mixing bowl, thoroughly combine the flour, tahini, cornstarch, baking powder, salt, black pepper, vodka, soy sauce, onion powder, garlic powder, cayenne pepper and red pepper flakes.

Brush the cauliflower florets with the sesame oil. Arrange the cauliflower florets in a single layer in the prepared baking pan. Bake the cauliflower for about 20 minutes.

Dip the cauliflower florets in the batter and bake for a further 20 minutes. Bon appétit!

**Per serving:** Calories: 247; Fat: 11.9g; Carbs: 31.4g; Protein: 5.2g

## 363. Chard Wraps with Herb-Walnut Pesto

(Ready in about 10 minutes | Servings 6)

### Ingredients

1 teaspoon garlic, peeled
1/2 cup walnuts, toasted
1 tablespoon tahini
1 tablespoon fresh parsley leaves, chopped
1 tablespoon fresh mint leaves, chopped

1 tablespoon fresh cilantro leaves, chopped
Sea salt and ground black pepper, to taste
6 large Swiss chard leaves, rinsed and dried

### Directions

Mix the garlic, walnuts, tahini, herbs and spices in a high-speed blender or food processor. Blend or until your desired consistency is reached.

Spoon the mixture into Swiss chard leaves, wrap them and serve immediately.

Bon appétit!

**Per serving:** Calories: 74; Fat: 5.8g; Carbs: 4.4g; Protein: 2.6g

## 364. 5-Minute Queso Dip

(Ready in about 10 minutes | Servings 6)

### Ingredients

1 cup cashews
1 clove garlic, chopped
1/2 cup water

1 tablespoon harissa
Sea salt, to taste

### Directions

Place all the ingredients in a high-speed blender or food processor.

Process until creamy and uniform.

Serve with your favorite dippers. Bon appétit!

**Per serving:** Calories: 112; Fat: 8.7g; Carbs: 6.3g; Protein: 3.6g

## 365. Asian-Style Mushrooms

(Ready in about 25 minutes | Servings 7)

### Ingredients

8 ounces tempeh, crumbled
1 tablespoon tahini
2 tablespoons soy sauce
1 teaspoon agave syrup
1 tablespoon rice vinegar
1 teaspoon paprika

2 tablespoons fresh cilantro, chopped
1 tablespoon fresh mint, chopped
1/2 cup breadcrumbs
1 tablespoon sesame oil
20 button mushrooms

### Directions

Thoroughly combine the tempeh, tahini, soy sauce, agave syrup, vinegar, paprika, cilantro and mint.

Divide the mixture between your mushrooms. Top them with breadcrumbs. Brush your mushrooms with the sesame oil.

Bake the mushrooms in the preheated oven at 350 degrees F for about 20 minutes or until tender and cooked through. Bon appétit!

**Per serving:** Calories: 133; Fat: 7.8g; Carbs: 8.8g; Protein: 8.6g

## 366. Provençal Eggplant Chips

(Ready in about 30 minutes | Servings 5)

### Ingredients

1 ½ pounds eggplant, cut into 1/8-inch-thick slices
1 tablespoon Herbes de Provence

1/2 black pepper
1/2 teaspoon garlic powder
2 tablespoons olive oil

### Directions

Toss the eggplant with the sea salt until well coated. Then, place them in a colander and let it sit for about 15 minutes; drain, rinse and pat dry with kitchen towels.

Toss the eggplant with the remaining ingredients.

Lay the eggplant slices in a single layer on a parchment-lined baking pan.

Bake at 420 degrees F for about 12 minutes until crisp and golden. Bon appétit!

**Per serving:** Calories: 86; Fat: 5.6g; Carbs: 8.2g; Protein: 1.4g

# SAUCES & CONDIMENTS

# 367. Classic Barbecue Sauce

(Ready in about 5 minutes | Servings 20)

## Ingredients

1 cup brown sugar
1 cup ketchup
1/4 cup wine vinegar
1/3 cup water

1 tablespoon soy sauce
2 tablespoon mustard powder
1 teaspoon black pepper
2 teaspoons sea salt

## Directions

Mix all the ingredients in your blender or food processor.

Blend until uniform and smooth.

Bon appétit!

**Per serving:** Calories: 36; Fat: 0.3g; Carbs: 8.6g; Protein: 0.2g

# 368. Garden Herb Mustard

(Ready in about 35 minutes | Servings 10)

## Ingredients

1/2 cup mustard powder
5 tablespoons mustard seeds, ground
1/4 cup water
1/4 cup beer

2 tablespoons sherry vinegar
1 ½ teaspoons coarse sea salt
1 tablespoon agave syrup
1 tablespoon dried cilantro
1 tablespoon dried basil

## Directions

Thoroughly combine the mustard powder, ground mustard seeds, water and beer in a mixing bowl; let it stand for about 30 minutes.

Add in the remaining ingredients and stir to combine well.

Let it sit at least 12 hours before serving. Bon appétit!

**Per serving:** Calories: 34; Fat: 1.6g; Carbs: 3.5g; Protein: 1.3g

# 369. Classic Homemade Ketchup

(Ready in about 25 minutes | Servings 10)

## Ingredients

4 ounces canned tomato paste
2 tablespoons agave syrup
1/4 cup red wine vinegar

1/4 cup water
1/2 teaspoon kosher salt
1/4 teaspoon garlic powder

## Directions

Preheat a saucepan over medium flame. Then, add all the ingredients to a saucepan and bring it to a boil.

Turn the heat to a simmer; let it simmer, stirring continuously, for about 20 minutes or until the sauce has thickened.

Store in a glass jar in your refrigerator. Bon appétit!

**Per serving:** Calories: 24; Fat: 0g; Carbs: 5.5g; Protein: 0.5g

# 370. Cashew, Lime and Dill Sauce

(Ready in about 25 minutes | Servings 8)

## Ingredients

1 cup raw cashews
1/2 cup water
2 tablespoons dill

1 tablespoon lime juice
Sea salt and red pepper, to taste

## Directions

Place all the ingredients in the bowl of your food processor or high-speed blender until smooth, uniform and creamy.

Season to taste and serve with crudités.

**Per serving:** Calories: 24; Fat: 0g; Carbs: 5.5g; Protein: 0.5g

# 371. Ligurian Walnut Sauce

(Ready in about 30 minutes | Servings 4)

## Ingredients

1/2 cup almond milk
1 slice white bread, crusts removed
1 (about 50 halves) cup raw walnuts
1/2 teaspoon garlic powder
1 teaspoon onion powder

1 teaspoon smoked paprika
2 tablespoons olive oil
1 tablespoon basil, chopped
3 curry leaves
Sea salt and ground black pepper, to taste

## Directions

Put the almond milk and bread in a bowl and let it soak well.

Transfer the soaked bread to the bowl of your food processor or high-speed blender; add in the remaining ingredients.

Process until smooth, uniform and creamy.

Serve with pasta or zucchini noodles. Bon appétit!

**Per serving:** Calories: 263; Fat: 24.1g; Carbs: 9g; Protein: 5.5g

# 372. Chia, Maple and Dijon Sauce

(Ready in about 10 minutes | Servings 4)

## Ingredients

2 tablespoons chia seeds
5 tablespoons extra-virgin olive oil
1 ½ tablespoons maple syrup

2 teaspoons Dijon mustard
1 tablespoon red wine vinegar
Sea salt and ground black pepper, to taste

## Directions

Put all the ingredients into a mixing bowl; whisk to combine and emulsify.

Let it sit for 15 minutes so the chia can expand. Bon appétit!

**Per serving:** Calories: 126; Fat: 9g; Carbs: 8.3g; Protein: 1.5g

# 373. Garlic Cilantro Dressing

(Ready in about 10 minutes | Servings 6)

## Ingredients

1/2 cup almonds
1/2 cup water
1 bunch cilantro
1 red chili pepper, chopped
2 cloves garlic, crushed

2 tablespoons fresh lime juice
1 teaspoon lime zest
Sea salt and ground black pepper
5 tablespoons extra-virgin olive oil

## Directions

Place the almonds and water in your blender and mix until creamy and smooth.

Add in the cilantro, chili pepper, garlic, lime juice, lime zest, salt and black pepper; blitz until everything is well combined.

Then, gradually add in the olive oil and mix until smooth. Store in your refrigerator for up to 5 days. Bon appétit!

**Per serving:** Calories: 181; Fat: 18.2g; Carbs: 4.8g; Protein: 3g

# 374. Classic Ranch Dressing

(Ready in about 10 minutes | Servings 8)

## Ingredients

1 cup vegan mayonnaise
1/4 almond milk, unsweetened
1 teaspoon sherry vinegar
1/2 teaspoon kosher salt
1/4 teaspoon black pepper
2 cloves garlic, minced
1/2 teaspoon dried chives
1/2 teaspoon dried dill weed
1 teaspoon dried parsley flakes
1/2 teaspoon onion powder
1/3 teaspoon paprika

## Directions

Using a wire whisk, thoroughly combine all the ingredients in a bowl.

Cover and place in your refrigerator until ready to serve.

Bon appétit!

**Per serving:** Calories: 191; Fat: 20.2g; Carbs: 0.8g; Protein: 0.5g

# 375. Coriander Tahini Sauce

(Ready in about 10 minutes | Servings 6)

## Ingredients

1/4 cup cashews, soaked overnight and drained
1/4 cup water
4 tablespoons tahini
1/4 cup fresh coriander leaves, roughly chopped
1 clove garlic, minced
Kosher salt and cayenne pepper, to taste

## Directions

Process the cashews and water in your blender until creamy and uniform.

Add in the remaining ingredients and continue to blend until everything is well incorporated.

Keep in your refrigerator for up to a week. Bon appétit!

**Per serving:** Calories: 91; Fat: 7.5g; Carbs: 4.5g; Protein: 2.9g

# 376. Lime Coconut Sauce

(Ready in about 10 minutes | Servings 7)

## Ingredients

1 teaspoon coconut oil
1 large garlic clove, minced
1 teaspoon fresh ginger, minced
1 cup coconut milk
1 lime, freshly squeezed and zested
A pinch of Himalayan rock salt

## Directions

In a small saucepan, melt the coconut oil over medium heat. Once hot, cook the garlic and ginger for about 1 minute or until aromatic.

Turn the heat to a simmer and add in the coconut milk, lime juice, lime zest and salt; continue to simmer for 1 minute or until heated through.

Bon appétit!

**Per serving:** Calories: 87; Fat: 8.8g; Carbs: 2.6g; Protein: 0.8g

# 377. Homemade Guacamole

(Ready in about 10 minutes | Servings 7)

## Ingredients

2 avocados, peeled, pitted
1 lemon, juiced
Sea salt and ground black pepper, to taste
1 small onion, diced
2 tablespoons chopped fresh cilantro
1 large tomato, diced

## Directions

Mash the avocados, together with the remaining ingredients in a mixing bowl.

Place the guacamole in your refrigerator until ready to serve. Bon appétit!

**Per serving:** Calories: 107; Fat: 8.6g; Carbs: 7.9g; Protein: 1.6g

# 378. Easiest Vegan Mayo Ever

(Ready in about 15 minutes | Servings 6)

## Ingredients

1/2 cup olive oil, at room temperature
1/4 cup rice milk, unsweetened, at room temperature
1 teaspoon yellow mustard
1 tablespoon fresh lemon juice
1/3 teaspoon kosher salt

## Directions

Blend the milk, mustard, lemon juice and salt using your high-speed blender.

While the machine is going, gradually add in the olive oil and continue to blend at a low speed until the mixture has thickened.

Store in your refrigerator for about 6 days. Bon appétit!

**Per serving:** Calories: 167; Fat: 18.1g; Carbs: 0.7g; Protein: 0.4g

# 379. Sunflower and Hemp Seed Butter

(Ready in about 15 minutes | Servings 16)

## Ingredients

2 cups sunflower seeds, hulled and roasted
4 tablespoons hemp seeds
2 tablespoons flaxseed meal
A pinch of salt
A pinch of grated nutmeg
2 dates, pitted

## Directions

Blitz the sunflower seeds in your food processor until a butter forms.

Add in the remaining ingredients and continue to blend until creamy and uniform.

Taste and adjust the flavor as needed. Bon appétit!

**Per serving:** Calories: 124; Fat: 10.6g; Carbs: 4.9g; Protein: 4.3g

## 380. Creamy Mustard Sauce

(Ready in about 35 minutes | Servings 4)

### Ingredients

1/2 plain hummus
1 teaspoon fresh garlic, minced
1 tablespoon deli mustard
1 tablespoon extra-virgin olive oil

1 tablespoon fresh lime juice
1 teaspoon red pepper flakes
1/2 teaspoon sea salt
1/4 teaspoon ground black pepper

### Directions

Thoroughly combine all ingredients in a mixing bowl.

Let it sit in your refrigerator for about 30 minutes before serving.

Bon appétit!

Per serving: Calories: 73; Fat: 4.2g; Carbs: 7.1g; Protein: 1.7g

## 381. Traditional Balkan-Style Ajvar

(Ready in about 30 minutes | Servings 6)

### Ingredients

4 red bell peppers
1 small eggplant
1 garlic clove, smashed
2 tablespoons olive oil

1 teaspoon white vinegar
Kosher salt and ground black pepper, to taste

### Directions

Grill the peppers and eggplant until they are soft and charred.

Place the peppers in a plastic bag and let them steam for about 15 minutes. Remove the skin, seeds and core of the peppers and eggplant.

Then, transfer them to the bowl of your food processor. Add in the garlic, olive oil, vinegar, salt and black pepper and continue to blend until well combined.

Store in the refrigerator for up to 1 week. Bon appétit!

Per serving: Calories: 93; Fat: 4.9g; Carbs: 11.1g; Protein: 1.8g

## 382. Amba (Mango Sauce)

(Ready in about 30 minutes | Servings 6)

### Ingredients

2 green-skinned mangos, peeled and pitted
1 onion, chopped
1 chili pepper, minced
2 garlic cloves, minced
1 tablespoon Himalayan salt

1 teaspoon ground turmeric
1/3 teaspoon ground cumin
1/2 teaspoon paprika
2 tablespoons soy sauce
2 tablespoons fresh lime juice

### Directions

Heat a medium saucepan over a moderately high heat. Bring 2 cups of water to a boil. Add in the mango followed by the onion, pepper and garlic and spices.

Turn the heat to a simmer and let it cook until the mango has softened or about 25 minutes.

Remove from the heat and stir in the soy sauce and fresh lime juice.

Then, purée the mixture in your blender until smooth and uniform. Store in your refrigerator for up to 1 month. Bon appétit!

Per serving: Calories: 93; Fat: 4.9g; Carbs: 11.1g; Protein: 1.8g

## 383. Dad's Homemade Ketchup

(Ready in about 30 minutes | Servings 12)

### Ingredients

2 tablespoons olive oil
1 onion, chopped
2 garlic cloves, chopped
1 teaspoon cayenne pepper
2 tablespoons tomato paste

30 ounces canned tomatoes, crushed
3 tablespoons brown sugar
1/4 cup apple cider vinegar
Salt and fresh ground black pepper, to taste

### Directions

In a medium saucepan, heat the olive oil over a moderately high heat. Sauté the onions until tender and aromatic.

Add in the garlic and continue to sauté for 1 minute or until fragrant.

Add in the remaining ingredients and bring to a simmer. Continue to cook for about 25 minutes.

Process the mixture in your blender until smooth and uniform. Bon appétit!

Per serving: Calories: 49; Fat: 2.4g; Carbs: 6.5g; Protein: 0.9g

## 384. Herb Avocado Salad Dressing

(Ready in about 10 minutes | Servings 6)

### Ingredients

1 medium-sized avocado, pitted, peeled and mashed
4 tablespoons extra-virgin olive oil
4 tablespoons almond milk
2 tablespoons cilantro, minced
2 tablespoons parsley, minced

1 lemon, juiced
2 garlic cloves, minced
1/2 teaspoon mustard seeds
1/2 teaspoon red pepper flakes
Kosher salt and cayenne pepper, to taste

### Directions

Mix all the above ingredients in your food processor or blender.

Blend until uniform, smooth and creamy. Bon appétit!

Per serving: Calories: 101; Fat: 9.4g; Carbs: 4.3g; Protein: 1.2g

## 385. Authentic French Remoulade

(Ready in about 10 minutes | Servings 9)

### Ingredients

1 cup vegan mayonnaise
1 tablespoon Dijon mustard
1 scallion, finely chopped
1 teaspoon garlic, minced
2 tablespoons capers, coarsely chopped

1 tablespoon hot sauce
1 tablespoon fresh lemon juice
1 tablespoon flat-leaf parsley, chopped

### Directions

Thoroughly combine all the ingredients in your food processor or blender.

Blend until uniform and creamy.

Bon appétit!

Per serving: Calories: 121; Fat: 10.4g; Carbs: 1.3g; Protein: 6.2g

## 386. Authentic Béchamel Sauce

(Ready in about 10 minutes | Servings 5)

### Ingredients

2 tablespoons soy butter
2 tablespoons all-purpose flour
1 ½ cups oat milk
Coarse sea salt, to taste
1/4 teaspoon turmeric powder
1/4 teaspoon ground black pepper, to taste
A pinch of grated nutmeg

### Directions

Melt the soy butter in a sauté pan over a moderate flame. Add in the flour and continue to cook, whisking continuously to avoid lumps.

Pour the milk and continue whisking for about 4 minutes until the sauce has thickened.

Add in the spices and stir to combine well. Bon appétit!

**Per serving:** Calories: 89; Fat: 6.1g; Carbs: 5.9g; Protein: 2.7g

## 387. Perfect Hollandaise Sauce

(Ready in about 15 minutes | Servings 6)

### Ingredients

1/2 cup cashews, soaked and drained
1 cup almond milk
2 tablespoons fresh lemon juice
3 tablespoons coconut oil
3 tablespoons nutritional yeast
Sea salt and ground white pepper, to taste
A pinch of grated nutmeg
1/2 teaspoon red pepper flakes, crushed

### Directions

Puree all the ingredients in a high-speed blender or food processor.

Then, heat the mixture in a small saucepan over low-medium heat; cook, stirring occasionally, until the sauce has reduced and thickened.

Bon appétit!

**Per serving:** Calories: 145; Fat: 12.6g; Carbs: 6.1g; Protein: 3.3g

## 388. Mexican-Style Chili Sauce

(Ready in about 5 minutes | Servings 5)

### Ingredients

10 ounces canned tomato sauce
2 tablespoons apple cider vinegar
2 tablespoons brown sugar
1 Mexican chili pepper, minced
1/2 teaspoon dried Mexican oregano
1/4 teaspoon ground allspices
Sea salt and ground black pepper, to taste

### Directions

In a mixing bowl, thoroughly combine all the ingredients.

Store in a glass jar in your refrigerator.

Bon appétit!

**Per serving:** Calories: 35; Fat: 0.2g; Carbs: 7.1g; Protein: 0.8g

## 389. Basic Tomato Sauce

(Ready in about 25 minutes | Servings 8)

### Ingredients

2 tablespoons olive oil
1 shallot, chopped
2 cloves garlic, minced
1 red chili pepper, seeded and minced
20 ounces canned tomatoes, puréed
2 tablespoons tomato paste
1 teaspoon cayenne pepper
1/2 teaspoon coarse sea salt

### Directions

In a medium saucepan, heat the olive oil over a moderately high heat. Sauté the shallot until tender and aromatic.

Add in the garlic and chili pepper; continue to sauté for 1 minute or until fragrant.

Add in the tomatoes, tomato paste, cayenne pepper and salt; turn the heat to a simmer. Continue to cook for about 22 minutes.

Bon appétit!

**Per serving:** Calories: 49; Fat: 3.6g; Carbs: 4.3g; Protein: 0.9g

## 390. Turkish Biber Salçası

(Ready in about 1 hour 25 minutes | Servings 16)

### Ingredients

4 sweet red peppers
4 red chili peppers
Juice of 1/2 lemon juice
2 tablespoons olive oil
1 teaspoon sea salt
1/2 teaspoon freshly ground black pepper

### Directions

Place the peppers directly over a low gas flame; roast the peppers for about 8 minutes until they are charred on all sides.

Let the peppers steam in a plastic bag or covered bowl for about 30 minutes. Remove the blackened skin and core and transfer the flesh to your food processor

Blitz until a smooth paste forms.

Heat the prepared paste in a saucepan; add in the remaining ingredients and stir to combine well. Turn the heat to a simmer and let it cook, partially covered, for about 45 minutes or until the sauce has thickened.

Store in your refrigerator for up to 4 weeks. Bon appétit!

**Per serving:** Calories: 39; Fat: 1.8g; Carbs: 4.8g; Protein: 0.7g

# 391. Italian Salsa al Pepe Verde

(Ready in about 15 minutes | Servings 6)

## Ingredients

3 tablespoons vegan butter
3 tablespoons all-purpose flour
1 ½ cups almond milk, unsweetened
1 cup vegetable broth

2 tablespoons green peppercorns, freshly cracked
Sea salt, to taste
1 tablespoon sherry wine

## Directions

In a saucepan, melt the butter over a moderate heat. Once hot, add in the flour and turn the heat to a simmer.

Gradually add in the milk and continue to cook for a few minutes more, whisking constantly to avoid the lumps.

Add in the broth, green peppercorns and salt. Continue to cook on low until the sauce has thickened. Add in the wine and continue to simmer for a few minutes more. Bon appétit!

**Per serving:** Calories: 153; Fat: 10.1g; Carbs: 13.3g; Protein: 2.6g

# 392. Sunflower Seed Pasta Sauce

(Ready in about 10 minutes | Servings 3)

## Ingredients

1/2 cup sunflower seeds, soaked overnight
1/2 cup almond milk, unsweetened
2 tablespoons lemon juice
1 teaspoon granulated garlic

1/4 teaspoon dried oregano
1/2 teaspoon dried basil
1 teaspoon dried dill
Sea salt and ground black pepper, to taste

## Directions

Place all the ingredients in the bowl of your food processor or a high-speed blender.

Puree until the sauce is uniform and smooth.

Serve the sauce over the cooked pasta or vegetable noodles. Bon appétit!

**Per serving:** Calories: 164; Fat: 13.1g; Carbs: 7.6g; Protein: 6.2g

# 393. Healthy Grandma's Applesauce

(Ready in about 30 minutes | Servings 12)

## Ingredients

3 pounds cooking apples, peeled, cored and diced
1/2 cup water
8 fresh dates, pitted
2 tablespoons lemon juice

A pinch of salt
A pinch of grated nutmeg
1/4 teaspoon ground cloves
1/2 teaspoon ground cinnamon

## Directions

Add the apples and water to a heavy-bottomed pot and cook for about 20 minutes.

Meanwhile, mix your dates and 1/2 cup water using a high-speed blender. Process until completely smooth.

Then, mash the cooked apples with a potato masher; stir the pureed dates into the mashed apples and stir to combine well.

Continue to simmer until the applesauce has thickened to your desired consistency. Add in the lemon juice and spices and stir until everything is well incorporated. Bon appétit!

**Per serving:** Calories: 73; Fat: 0.2g; Carbs: 19.3g; Protein: 0.4g

# 394. Homemade Chocolate Sauce

(Ready in about 10 minutes | Servings 9)

## Ingredients

5 tablespoons coconut oil, melted
3 tablespoons agave syrup
3 tablespoons cacao powder
A pinch of grated nutmeg

A pinch of kosher salt
1/2 teaspoon cinnamon powder
1/2 teaspoon vanilla paste

## Directions

Thoroughly combine all the ingredients using a wire whisk.

Store the chocolate sauce in your refrigerator. To soften the sauce, heat it up over low heat just before serving.

Bon appétit!

**Per serving:** Calories: 95; Fat: 7.6g; Carbs: 7.5g; Protein: 0.2g

# 395. Favorite Cranberry Sauce

(Ready in about 15 minutes | Servings 8)

## Ingredients

1/2 cup brown sugar
1/2 cup water
8 ounces cranberries, fresh or frozen

A pinch of allspice
A pinch of sea salt
1 tablespoon crystallized ginger

## Directions

In a heavy-bottomed saucepan, bring the sugar and water to a rolling boil.

Stir until the sugar has dissolved.

Add in the cranberries, followed by the remaining ingredients. Turn the heat to a simmer and continue to cook for 10 to 12 minutes or until the cranberries burst.

Let it cool at room temperature. Store in a glass jar in your refrigerator. Bon appétit!

**Per serving:** Calories: 62; Fat: 0.6g; Carbs: 16g; Protein: 0.2g

# 396. Traditional Russian Chrain

(Ready in about 40 minutes | Servings 12)

## Ingredients

1 cup boiled water
6 ounces raw beets, peeled
1 tablespoon brown salt

9 ounces raw horseradish, peeled
1 tablespoon olive oil
1/2 cup apple cider vinegar

## Directions

In a heavy-bottomed saucepan, bring the water a boil. Then, cook the beets for about 35 minutes or until they have softened.

Remove the skins and transfer the beets to a food processor. Add in the remaining ingredients and blend until well combined.

Bon appétit!

**Per serving:** Calories: 28; Fat: 1.3g; Carbs: 3.8g; Protein: 0.5g

## 397. French Mignonette Sauce

(Ready in about 15 minutes | Servings 6)

### Ingredients

3/4 cup red wine vinegar
2 teaspoons mixed peppercorns, freshly cracked

1 small eschalot, finely chopped
Sea salt, to taste

### Directions

Combine the vinegar, peppercorns and eschalot in a mixing bowl. Season with salt.

Let it stand at least 15 minutes. Serve with grilled oyster mushrooms.

Bon appétit!

**Per serving:** Calories: 14; Fat: 0g; Carbs: 1.9g; Protein: 0.2g

## 398. Smoked Cheese Sauce

(Ready in about 10 minutes | Servings 6)

### Ingredients

1/2 cup raw cashews, soaked and drained
4 tablespoons water
2 tablespoons raw tahini
Fresh juice of 1/2 lemon
1 tablespoon apple cider vinegar

2 carrots, cooked
1 teaspoon smoked paprika
Sea salt, to taste
1 clove garlic
1 teaspoon fresh dill weed
1/2 cup frozen corn kernels, thawed and squeezed

### Directions

Process the cashews and water in your blender until creamy and uniform.

Add in the remaining ingredients and continue to blend until everything is well incorporated.

Keep in your refrigerator for up to a week. Bon appétit!

**Per serving:** Calories: 107; Fat: 7.3g; Carbs: 8.8g; Protein: 3.3g

## 399. Easy Homemade Pear Sauce

(Ready in about 30 minutes | Servings 8)

### Ingredients

2 pounds pears, peeled, cored and diced
1/4 cup water
1/4 cup brown sugar
1/2 teaspoon fresh ginger, minced

1/2 teaspoon ground cloves
1 teaspoon ground cinnamon
1 teaspoon fresh lime juice
1 teaspoon cider vinegar
1 teaspoon vanilla paste

### Directions

Add the apples, water and sugar to a heavy-bottomed pot and cook for about 20 minutes.

Then, mash the cooked pears with a potato masher. Add in the remaining ingredients.

Continue to simmer until the pear sauce has thickened to your desired consistency.

Bon appétit!

**Per serving:** Calories: 76; Fat: 0.3g; Carbs: 19.2g; Protein: 0.6g

## 400. Country-Style Mustard

(Ready in about 5 minutes | Servings 16)

### Ingredients

1/3 cup mustard seeds
1/2 cup wine vinegar
1 Medjool date, pitted

1 teaspoon olive oil
1/2 teaspoon Himalayan rock salt

### Directions

Soak the mustard seeds for at least 12 hours.

Then, mix all the ingredients in a high-speed blender until creamy and uniform.

Store in a glass jar in your refrigerator. Bon appétit!

**Per serving:** Calories: 24; Fat: 1.6g; Carbs: 1.7g; Protein: 0.6g

## 401. Thai-Style Coconut Sauce

(Ready in about 10 minutes | Servings 4)

### Ingredients

1 tablespoon coconut oil
1 teaspoon garlic, minced
1 teaspoon fresh ginger, minced
1 lemon, juiced and zested
1 teaspoon turmeric powder

1/2 cup coconut milk
1 tablespoon soy sauce
1 teaspoon coconut sugar, or more to taste
A pinch of salt
A pinch of grated nutmeg

### Directions

In a small saucepan, melt the coconut oil over medium heat. Once hot, cook the garlic and ginger for about 1 minute or until aromatic.

Turn the heat to a simmer and add in the lemon, turmeric, coconut milk, soy sauce, coconut sugar, salt and nutmeg; continue to simmer for 1 minute or until heated through.

Bon appétit!

**Per serving:** Calories: 68; Fat: 5.1g; Carbs: 4.7g; Protein: 1.4g

## 402. Simple Aquafaba Mayo

(Ready in about 10 minutes | Servings 12)

### Ingredients

1/2 cup aquafaba
1 ¼ cups canola oil
1 teaspoon yellow mustard
1/2 teaspoon kosher salt

2 tablespoons lemon juice
1/2 teaspoon garlic powder
1/4 teaspoon dried dill

### Directions

Blend the aquafaba at high speed using an immersion blender or a high-speed blender.

While the machine is going, gradually add in the oil and continue to blend until the mixture has thickened.

Add in the mustard, salt, lemon juice, garlic powder and dill.

Store in your refrigerator for up to 2 weeks. Enjoy!

**Per serving:** Calories: 200; Fat: 22.7g; Carbs: 0.3g; Protein: 0g

## 403. Classic Velouté Sauce

(Ready in about 10 minutes | Servings 5)

### Ingredients

2 tablespoons vegan butter
2 tablespoons all-purpose flour
1 ½ cups vegetable stock
1/4 teaspoon white pepper

### Directions

Melt the vegan butter in a saucepan over a moderate flame. Add in the flour and continue to cook, whisking continuously to avoid lumps.

Gradually and slowly pour in the vegetable stock and continue whisking for about 5 minutes until the sauce has thickened.

Add in white pepper and stir to combine well. Bon appétit!

Per serving: Calories: 65; Fat: 5.2g; Carbs: 2.4g; Protein: 1.9g

## 404. Classic Espagnole Sauce

(Ready in about 55 minutes | Servings 6)

### Ingredients

3 tablespoons vegan butter
4 tablespoons rice flour
1/2 cup mirepoix
1 teaspoon garlic cloves, chopped
3 cups vegetable broth
1/4 cup canned tomatoes, puréed
1 bay laurel
1 teaspoon thyme
Sea salt and black pepper, to taste

### Directions

Melt the vegan butter in a saucepan over a moderately high heat. Then, add in the flour and cook, stirring continuously, for about 8 minutes or until brown.

Then, sauté the mirepoix for about 5 minutes or until tender and fragrant.

Now, add in the mirepoix, garlic, vegetable broth, canned tomatoes and spices. Turn the heat to a bare simmer. Let it simmer for about 40 minutes.

Pour the sauce through a fine-mesh sieve into a bowl. Enjoy!

Per serving: Calories: 99; Fat: 6.6g; Carbs: 6.9g; Protein: 3.1g

## 405. Authentic Mediterranean Aïoli

(Ready in about 10 minutes | Servings 16)

### Ingredients

4 tablespoons aquafaba
1 teaspoon fresh lemon juice
1 teaspoon apple cider vinegar
1 teaspoon Dijon mustard
1 teaspoon garlic, crushed
Coarse sea salt and ground white pepper, to taste
1 cup olive oil
1/4 teaspoon dried dill

### Directions

Place the aquafaba, lemon juice, vinegar, mustard, garlic, salt and pepper in the bowl of your food blender. Mix for 30 to 40 seconds.

Slowly and gradually, pour in the oil and continue to blend until the sauce has thickened.

Sprinkle dried dill over the top of your sauce. Store in your refrigerator until ready to serve. Bon appétit!

Per serving: Calories: 122; Fat: 13.6g; Carbs: 0.4g; Protein: 0.1g

## 406. Vegan Barbecue Sauce

(Ready in about 25 minutes | Servings 10)

### Ingredients

1 cup tomato paste
2 tablespoons apple cider vinegar
2 tablespoons lime juice
1 tablespoon brown sugar
1 tablespoon mustard powder
1 teaspoon red pepper flakes, crushed
1 teaspoon onion powder
1 teaspoon garlic powder
1 teaspoon chili powder
2 tablespoons vegan Worcestershire
1/2 cup water

### Directions

Thoroughly combine all the ingredients in a saucepan over medium-high heat. Bring to a rolling boil.

Turn the heat to a bare simmer.

Let it simmer for about 20 minutes or until the sauce has reduced and thickened.

Place in your refrigerator for up to 3 weeks. Bon appétit!

Per serving: Calories: 32; Fat: 0.2g; Carbs: 7.4g; Protein: 1.3g

## 407. Classic Béarnaise Sauce

(Ready in about 30 minutes | Servings 8)

### Ingredients

4 tablespoons soy butter non-dairy
2 tablespoons all-purpose flour
1 teaspoon garlic, minced
1 cup soy milk
1 tablespoon fresh lime juice
1/4 teaspoon turmeric powder
Kosher salt and ground black pepper, to taste
1 tablespoon fresh parsley, chopped

### Directions

Melt the butter in a saucepan over a moderately high heat. Then, add in the flour and cook, stirring continuously, for about 8 minutes or until brown.

Then, sauté the garlic for about 30 seconds or until fragrant.

Now, add in the milk, fresh lime juice, turmeric, salt and black pepper. Turn the heat to a bare simmer. Let it simmer for about 20 minutes.

Top with fresh parsley just before serving. Bon appétit!

Per serving: Calories: 82; Fat: 6.8g; Carbs: 3.8g; Protein: 1.4g

## 408. Perfect Cheese Sauce

(Ready in about 30 minutes | Servings 8)

### Ingredients

1 ½ cups cashews
1/2 cup water
1 teaspoon apple cider vinegar
1 teaspoon lime juice
1/2 teaspoon granulated garlic
Sea salt and cayenne pepper, to taste
1 tablespoon coconut oil
1/4 cup nutritional yeast

### Directions

Process the cashews and water in your blender until creamy and uniform.

Add in the remaining ingredients and continue to blend until everything is well incorporated.

Keep in your refrigerator for up to a week. Bon appétit!

Per serving: Calories: 172; Fat: 12.6g; Carbs: 10g; Protein: 6.8g

# 409. Easy Raw Pasta Sauce

(Ready in about 10 minutes | Servings 4)

## Ingredients

1 pound ripe tomatoes, cored
1 small onion, peeled
1 small garlic clove, minced
1 tablespoon fresh parsley leaves
1 tablespoon fresh basil leaves
1 tablespoon fresh rosemary leaves
4 tablespoons extra-virgin olive oil
Sea salt and ground black pepper, to taste

## Directions

Blend all the ingredients in your food processor or blender until well combined.

Serve with warm pasta or zoodles (zucchini noodles). Bon appétit!

**Per serving:** Calories: 80; Fat: 6.3g; Carbs: 5.4g; Protein: 1.4g

# 410. Basic Basil Pesto

(Ready in about 10 minutes | Servings 8)

## Ingredients

1 cup fresh basil, packed
4 tablespoons pine nuts
2 cloves garlic, peeled
1 tablespoon fresh lime juice
2 tablespoons nutritional yeast
2 tablespoons extra-virgin olive oil
Sea salt, to taste
4 tablespoons water

## Directions

In your food processor, place all ingredients, except for the oil. Process until well combined.

Continue to blend, gradually adding the oil, until the mixture comes together. Bon appétit!

**Per serving:** Calories: 42; Fat: 3.5g; Carbs: 1.4g; Protein: 1.2g

# 411. Classic Alfredo Sauce

(Ready in about 10 minutes | Servings 4)

## Ingredients

2 tablespoons olive oil
2 cloves garlic, minced
2 tablespoons rice flour
1 ½ cups rice milk, unsweetened
Sea salt and ground black pepper, to taste
1/2 teaspoon red pepper flakes, crushed
4 tablespoons tahini
2 tablespoons nutritional yeast

## Directions

In a large saucepan, heat the olive oil over a moderate heat. Once hot, sauté the garlic for about 30 seconds or until fragrant.

Add in the rice flour and turn the heat to a simmer. Gradually add in the milk and continue to cook for a few minutes more, whisking constantly to avoid the lumps.

Add in the salt, black pepper, red pepper flakes, tahini and nutritional yeast.

Continue to cook on low until the sauce has thickened.

Store in an airtight container in your refrigerator for up to four days. Bon appétit!

**Per serving:** Calories: 245; Fat: 17.9g; Carbs: 14.9g; Protein: 8.2g

# 412. Sophisticated Cashew Mayonnaise

(Ready in about 10 minutes | Servings 12)

## Ingredients

3/4 cup raw cashews, soaked overnight and drained
2 tablespoons fresh lime juice
1/4 cup water
1/2 teaspoon deli mustard
1 teaspoon maple syrup
1/4 teaspoon garlic powder
1/4 teaspoon dried dill weed
1/2 teaspoon sea salt

## Directions

Blitz all the ingredients using a high-speed blender or food processor until smooth, creamy and uniform.

Add more spices, if needed.

Place in your refrigerator until ready to serve. Bon appétit!

**Per serving:** Calories: 159; Fat: 12.4g; Carbs: 9.2g; Protein: 5.2g

# 413. Cinnamon Vanilla Sunflower Butter

(Ready in about 10 minutes | Servings 16)

## Ingredients

2 cups roasted sunflower seeds, hulled
1/2 cup maple syrup
1 teaspoon vanilla extract
1 teaspoon cinnamon powder
A pinch of grated nutmeg
A pinch of sea salt

## Directions

Blitz the sunflower seeds in your food processor until a butter forms.

Add in the remaining ingredients and continue to blend until creamy, smooth and uniform.

Taste and adjust the flavor as needed. Bon appétit!

**Per serving:** Calories: 129; Fat: 9g; Carbs: 10.1g; Protein: 3.6g

# 414. Spicy Homemade Ketchup

(Ready in about 25 minutes | Servings 12)

## Ingredients

2 tablespoons sunflower oil
4 tablespoons shallots, chopped
2 cloves garlic, crushed
30 ounces canned tomatoes, crushed
1/4 cup brown sugar
1/4 cup white vinegar
1 teaspoon hot sauce
1/4 teaspoon allspice

## Directions

In a medium saucepan, heat the oil over a moderately high heat. Sauté the shallots until tender and aromatic.

Add in the garlic and continue to sauté for 1 minute or until fragrant.

Add in the remaining ingredients and bring to a simmer. Continue to simmer for 22 to 25 minutes.

Process the mixture in your blender until smooth and uniform. Bon appétit!

**Per serving:** Calories: 49; Fat: 2.5g; Carbs: 5.3g; Protein: 0.7g

## 415. Tomato Sauce with Garlic and Herbs

(Ready in about 25 minutes | Servings 12)

### Ingredients

3 tablespoons olive oil
4 garlic cloves, minced
1 teaspoon dried parsley flakes
1 teaspoon dried rosemary
1 teaspoon dried basil

Kosher salt and black pepper, to taste
1 teaspoon red pepper flakes, crushed
1 (28-ounce) can tomatoes, crushed

### Directions

In a medium saucepan, heat the olive oil over a moderately high heat. Sauté the garlic for 1 minute or until aromatic.

Add in the herbs, spices and tomatoes and turn the heat to a simmer. Continue to simmer for about 22 minutes.

Bon appétit!

Per serving: Calories: 44; Fat: 3.5g; Carbs: 3.1g; Protein: 0.7g

## 416. Traditional French Sauce

(Ready in about 10 minutes | Servings 9)

### Ingredients

1 cup vegan mayonnaise
1 tablespoon fresh basil leaves, chopped
1 tablespoon fresh parsley leaves, chopped
1 tablespoon fresh scallions, chopped

3 small cornichon pickles, coarsely chopped
2 tablespoons capers, coarsely chopped
2 teaspoons fresh lemon juice
1 teaspoon Dijon mustard
Sea salt and ground black pepper, to taste

### Directions

Thoroughly combine all ingredients in your food processor or blender.

Blend until uniform and creamy.

Bon appétit!

Per serving: Calories: 92; Fat: 8.5g; Carbs: 2.2g; Protein: 1.7g

## 417. Easy Tofu Hollandaise

(Ready in about 15 minutes | Servings 12)

### Ingredients

1/4 cup vegan butter, at room temperature
1 cup silken tofu
1 cup unsweetened rice milk

Sea salt and ground black pepper, to taste
1/4 cup nutritional yeast
1/2 teaspoon turmeric powder
2 tablespoons fresh lime juice

### Directions

Puree all the ingredients in a high-speed blender or food processor.

Then, heat the mixture in a small saucepan over low-medium heat; cook, stirring occasionally, until the sauce has reduced and thickened. Bon appétit!

Per serving: Calories: 82; Fat: 4.9g; Carbs: 6.4g; Protein: 2.9g

## 418. Hot Pepper Sauce

(Ready in about 1 hour 20 minutes | Servings 6)

### Ingredients

2 sweet red peppers
2 red chili peppers
2 tablespoons olive oil
2 garlic cloves, crushed

1 cup cream of onion soup
1/2 teaspoon cayenne pepper
Black pepper, to taste

### Directions

Place the peppers directly over a low gas flame; roast the peppers for about 8 minutes until they are charred on all sides.

Let the peppers steam in a plastic bag or covered bowl for about 30 minutes. Remove the blackened skin and core and transfer the flesh to your food processor

Blitz until a smooth paste forms.

Heat the prepared paste in a saucepan; add in the remaining ingredients and stir to combine well. Turn the heat to a simmer and let it cook, partially covered, for about 40 minutes or until the sauce has reduced to your desired consistency. Bon appétit!

Per serving: Calories: 71; Fat: 5.5g; Carbs: 5.4g; Protein: 1.1g

## 419. Spinach and Pistachio Pesto

(Ready in about 10 minutes | Servings 10)

### Ingredients

2 cups baby spinach
1 teaspoon dried parsley flakes
1/2 teaspoon dried oregano
1/2 teaspoon dried savory
1/2 cup pistachio, hulled

2 cloves garlic, peeled
1/3 cup extra-virgin olive oil
Kosher salt and ground black pepper, to taste
1/2 lemon, freshly squeezed

### Directions

In your food processor, place all ingredients, except for the oil. Process until well combined.

While the machine is running, gradually pour in the olive oil until the mixture comes together.

Serve with pasta or pita. Bon appétit!

Per serving: Calories: 102; Fat: 9.9g; Carbs: 2.7g; Protein: 1.5g

## 420. Spicy Home-Style Mayonnaise

(Ready in about 10 minutes | Servings 8)

### Ingredients

2 tablespoons apple cider vinegar
1/2 teaspoon agave syrup
1/2 teaspoon stone-ground mustard

1/2 cup olive oil
1/4 cup almonds
1/2 teaspoon sea salt
1/2 teaspoon hot sauce

### Directions

Blend the vinegar and agave syrup at high speed using an immersion blender or a high-speed blender.

While the machine is going, gradually add in the olive oil and continue to blend until the mixture has thickened.

Add in the mustard, almonds, salt and hot sauce and blend to combine well.

Store in your refrigerator for up to 2 weeks. Enjoy!

Per serving: Calories: 129; Fat: 13.6g; Carbs: 0.4g; Protein: 0g

## 421. French-Style White Sauce

(Ready in about 10 minutes | Servings 6)

### Ingredients

3 tablespoons dairy-free butter
3 tablespoons rice flour
1 ½ cups rice milk
A pinch of salt
A pinch of grated nutmeg

### Directions

Melt the butter in a sauté pan over a moderate flame. Add in the flour and continue to cook, whisking continuously to avoid lumps.

Pour the milk and continue whisking for about 4 minutes until the sauce has thickened.

Add in the spices and stir to combine well. Bon appétit!

**Per serving:** Calories: 141; Fat: 6.8g; Carbs: 16.4g; Protein: 2.9g

## 422. Spicy Cheese Sauce

(Ready in about 10 minutes | Servings 8)

### Ingredients

1/2 cup sunflower seeds, soaked overnight and drained
1/2 cup raw cashews, soaked overnight and drained
1 cup water
2 tablespoons lemon juice
1 tablespoon coconut oil
1/4 cup nutritional yeast
1 teaspoon hot sauce
1 teaspoon garlic powder
1/2 teaspoon curry powder
Kosher salt and ground white pepper, to season

### Directions

Process the sunflower seeds, cashews and water in your blender until creamy and uniform.

Add in the remaining ingredients and continue to blend until everything is well incorporated.

Keep in your refrigerator for up to a week. Bon appétit!

**Per serving:** Calories: 125; Fat: 9.5g; Carbs: 6.2g; Protein: 5.3g

## 423. Easy Caramel Sauce

(Ready in about 20 minutes | Servings 12)

### Ingredients

1 ½ cups granulated sugar
1/2 cup water
1 cup coconut cream
3 tablespoons coconut oil
A pinch of salt
A pinch of ground allspice
1 teaspoon vanilla essence

### Directions

In a saucepan, place the sugar and water over medium-low heat; let it cook until the sugar has dissolved.

Turn the heat to medium and continue to cook for 9 to 11 minutes or until the sugar turns into a thick, brown liquid.

Remove from the heat and stir in the coconut cream, coconut oil, salt, allspices and vanilla essence.

Cook for a few more minutes over a moderate heat until the sauce is smooth. The caramel sauce thickens as it cools.

Store in your refrigerator for up to one month. Bon appétit!

**Per serving:** Calories: 192; Fat: 10.4g; Carbs: 26.2g; Protein: 0.7g

## 424. Red Pepper and Tomato Sauce

(Ready in about 1 hour 20 minutes | Servings 6)

### Ingredients

1 pound red peppers
2 tablespoons olive oil
1 shallot, chopped
2 garlic cloves, minced
1 pound tomatoes, chopped
1/2 cup vegetable broth
1 teaspoon cayenne pepper
1 teaspoon dried basil
1/2 teaspoon dried oregano
2 tablespoons red wine
Sea salt and freshly ground pepper, to taste

### Directions

Place the peppers directly over a low gas flame; roast the peppers for about 8 minutes until they are charred on all sides.

Let the peppers steam in a plastic bag or covered bowl for about 30 minutes. Remove the blackened skin and core and transfer the flesh to your food processor

Blitz until a smooth paste forms.

Heat the prepared paste in a saucepan; add in the remaining ingredients and stir to combine well. Turn the heat to a simmer and let it cook, partially covered, for about 40 minutes or until the sauce has reduced to your desired consistency.

Bon appétit!

**Per serving:** Calories: 92; Fat: 5.1g; Carbs: 10.6g; Protein: 2.6g

## 425. Kale and Hemp Seed Pesto

(Ready in about 10 minutes | Servings 10)

### Ingredients

1/2 cup hemp seeds, hulled
1/2 cup raw cashews
2 cloves garlic, minced
1 cup fresh kale
1/2 cup fresh basil
1/2 cup fresh parsley
3 tablespoons nutritional yeast
1 tablespoon fresh lemon juice
1 teaspoon sherry vinegar
Sea salt and ground black pepper, to taste
1/4 cup olive oil

### Directions

In your food processor, place all ingredients, except for the oil. Process until well combined.

While the machine is running, gradually pour in the olive oil until the sauce is uniform and creamy.

Serve with pasta, crackers or breadsticks. Bon appétit!

**Per serving:** Calories: 140; Fat: 11.9g; Carbs: 5.5g; Protein: 4.2g

# 426. Mediterranean Herb Ketchup

(Ready in about 30 minutes | Servings 8)

## Ingredients

1 tablespoon olive oil
16 ounces tomato paste
3 tablespoons brown sugar
1 teaspoon kosher salt
1/4 teaspoon ground cloves
1/4 teaspoon ground allspice
1 teaspoon dried basil
1 teaspoon dried oregano

1 teaspoon dried rosemary
1 teaspoon garlic powder
1 teaspoon onion powder
1 teaspoon porcini powder
3 tablespoons apple cider vinegar
1/4 cup water

## Directions

In a medium saucepan, heat the olive oil until sizzling.

Add in the remaining ingredients and bring to a simmer. Continue to simmer for about 25 minutes.

Process the mixture in your blender until smooth and uniform. Bon appétit!

**Per serving:** Calories: 42; Fat: 1.8g; Carbs: 5.8g; Protein: 0.8g

# 427. Almond and Sunflower Seed Mayo

(Ready in about 10 minutes | Servings 12)

## Ingredients

1/4 cup raw sunflower seeds, hulled
1/2 cup raw almonds
3/4 cup water
1/2 teaspoon onion powder
1/2 teaspoon garlic powder

1/4 teaspoon dried dill
1/2 teaspoon sea salt
1 cup sunflower seed oil
2 tablespoons fresh lime juice
1 tablespoon apple cider vinegar

## Directions

Process all the ingredients, except for the oil, in your blender or food processor until well combined.

Then, gradually add in the oil and continue to blend at low speed until smooth and creamy.

Add more spices, if needed.

Place in your refrigerator until ready to serve. Bon appétit!

**Per serving:** Calories: 109; Fat: 9.2g; Carbs: 4.4g; Protein: 3.7g

# DESSERTS

## 428. Homemade Chocolates with Coconut and Raisins

(Ready in about 10 minutes + chilling time | Servings 20)

### Ingredients

1/2 cup cacao butter, melted
1/3 cup peanut butter
1/4 cup agave syrup
A pinch of grated nutmeg
A pinch of coarse salt

1/2 teaspoon vanilla extract
1 cup dried coconut, shredded
6 ounces dark chocolate, chopped
3 ounces raisins

### Directions

Thoroughly combine all the ingredients, except for the chocolate, in a mixing bowl.

Spoon the mixture into molds. Leave to set hard in a cool place.

Melt the dark chocolate in your microwave. Pour in the melted chocolate until the fillings are covered. Leave to set hard in a cool place.

Enjoy!

**Per serving:** Calories: 130; Fat: 9.1g; Carbs: 12.1g; Protein: 1.3g

## 429. Easy Mocha Fudge

(Ready in about 1 hour 10 minutes | Servings 20)

### Ingredients

1 cup cookies, crushed
1/2 cup almond butter
1/4 cup agave nectar
6 ounces dark chocolate, broken into chunks

1 teaspoon instant coffee
A pinch of grated nutmeg
A pinch of salt

### Directions

Line a large baking sheet with parchment paper.

Melt the chocolate in your microwave and add in the remaining ingredients; stir to combine well.

Scrape the batter into a parchment-lined baking sheet. Place it in your freezer for at least 1 hour to set.

Cut into squares and serve. Bon appétit!

**Per serving:** Calories: 105; Fat: 5.6g; Carbs: 12.9g; Protein: 1.1g

## 430. Almond and Chocolate Chip Bars

(Ready in about 40 minutes | Servings 10)

### Ingredients

1/2 cup almond butter
1/4 cup coconut oil, melted
1/4 cup agave syrup
1 teaspoon vanilla extract
1/4 teaspoon sea salt
1/4 teaspoon grated nutmeg
1/2 teaspoon ground cinnamon

2 cups almond flour
1/4 cup flaxseed meal
1 cup vegan chocolate, cut into chunks
1 1/3 cups almonds, ground
2 tablespoons cacao powder
1/4 cup agave syrup

### Directions

In a mixing bowl, thoroughly combine the almond butter, coconut oil, 1/4 cup of agave syrup, vanilla, salt, nutmeg and cinnamon.

Gradually stir in the almond flour and flaxseed meal and stir to combine. Add in the chocolate chunks and stir again.

In a small mixing bowl, combine the almonds, cacao powder and agave syrup. Now, spread the ganache onto the cake. Freeze for about 30 minutes, cut into bars and serve well chilled. Enjoy!

**Per serving:** Calories: 295; Fat: 17g; Carbs: 35.2g; Protein: 1.7g

## 431. Almond Butter Cookies

(Ready in about 45 minutes | Servings 10)

### Ingredients

3/4 cup all-purpose flour
1/2 teaspoon baking soda
1/4 teaspoon kosher salt
1 flax egg
1/4 cup coconut oil, at room temperature

2 tablespoons almond milk
1/2 cup brown sugar
1/2 cup almond butter
1/2 teaspoon ground cinnamon
1/2 teaspoon vanilla

### Directions

In a mixing bowl, combine the flour, baking soda and salt.

In another bowl, combine the flax egg, coconut oil, almond milk, sugar, almond butter, cinnamon and vanilla. Stir the wet mixture into the dry ingredients and stir until well combined.

Place the batter in your refrigerator for about 30 minutes. Shape the batter into small cookies and arrange them on a parchment-lined cookie pan.

Bake in the preheated oven at 350 degrees F for approximately 12 minutes. Transfer the pan to a wire rack to cool at room temperature. Bon appétit!

**Per serving:** Calories: 197; Fat: 15.8g; Carbs: 12.5g; Protein: 2.1g

## 432. Peanut Butter Oatmeal Bars

(Ready in about 25 minutes | Servings 20)

### Ingredients

1 cup vegan butter
3/4 cup coconut sugar
2 tablespoons applesauce
1 ¾ cups old-fashioned oats
1 teaspoon baking soda

A pinch of sea salt
A pinch of grated nutmeg
1 teaspoon pure vanilla extract
1 cup oat flour
1 cup all-purpose flour

### Directions

Begin by preheating your oven to 350 degrees F.

In a mixing bowl, thoroughly combine the dry ingredients. In another bowl, combine the wet ingredients.

Then, stir the wet mixture into the dry ingredients; mix to combine well.

Spread the batter mixture in a parchment-lined square baking pan. Bake in the preheated oven for about 20 minutes. Enjoy!

**Per serving:** Calories: 161; Fat: 10.3g; Carbs: 17.5g; Protein: 2.9g

## 433. Vanilla Halvah Fudge

(Ready in about 10 minutes + chilling time | Servings 16)

### Ingredients

1/2 cup cocoa butter
1/2 cup tahini
8 dates, pitted
1/4 teaspoon ground cloves
A pinch of grated nutmeg
A pinch coarse salt
1 teaspoon vanilla extract

### Directions

Line a square baking pan with parchment paper.

Mix the ingredients until everything is well incorporated.

Scrape the batter into the parchment-lined pan. Place in your freezer until ready to serve. Bon appétit!

**Per serving:** Calories: 106; Fat: 9.8g; Carbs: 4.5g; Protein: 1.4g

## 434. Raw Chocolate Mango Pie

(Ready in about 10 minutes + chilling time | Servings 16)

### Ingredients

Avocado layer:
3 ripe avocados, pitted and peeled
A pinch of sea salt
A pinch of ground anise
1/2 teaspoon vanilla paste
2 tablespoons coconut milk
5 tablespoons agave syrup
1/3 cup cocoa powder
Crema layer:
1/3 cup almond butter
1/2 cup coconut cream
1 medium mango, peeled
1/2 coconut flakes
2 tablespoons agave syrup

### Directions

In your food processor, blend the avocado layer until smooth and uniform; reserve.

Then, blend the other layer in a separate bowl. Spoon the layers in a lightly oiled baking pan.

Transfer the cake to your freezer for about 3 hours. Store in your freezer. Bon appétit!

**Per serving:** Calories: 196; Fat: 16.8g; Carbs: 14.1g; Protein: 1.8g

## 435. Chocolate N'ice Cream

(Ready in about 10 minutes | Servings 1)

### Ingredients

2 frozen bananas, peeled and sliced
2 tablespoons coconut milk
1 teaspoon carob powder
1 teaspoon cocoa powder
A pinch of grated nutmeg
1/8 teaspoon ground cardamom
1/8 teaspoon ground cinnamon
1 tablespoon chocolate curls

### Directions

Place all the ingredients in the bowl of your food processor or high-speed blender.

Blitz the ingredients until creamy or until your desired consistency is achieved.

Serve immediately or store in your freezer. Bon appétit!

**Per serving:** Calories: 349; Fat: 2.8; Carbs: 84.1g; Protein: 4.8g

## 436. Raw Raspberry Cheesecake

(Ready in about 15 minutes + chilling time | Servings 9)

### Ingredients

Crust:
2 cups almonds
1 cup fresh dates, pitted
1/4 teaspoon ground cinnamon
Filling:
2 cups raw cashews, soaked overnight and drained
14 ounces blackberries, frozen
1 tablespoon fresh lime juice
1/4 teaspoon crystallized ginger
1 can coconut cream
8 fresh dates, pitted

### Directions

In your food processor, blend the crust ingredients until the mixture comes together; press the crust into a lightly oiled springform pan.

Then, blend the filling layer until completely smooth. Spoon the filling onto the crust, creating a flat surface with a spatula.

Transfer the cake to your freezer for about 3 hours. Store in your freezer.

Garnish with organic citrus peel. Bon appétit!

**Per serving:** Calories: 385; Fat: 22.9; Carbs: 41.1g; Protein: 10.8g

## 437. Mini Lemon Tarts

(Ready in about 15 minutes + chilling time | Servings 9)

### Ingredients

1 cup cashews
1 cup dates, pitted
1/2 cup coconut flakes
1/2 teaspoon anise, ground
3 lemons, freshly squeezed
1 cup coconut cream
2 tablespoons agave syrup

### Directions

Brush a muffin tin with a nonstick cooking oil.

Blend the cashews, dates, coconut and anise in your food processor or a high-speed blender. Press the crust into the peppered muffin tin.

Then, blend the lemon, coconut cream and agave syrup. Spoon the cream into the muffin tin.

Store in your freezer. Bon appétit!

**Per serving:** Calories: 257; Fat: 16.5; Carbs: 25.4g; Protein: 4g

## 438. Fluffy Coconut Blondies with Raisins

(Ready in about 30 minutes | Servings 9)

### Ingredients

1 cup coconut flour
1 cup all-purpose flour
1/2 teaspoon baking powder
1/4 teaspoon salt
1 cup desiccated coconut, unsweetened
3/4 cup vegan butter, softened
1 ½ cups brown sugar
3 tablespoons applesauce
1/2 teaspoon vanilla extract
1/2 teaspoon ground anise
1 cup raisins, soaked for 15 minutes

### Directions

Start by preheating your oven to 350 degrees F. Brush a baking pan with a nonstick cooking oil.

Thoroughly combine the flour, baking powder, salt and coconut. In another bowl, mix the butter, sugar, applesauce, vanilla and anise. Stir the butter mixture into the dry ingredients; stir to combine well.

Fold in the raisins. Press the batter into the prepared baking pan.

Bake for approximately 25 minutes or until it is set in the middle. Place the cake on a wire rack to cool slightly.

Bon appétit!

**Per serving:** Calories: 365; Fat: 18.5; Carbs: 49g; Protein: 2.1g

## 439. Easy Chocolate Squares

(Ready in about 1 hour 10 minutes | Servings 20)

### Ingredients

1 cup cashew butter
1 cup almond butter
1/4 cup coconut oil, melted
1/4 cup raw cacao powder
2 ounces dark chocolate
4 tablespoons agave syrup
1 teaspoon vanilla paste
1/4 teaspoon ground cinnamon
1/4 teaspoon ground cloves

### Directions

Process all the ingredients in your blender until uniform and smooth.

Scrape the batter into a parchment-lined baking sheet. Place it in your freezer for at least 1 hour to set.

Cut into squares and serve. Bon appétit!

**Per serving:** Calories: 187; Fat: 13.8g; Carbs: 15.1g; Protein: 2.9g

## 440. Chocolate and Raisin Cookie Bars

(Ready in about 40 minutes | Servings 10)

### Ingredients

1/2 cup peanut butter, at room temperature
1 cup agave syrup
1 teaspoon pure vanilla extract
1/4 teaspoon kosher salt
2 cups almond flour
1 teaspoon baking soda
1 cup raisins
1 cup vegan chocolate, broken into chunks

### Directions

In a mixing bowl, thoroughly combine the peanut butter, agave syrup, vanilla and salt.

Gradually stir in the almond flour and baking soda and stir to combine. Add in the raisins and chocolate chunks and stir again.

Freeze for about 30 minutes and serve well chilled. Enjoy!

**Per serving:** Calories: 267; Fat: 2.9g; Carbs: 61.1g; Protein: 2.2g

## 441. Almond Granola Bars

(Ready in about 25 minutes | Servings 12)

### Ingredients

1/2 cup spelt flour
1/2 cup oat flour
1 cup rolled oats
1 teaspoon baking powder
1/2 teaspoon cinnamon
1/2 teaspoon ground cardamom
1/4 teaspoon freshly grated nutmeg
1/8 teaspoon kosher salt
1 cup almond milk
3 tablespoons agave syrup
1/2 cup peanut butter
1/2 cup applesauce
1/2 teaspoon pure almond extract
1/2 teaspoon pure vanilla extract
1/2 cup almonds, slivered

### Directions

Begin by preheating your oven to 350 degrees F.

In a mixing bowl, thoroughly combine the flour, oats, baking powder and spices. In another bowl, combine the wet ingredients.

Then, stir the wet mixture into the dry ingredients; mix to combine well. Fold in the slivered almonds.

Scrape the batter mixture into a parchment-lined baking pan. Bake in the preheated oven for about 20 minutes. Let it cool on a wire rack. Cut into bars and enjoy!

**Per serving:** Calories: 147; Fat: 5.9g; Carbs: 21.7g; Protein: 5.2g

## 442. Fluffy Coconut Cookies

(Ready in about 40 minutes | Servings 10)

### Ingredients

1/2 cup oat flour
1/2 cup all-purpose flour
1/2 teaspoon baking soda
A pinch of salt
1/4 teaspoon grated nutmeg
1/2 teaspoon ground cloves
1/2 teaspoon ground cinnamon
4 tablespoons coconut oil
2 tablespoons oat milk
1/2 cup coconut sugar
1/2 cup coconut flakes, unsweetened

### Directions

In a mixing bowl, combine the flour, baking soda and spices.

In another bowl, combine the coconut oil, oat milk, sugar and coconut. Stir the wet mixture into the dry ingredients and stir until well combined.

Place the batter in your refrigerator for about 30 minutes. Shape the batter into small cookies and arrange them on a parchment-lined cookie pan.

Bake in the preheated oven at 330 degrees F for approximately 10 minutes. Transfer the pan to a wire rack to cool at room temperature. Bon appétit!

**Per serving:** Calories: 136; Fat: 7.3g; Carbs: 15.6g; Protein: 1.6g

## 443. Raw Walnut and Berry Cake

(Ready in about 10 minutes + chilling time | Servings 8)

### Ingredients

Crust:
1 ½ cups walnuts, ground
2 tablespoons maple syrup
1/4 cup raw cacao powder
1/4 teaspoon ground cinnamon
A pinch of coarse salt

A pinch of freshly grated nutmeg
Berry layer:
6 cups mixed berries
2 frozen bananas
1/2 cup agave syrup

### Directions

In your food processor, blend the crust ingredients until the mixture comes together; press the crust into a lightly oiled baking pan.

Then, blend the berry layer. Spoon the berry layer onto the crust, creating a flat surface with a spatula.

Transfer the cake to your freezer for about 3 hours. Store in your freezer. Bon appétit!

**Per serving:** Calories: 244; Fat: 10.2g; Carbs: 39g; Protein: 3.8g

## 444. Chocolate Dream Balls

(Ready in about 10 minutes + chilling time | Servings 8)

### Ingredients

3 tablespoons cocoa powder
8 fresh dates, pitted and soaked for 15 minutes
2 tablespoons tahini, at room temperature

1/2 teaspoon ground cinnamon
1/2 cup vegan chocolate, broken into chunks
1 tablespoon coconut oil, at room temperature

### Directions

Add the cocoa powder, dates, tahini and cinnamon to the bowl of your food processor. Process until the mixture forms a ball.

Use a cookie scoop to portion the mixture into 1-ounce portions. Roll the balls and refrigerate them for at least 30 minutes.

Meanwhile, microwave the chocolate until melted; add in the coconut oil and whisk to combine well.

Dip the chocolate balls in the coating and store them in your refrigerator until ready to serve. Bon appétit!

**Per serving:** Calories: 107; Fat: 7.2g; Carbs: 10.8g; Protein: 1.8g

## 445. Last-Minute Macaroons

(Ready in about 15 minutes | Servings 10)

### Ingredients

3 cups coconut flakes, sweetened
9 ounces canned coconut milk, sweetened

1 teaspoon ground anise
1 teaspoon vanilla extract

### Directions

Begin by preheating your oven to 325 degrees F. Line the cookie sheets with parchment paper.

Thoroughly combine all the ingredients until everything is well incorporated.

Use a cookie scoop to drop mounds of the batter onto the prepared cookie sheets.

Bake for about 11 minutes until they are lightly browned. Bon appétit!

**Per serving:** Calories: 125; Fat: 7.2g; Carbs: 14.3g; Protein: 1.1g

## 446. Old-Fashioned Ratafias

(Ready in about 20 minutes | Servings 8)

### Ingredients

2 ounces all-purpose flour
2 ounces almond flour
1 teaspoon baking powder
2 tablespoons applesauce

5 ounces caster sugar
1 ½ ounces vegan butter
4 drops of ratafia essence

### Directions

Start by preheating your oven to 330 degrees F. Line a cookie sheet with parchment paper.

Thoroughly combine all the ingredients until everything is well incorporated.

Use a cookie scoop to drop mounds of the batter onto the prepared cookie sheet.

Bake for about 15 minutes until they are lightly browned. Bon appétit!

**Per serving:** Calories: 272; Fat: 16.2g; Carbs: 28.6g; Protein: 5.8g

## 447. Jasmine Rice Pudding with Dried Apricots

(Ready in about 20 minutes | Servings 4)

### Ingredients

1 cup jasmine rice, rinsed
1 cup water
1 cup almond milk
1/2 cup brown sugar
A pinch of salt
A pinch of grated nutmeg

1/2 cup dried apricots, chopped
1/4 teaspoon cinnamon powder
1 teaspoon vanilla extract

### Directions

Add the rice and water to a saucepan. Cover the saucepan and bring the water to a boil.

Turn the heat to low; let it simmer for another 10 minutes until all the water is absorbed.

Then, add in the remaining ingredients and stir to combine. Let it simmer for 10 minutes more or until the pudding has thickened. Bon appétit!

**Per serving:** Calories: 300; Fat: 2.2g; Carbs: 63.6g; Protein: 5.6g

## 448. Everyday Energy Bars

(Ready in about 35 minutes | Servings 16)

### Ingredients

1 cup vegan butter
1 cup brown sugar
2 tablespoons agave syrup
2 cups old-fashioned oats
1/2 cup almonds, slivered
1/2 cup walnuts, chopped
1/2 cup dried currants
1/2 cup pepitas

### Directions

Begin by preheating your oven to 320 degrees F. Line a baking pan with parchment paper or Silpat mat.

Thoroughly combine all the ingredients until everything is well incorporated.

Spread the mixture onto the prepared baking pan using a wide spatula.

Bake for about 33 minutes or until golden brown. Cut into bars using a sharp knife and enjoy!

**Per serving:** Calories: 285; Fat: 17.1g; Carbs: 30g; Protein: 5.1g

## 449. Raw Coconut Ice Cream

(Ready in about 10 minutes + chilling time | Servings 2)

### Ingredients

4 over-ripe bananas, frozen
4 tablespoons coconut milk
6 fresh dates, pitted
1/4 teaspoon pure coconut extract
1/2 teaspoon pure vanilla extract
1/2 cup coconut flakes

### Directions

Place all the ingredients in the bowl of your food processor or high-speed blender.

Blitz the ingredients until creamy or until your desired consistency is achieved.

Serve immediately or store in your freezer.

Bon appétit!

**Per serving:** Calories: 388; Fat: 7.7g; Carbs: 82g; Protein: 4.8g

## 450. Chocolate Hazelnut Fudge

(Ready in about 1 hour 10 minutes | Servings 20)

### Ingredients

1 cup cashew butter
1 cup fresh dates, pitted
1/4 cup cocoa powder
1/4 teaspoon ground cloves
1 teaspoon matcha powder
1 teaspoon vanilla extract
1/2 cup hazelnuts, coarsely chopped

### Directions

Process all ingredients in your blender until uniform and smooth.

Scrape the batter into a parchment-lined baking sheet. Place it in your freezer for at least 1 hour to set.

Cut into squares and serve. Bon appétit!

**Per serving:** Calories: 127; Fat: 9g; Carbs: 10.7g; Protein: 2.4g

## 451. Oatmeal Squares with Cranberries

(Ready in about 25 minutes | Servings 20)

### Ingredients

1 ½ cups rolled oats
1/2 cup brown sugar
1 teaspoon baking soda
A pinch of coarse salt
A pinch of grated nutmeg
1/2 teaspoon cinnamon
2/3 cup peanut butter
1 medium banana, mashed
1/3 cup oat milk
1 teaspoon vanilla extract
1/2 cup dried cranberries

### Directions

Begin by preheating your oven to 350 degrees F.

In a mixing bowl, thoroughly combine the dry ingredients. In another bowl, combine the wet ingredients.

Then, stir the wet mixture into the dry ingredients; mix to combine well.

Spread the batter mixture in a parchment-lined baking pan. Bake in the preheated oven for about 20 minutes.

Let it cool on a wire rack. Cut into squares and enjoy!

**Per serving:** Calories: 101; Fat: 2.5g; Carbs: 17.2g; Protein: 2.8g

## 452. Classic Bread Pudding with Sultanas

(Ready in about 2 hours | Servings 4)

### Ingredients

10 ounces day-old bread, cut into cubes
2 cups coconut milk
1/2 cup coconut sugar
1 teaspoon vanilla extract
1/2 teaspoon ground cloves
1/2 teaspoon ground cinnamon
1/2 cup Sultanas

### Directions

Place the bread cubes in a lightly oiled baking dish.

Now, blend the milk, sugar, vanilla, ground cloves and cinnamon until creamy and smooth.

Spoon the mixture all over the bread cubes, pressing them with a wide spatula to soak well; fold in Sultanas and set aside for about 1 hour.

Bake in the preheated oven at 350 degrees F for about 1 hour or until the top of your pudding is golden brown.

Bon appétit!

**Per serving:** Calories: 377; Fat: 6.5g; Carbs: 72g; Protein: 10.7g

## 453. Decadent Hazelnut Halvah

(Ready in about 10 minutes | Servings 16)

### Ingredients

1/2 cup tahini
1/2 cup almond butter
1/4 cup coconut oil, melted
4 tablespoons agave nectar
1/2 teaspoon pure almond extract
1/2 teaspoon pure vanilla extract
1/8 teaspoon salt
1/8 teaspoon freshly grated nutmeg
1/2 cup hazelnuts, chopped

### Directions

Line a square baking pan with parchment paper.

Mix the ingredients, except for the hazelnuts, until everything is well incorporated.

Scrape the batter into the parchment-lined pan. Press the hazelnuts into the batter.

Place in your freezer until ready to serve. Bon appétit!

**Per serving:** Calories: 169; Fat: 15.5g; Carbs: 6.6g; Protein: 1.9g

## 454. Orange Mini Cheesecakes

(Ready in about 10 minutes + chilling time | Servings 12)

### Ingredients

Crust:
1 cup raw almonds
1 cup fresh dates, pitted
Topping:
1/2 cup raw sunflower seeds, soaked overnight and drained
1 cup raw cashew nuts, soaked overnight and drained
1 orange, freshly squeezed
1/4 cup coconut oil, softened
1/2 cup dates, pitted
Garnish:
2 tablespoons caramel topping

### Directions

In your food processor, blend the crust ingredients until the mixture comes together; press the crust into a lightly greased muffin tin.

Then, blend the topping ingredients until creamy and smooth. Spoon the topping mixture onto the crust, creating a flat surface with a spatula.

Place these mini cheesecakes in your freezer for about 3 hours. Garnish with caramel topping. Bon appétit!

**Per serving:** Calories: 226; Fat: 15.9g; Carbs: 19.8g; Protein: 5.1g

## 455. Berry Compote with Red Wine

(Ready in about 15 minutes | Servings 4)

### Ingredients

4 cups mixed berries, fresh or frozen
1 cup sweet red wine
1 cup agave syrup
1/2 teaspoon star anise
1 cinnamon stick
3-4 cloves
A pinch of grated nutmeg
A pinch of sea salt

### Directions

Add all ingredients to a saucepan. Cover with water by 1 inch. Bring to a boil and immediately reduce the heat to a simmer.

Let it simmer for 9 to 11 minutes. Allow it to cool completely.

Bon appétit!

**Per serving:** Calories: 260; Fat: 0.5g; Carbs: 64.1g; Protein: 1.1g

## 456. Turkish Irmik Helvasi

(Ready in about 35 minutes | Servings 8)

### Ingredients

1 cup semolina flour
1/2 cup coconut, shredded
1/2 teaspoon baking powder
A pinch of salt
1 teaspoon pure vanilla extract
1 cup vegan butter
1 cup coconut milk
1/2 cup walnuts, ground

### Directions

Thoroughly combine the flour, coconut, baking powder, salt and vanilla. Add in the butter and milk; mix to combine.

Fold in the walnuts and let it rest for about 1 hour.

Bake in the preheated oven at 350 degrees F for approximately 30 minutes or until a tester inserted in the center of the cake comes out dry and clean.

Transfer to a wire rack to cool completely before slicing and serving. Bon appétit!

**Per serving:** Calories: 349; Fat: 29.1g; Carbs: 18.1g; Protein: 4.7g

## 457. Traditional Greek Koufeto

(Ready in about 15 minutes | Servings 8)

### Ingredients

1 pound pumpkin
8 ounces brown sugar
1 vanilla bean
3-4 cloves
1 cinnamon stick
1 cup almonds, slivered and lightly toasted

### Directions

Bring the pumpkin and brown sugar to a boil; add in the vanilla, cloves and cinnamon.

Stir continuously to prevent from sticking.

Cook until your Koufeto has thickened; fold in the almonds; let it cool completely. Enjoy!

**Per serving:** Calories: 203; Fat: 6.8g; Carbs: 34.1g; Protein: 3.4g

## 458. Tangy Fruit Salad with Lemon Dressing

(Ready in about 15 minutes | Servings 4)

### Ingredients

Salad:
1/2 pound mixed berries
1/2 pound apples, cored and diced
8 ounces red grapes
2 kiwis, peeled and diced
2 large oranges, peeled and sliced
2 bananas, sliced
Lemon Dressing:
2 tablespoons fresh lemon juice
1 teaspoon fresh ginger, peeled and minced
4 tablespoons agave syrup

### Directions

Mix all the ingredients for the salad until well combined.

Then, in a small mixing bowl, whisk all the lemon dressing ingredients.

Dress your salad and serve well chilled. Bon appétit!

**Per serving:** Calories: 223; Fat: 0.8g; Carbs: 56.1g; Protein: 2.4g

# 459. German-Style Apple Crumble

(Ready in about 50 minutes | Servings 8)

## Ingredients

4 apples, cored, peeled and sliced
1/2 cup brown sugar
1 cup all-purpose flour
1/2 cup coconut flour
2 tablespoons flaxseed meal
1 teaspoon baking powder
1/2 teaspoon baking soda
A pinch of sea salt
A pinch of freshly grated nutmeg
1/2 teaspoon ground cinnamon
1/2 teaspoon ground anise
1/2 teaspoon pure vanilla extract
1/2 teaspoon pure coconut extract
1 cup coconut milk
1/2 cup coconut oil, softened

## Directions

Arrange the apples on the bottom of a lightly oiled baking pan. Sprinkle brown sugar over them.

In a mixing bowl, thoroughly combine the flour, flaxseed meal, baking powder, baking soda, salt, nutmeg, cinnamon, anise, vanilla and coconut extract.

Add in the coconut milk and softened oil and mix until everything is well incorporated. Spread the topping mixture over the fruit layer.

Bake the apple crumble at 350 degrees F for about 45 minutes or until golden brown. Bon appétit!

Per serving: Calories: 376; Fat: 23.8g; Carbs: 41.3g; Protein: 3.3g

# 460. Vanilla Cinnamon Pudding

(Ready in about 25 minutes | Servings 4)

## Ingredients

1 cup basmati rice, rinsed
1 cup water
3 cups almond milk
12 dates, pitted
1 teaspoon vanilla paste
1 teaspoon ground cinnamon

## Directions

Add the rice, water and 1 ½ cups of milk to a saucepan. Cover the saucepan and bring the mixture to a boil.

Turn the heat to low; let it simmer for another 10 minutes until all the liquid is absorbed.

Then, add in the remaining ingredients and stir to combine. Let it simmer for 10 minutes more or until the pudding has thickened. Bon appétit!

Per serving: Calories: 332; Fat: 4.4g; Carbs: 64g; Protein: 9.9g

# 461. Mint Chocolate Cake

(Ready in about 45 minutes | Servings 16)

## Ingredients

1/2 cup vegan butter
1/2 cup brown sugar
2 chia eggs
3/4 cup all-purpose flour
1 teaspoon baking powder
A pinch of salt
A pinch of ground cloves
1 teaspoon ground cinnamon
1 teaspoon pure vanilla extract
1/3 cup coconut flakes
1 cup vegan chocolate chunks
A few drops peppermint essential oil

## Directions

In a mixing bowl, beat the vegan butter and sugar until fluffy.

Add in the chia eggs, flour, baking powder, salt, cloves, cinnamon and vanilla. Beat to combine well.

Add in the coconut and mix again.

Scrape the mixture into a lightly greased baking pan; bake at 350 degrees F for 35 to 40 minutes.

Melt the chocolate in your microwave and add in the peppermint essential oil; stir to combine well.

Afterwards, spread the chocolate ganache evenly over the surface of the cake. Bon appétit!

Per serving: Calories: 167; Fat: 7.1g; Carbs: 25.1g; Protein: 1.4g

# 462. Old-Fashioned Cookies

(Ready in about 45 minutes | Servings 12)

## Ingredients

1 cup all-purpose flour
1 teaspoon baking powder
A pinch of salt
A pinch of grated nutmeg
1/2 teaspoon ground cinnamon
1/4 teaspoon ground cardamom
1/2 cup peanut butter
2 tablespoons coconut oil, room temperature
2 tablespoons almond milk
1/2 cup brown sugar
1 teaspoon vanilla extract
1 cup vegan chocolate chips

## Directions

In a mixing bowl, combine the flour, baking powder and spices.

In another bowl, combine the peanut butter, coconut oil, almond milk, sugar and vanilla. Stir the wet mixture into the dry ingredients and stir until well combined.

Fold in the chocolate chips. Place the batter in your refrigerator for about 30 minutes. Shape the batter into small cookies and arrange them on a parchment-lined cookie pan.

Bake in the preheated oven at 350 degrees F for approximately 11 minutes. Transfer them to a wire rack to cool slightly before serving. Bon appétit!

Per serving: Calories: 167; Fat: 8.6g; Carbs: 19.6g; Protein: 2.7g

## 463. Coconut Cream Pie

(Ready in about 15 minutes + chilling time | Servings 12)

### Ingredients

Crust:
2 cups walnuts
10 fresh dates, pitted
2 tablespoons coconut oil at room temperature
1/4 teaspoon groin cardamom
1/2 teaspoon ground cinnamon
1 teaspoon vanilla extract

Filling:
2 medium over-ripe bananas
2 frozen bananas
1 cup full-fat coconut cream, well-chilled
1/3 cup agave syrup
Garnish:
3 ounces vegan dark chocolate, shaved

### Directions

In your food processor, blend the crust ingredients until the mixture comes together; press the crust into a lightly oiled baking pan.

Then, blend the filling layer. Spoon the filling onto the crust, creating a flat surface with a spatula.

Transfer the cake to your freezer for about 3 hours. Store in your freezer.

Garnish with chocolate curls just before serving. Bon appétit!

Per serving: Calories: 295; Fat: 21.1g; Carbs: 27.1g; Protein: 3.8g

## 464. Easy Chocolate Candy

(Ready in about 35 minutes | Servings 8)

### Ingredients

10 ounces dark chocolate, broken into chunks
6 tablespoons coconut milk, warm
1/4 teaspoon ground cinnamon

1/4 teaspoon ground anise
1/2 teaspoon vanilla extract
1/4 cup cacao powder, unsweetened

### Directions

Thoroughly combine the chocolate, warm coconut milk, cinnamon, anise and vanilla until everything is well incorporated.

Use a cookie scoop to portion the mixture into 1-ounce portions. Roll the balls with your hands and refrigerate them for at least 30 minutes.

Dip the chocolate balls in the cacao powder and store them in your refrigerator until ready to serve. Bon appétit!

Per serving: Calories: 232; Fat: 15.5g; Carbs: 19.6g; Protein: 3.4g

## 465. Mom's Raspberry Cobbler

(Ready in about 50 minutes | Servings 7)

### Ingredients

1 pound fresh raspberries
1/2 teaspoon fresh ginger, peeled and minced
1/2 teaspoon lime zest
2 tablespoons brown sugar
1 cup all-purpose flour
1 teaspoon baking powder
1/4 teaspoon sea salt

2 ounces agave syrup
1/4 teaspoon ground cloves
1/2 teaspoon ground cinnamon
1/8 teaspoon freshly grated nutmeg
1/2 cup coconut cream
1/2 cup coconut milk

### Directions

Arrange the raspberries on the bottom of a lightly oiled baking pan. Sprinkle ginger, lime zest and brown sugar over them.

In a mixing bowl, thoroughly combine the flour, baking powder, salt, agave syrup, ground cloves, cinnamon and nutmeg.

Add in the coconut cream and milk and mix until everything is well incorporated. Spread the topping mixture over the raspberry layer.

Bake your cobbler at 350 degrees F for about 45 minutes or until golden brown. Bon appétit!

Per serving: Calories: 227; Fat: 10.6g; Carbs: 32.1g; Protein: 3.6g

## 466. Autumn Pear Crisp

(Ready in about 50 minutes | Servings 8)

### Ingredients

4 pears, peeled, cored and sliced
1 tablespoon fresh lemon juice
1/2 teaspoon ground cinnamon
1/2 teaspoon ground anise

1 cup brown sugar
1 ¼ cups quick-cooking oats
1/2 cup water
1/2 teaspoon baking powder
1/2 cup coconut oil, melted
1 teaspoon pure vanilla extract

### Directions

Start by preheating your oven to 350 degrees F.

Arrange the pears on the bottom of a lightly oiled baking pan. Sprinkle lemon juice, cinnamon, anise and 1/2 cup of brown sugar over them.

In a mixing bowl, thoroughly combine the quick-cooking oats, water, 1/2 of the brown sugar, baking powder, coconut oil and vanilla extract.

Spread the topping mixture over the fruit layer.

Bake in the preheated oven for about 45 minutes or until golden brown. Bon appétit!

Per serving: Calories: 289; Fat: 15.4g; Carbs: 35.5g; Protein: 4.4g

## 467. Famous Haystack Cookies

(Ready in about 20 minutes | Servings 9)

### Ingredients

1 cup instant oats
1/2 cup almond butter
2 ounces almonds, ground
1/4 cup cocoa powder, unsweetened
1/2 teaspoon vanilla

1/2 teaspoon ground cinnamon
1/2 teaspoon ground anise
1/4 cup almond milk
3 tablespoons vegan butter
1 cup brown sugar

### Directions

In mixing bowl, thoroughly combine the oats, almond butter, ground almonds, cocoa, vanilla, cinnamon and anise; reserve.

In a medium saucepan, bring the milk, butter and sugar to a boil. Let it boil for approximately 1 minute, stirring frequently.

Pour the milk/butter mixture over the oat mixture; stir to combine well.

Drop by teaspoonfuls onto a parchment-lined cookie sheet and let them cool completely. Enjoy!

Per serving: Calories: 332; Fat: 18.4g; Carbs: 38.5g; Protein: 5.1g

# 468. Double Chocolate Brownies

(Ready in about 25 minutes | Servings 9)

## Ingredients

1/2 cup vegan butter, melted
2 tablespoons applesauce
1/2 cup all-purpose flour
1/2 cup almond flour
1 teaspoon baking powder
2/3 cup brown sugar

1/2 teaspoon vanilla extract
1/3 cup cocoa powder
A pinch of sea salt
A pinch of freshly grated nutmeg
1/4 cup chocolate chips

## Directions

Start by preheating your oven to 350 degrees F.

In a mixing bowl, whisk the butter and applesauce until well combined. Then, stir in the remaining ingredients, whisking continuously to combine well.

Pour the batter into a lightly oiled baking pan. Bake in the preheated oven for about 25 minutes or until a tester inserted in the middle comes out clean. Bon appétit!

**Per serving:** Calories: 237; Fat: 14.4g; Carbs: 26.5g; Protein: 2.8g

# 469. Crispy Oat and Pecan Treats

(Ready in about 25 minutes | Servings 10)

## Ingredients

1 cup all-purpose flour
2 ½ cups instant oats
1 teaspoon baking soda
A pinch of coarse salt
1 cup brown sugar
1/2 cup coconut oil, room temperature
4 tablespoons agave syrup

1 teaspoon vanilla extract
1/4 teaspoon ground cinnamon
1/4 teaspoon ground anise
1/4 teaspoon ground cloves
2 tablespoons applesauce
1/2 cup pecans, roughly chopped

## Directions

In a mixing bowl, thoroughly combine the flour, oats, baking soda and salt.

Then, whip the sugar with coconut oil and agave syrup. Add in the spices and applesauce. Add the wet mixture to the dry ingredients.

Fold in the pecans and stir to combine. Spread the batter onto a parchment-lined baking sheet.

Bake your cake at 350 degrees F for about 25 minutes or until the center is set. Let it cool and cut into bars. Bon appétit!

**Per serving:** Calories: 375; Fat: 16.3g; Carbs: 56g; Protein: 4.7g

# 470. Mom's Raspberry Cheesecake

(Ready in about 15 minutes + chilling time | Servings 9)

## Ingredients

Crust:
1 cup almond flour
1/2 cup macadamia nuts
1 cup dried desiccated coconut
1/2 teaspoon cinnamon
1/4 teaspoon grated nutmeg

Topping:
1 cup raw cashew nuts, soaked overnight and drained
1 cup raw sunflower seeds, soaked overnight and drained
1/4 cup coconut oil, at room temperature
1/2 cup pure agave syrup
1/2 cup freeze-dried raspberries

## Directions

In your food processor, blend the crust ingredients until the mixture comes together; press the crust into a lightly greased springform pan.

Then, blend the topping ingredients until creamy and smooth. Spoon the topping mixture onto the crust.

Place the cheesecake in your freezer for about 3 hours. Garnish with some extra raspberries and coconut flakes. Bon appétit!

**Per serving:** Calories: 355; Fat: 29.1g; Carbs: 20.1g; Protein: 6.6g

# 471. Chocolate-Glazed Cookies

(Ready in about 45 minutes | Servings 14)

## Ingredients

1/2 cup all-purpose flour
1/2 cup almond flour
1 teaspoon baking powder
A pinch of sea salt
A pinch of grated nutmeg
1/4 teaspoon ground cloves
1/2 cup cocoa powder

1/2 cup cashew butter
2 tablespoons almond milk
1 cup brown sugar
1 teaspoon vanilla paste
4 ounces vegan chocolate
1 ounce coconut oil

## Directions

In a mixing bowl, combine the flour, baking powder, salt, nutmeg, cloves and cocoa powder.

In another bowl, combine the cashew butter, almond milk, sugar and vanilla paste. Stir the wet mixture into the dry ingredients and stir until well combined.

Place the batter in your refrigerator for about 30 minutes. Shape the batter into small cookies and arrange them on a parchment-lined cookie pan.

Bake in the preheated oven at 330 degrees F for approximately 10 minutes. Transfer the pan to a wire rack to cool slightly.

Microwave the chocolate until melted; mix the melted chocolate with the coconut oil. Spread the glaze over your cookies and let it cool completely. Bon appétit!

**Per serving:** Calories: 177; Fat: 12.6g; Carbs: 16.2g; Protein: 1.7g

# 472. Caramel Bread Pudding

(Ready in about 2 hours | Servings 5)

## Ingredients

12 ounces stale bread, cut into cubes
3 cups almond milk
1/2 cup agave syrup
1/4 teaspoon coarse salt
1/4 teaspoon freshly grated nutmeg
1 teaspoon pure vanilla extract
1/2 teaspoon ground cinnamon
1 cup almonds, slivered
1 cup caramel sauce

## Directions

Place the bread cubes in a lightly oiled baking dish.

Now, blend the milk, agave syrup, coarse salt, freshly grated nutmeg, vanilla extract and cinnamon until creamy and smooth.

Spoon the mixture all over the bread cubes, pressing them with a wide spatula to soak well; fold in the almonds and set aside for about 1 hour.

Bake in the preheated oven at 350 degrees F for about 1 hour or until the top of your pudding is golden brown.

Spoon the caramel sauce over the bread pudding and serve at room temperature. Bon appétit!

**Per serving:** Calories: 386; Fat: 7.3g; Carbs: 69.3g; Protein: 10.8g

# 473. The Best Granola Bars Ever

(Ready in about 25 minutes | Servings 16)

## Ingredients

1 cup vegan butter
1 cup rolled oats
1 cup all-purpose flour
1 cup oat flour
1 teaspoon baking powder
A pinch of coarse sea salt
A pinch of freshly grated nutmeg
1/4 teaspoon ground cloves
1/4 teaspoon ground cardamom
1/4 teaspoon ground cinnamon
1 heaping cup packed dates, pitted
4 ounces raspberry preserves

## Directions

Begin by preheating your oven to 350 degrees F.

In a mixing bowl, thoroughly combine the dry ingredients. In another bowl, combine the wet ingredients.

Then, stir the wet mixture into the dry ingredients; mix to combine well.

Spread the batter mixture in a parchment-lined baking pan. Bake in the preheated oven for about 20 minutes.

Let it cool on a wire rack and then, cut into bars. Bon appétit!

**Per serving:** Calories: 227; Fat: 12.8g; Carbs: 25.5g; Protein: 3.7g

# 474. Old-Fashioned Fudge Penuche

(Ready in about 15 minutes | Servings 12)

## Ingredients

4 ounces dark vegan chocolate
1/2 cup almond milk
1 cup brown sugar
1/4 cup coconut oil, softened
1/2 cup walnuts, chopped
1/4 teaspoon ground cloves
1/2 teaspoon ground cinnamon

## Directions

Microwave the chocolate until melted.

In a saucepan, heat the milk and add the warm milk to the melted chocolate.

Add in the remaining ingredients and mix to combine well.

Pour the mixture into a well-greased pan and place it in your refrigerator until set. Bon appétit

**Per serving:** Calories: 156; Fat: 11.1g; Carbs: 13.6g; Protein: 1.5g

# 475. Easy Blueberry Cheesecakes

(Ready in about 10 minutes + chilling time | Servings 12)

## Ingredients

1 cup almonds, ground
1 ½ cups dates, pitted
1 ½ cups vegan cream cheese
1/4 cup coconut oil, softened
1/2 cup fresh or frozen blueberries

## Directions

In your food processor, blend the almonds and 1 cup of dates until the mixture comes together; press the crust into a lightly greased muffin tin.

Then, blend the remaining 1/2 cup of dates along with the vegan cheese, coconut oil and blueberries until creamy and smooth. Spoon the topping mixture onto the crust.

Place these mini cheesecakes in your freezer for about 3 hours. Bon appétit!

**Per serving:** Calories: 235; Fat: 17.8g; Carbs: 17.5g; Protein: 4.6g

# 476. Chocolate Rice Pudding

(Ready in about 40 minutes | Servings 4)

## Ingredients

3/4 cup white rice, rinsed
2 cups coconut milk
1/2 cup brown sugar
1/2 teaspoon vanilla extract
1/2 teaspoon ground cinnamon
1/2 teaspoon ground cloves
2 ounces vegan chocolate, broken into chunks

## Directions

Bring 1 ½ cups of water to a boil in a saucepan; stir the rice into a boiling water. Reduce the heat to low and simmer, covered, for 20 minutes.

Then, add in the milk, sugar, vanilla, cinnamon and cloves and stir to combine. Let it simmer for 15 minutes more or until the pudding has thickened.

Fold the chocolate chunks into the warm pudding and gently stir to combine. Bon appétit!

**Per serving:** Calories: 345; Fat: 10.8g; Carbs: 54.8g; Protein: 7.4g

## 477. Greek-Style Fruit Compote (Hosafi)

(Ready in about 20 minutes | Servings 4)

### Ingredients

3 peaches, pitted and sliced
4 apricots, halved and pitted
4 dried apricots
1 cup dried figs
1 cup sweet red wine

4 tablespoons agave syrup
3-4 cloves
1 cinnamon stick
1 vanilla bean
1 cup full-fat coconut yogurt

### Directions

Add the fruits, dried fruits, wine, agave syrup, cloves, cinnamon and vanilla to a saucepan. Cover with water by 1 inch. Bring to a boil and immediately reduce the heat to a simmer.

Let it simmer, partially covered, for 15 minutes. Allow it to cool completely.

Spoon into individual bowls and serve with well-chilled coconut yogurt. Bon appétit!

**Per serving:** Calories: 294; Fat: 1g; Carbs: 66.8g; Protein: 7.8g

## 478. Fruit and Almond Crisp

(Ready in about 45 minutes | Servings 8)

### Ingredients

4 cups peaches, pitted and sliced
3 cups plums, pitted and halved
1 tablespoon lemon juice, freshly squeezed
1 cup brown sugar
For the topping:
2 cups rolled oats
1/2 cup oat flour
1 teaspoon baking powder

4 tablespoons water
1/2 cup almonds, slivered
1/2 teaspoon vanilla extract
1/2 teaspoon almond extract
1/4 teaspoon ground cloves
1/4 teaspoon ground cinnamon
A pinch of kosher salt
A pinch of grated nutmeg
5 ounces coconut oil, softened

### Directions

Start by preheating your oven to 350 degrees F.

Arrange the fruits on the bottom of a lightly oiled baking pan. Sprinkle lemon juice and 1/2 cup of brown sugar over them.

In a mixing bowl, thoroughly combine the oats, oat flour, baking powder, water, almonds, vanilla, almond extract, ground cloves, cinnamon, salt, nutmeg and coconut oil.

Spread the topping mixture over the fruit layer.

Bake in the preheated oven for about 45 minutes or until golden brown. Bon appétit!

**Per serving:** Calories: 409; Fat: 19.1g; Carbs: 55.6g; Protein: 7.7g

## 479. French-Style Chocolate Custard

(Ready in about 10 minutes + chilling time | Servings 2)

### Ingredients

1/2 cup raw cashews, soaked and drained
1/4 cup vegan half-and-half
2 tablespoons agave syrup
4 tablespoons vegan chocolate chips

1/8 teaspoon coarse salt
1/8 teaspoon grated nutmeg
2 dollops coconut whipped cream

### Directions

Place the cashews in the bowl of your high-speed blender. Add in the remaining ingredients and blend until uniform and smooth.

Pour the mixture into 2 ramekins and refrigerate for at least 2 hours or until well-chilled.

Garnish with coconut whipped cream and serve. Bon appétit!

**Per serving:** Calories: 658; Fat: 50.2g; Carbs: 47g; Protein: 10.7g

## 480. Glazed Lemon Cookies

(Ready in about 45 minutes | Servings 16)

### Ingredients

1 cup almond flour
1/2 cup all-purpose flour
1/2 teaspoon baking powder
1/4 teaspoon coarse sea salt
3/4 cup coconut sugar
1/2 cup vegan butter
2 tablespoons coconut milk

2 tablespoons fresh lemon juice
1 teaspoon fresh lemon zest
For the glaze:
1 cup powdered sugar
2 tablespoons fresh lemon juice

### Directions

In a mixing bowl, thoroughly combine the flour, baking powder, sea salt and coconut sugar.

In another bowl, combine the butter, coconut milk, lemon juice and lemon zest. Stir the wet mixture into the dry ingredients and stir until well combined.

Place the dough in your refrigerator for about 30 minutes. Roll the dough into small cookies and arrange them on a parchment-lined cookie pan.

Bake in the preheated oven at 350 degrees F for approximately 13 minutes. Transfer the pan to a wire rack to cool slightly.

Meanwhile, whisk the powdered sugar and lemon juice to make the glaze. Drizzle the lemon glaze over the cooled cookies. Enjoy!

**Per serving:** Calories: 163; Fat: 8.8g; Carbs: 20.2g; Protein: 1.7g

## 481. Vanilla Ice Cream

(Ready in about 10 minutes + chilling time | Servings 4)

### Ingredients

1/2 cup raw cashews, soaked overnight and drained
1 cup coconut milk
1/4 cup agave syrup

A pinch of ground anise
A pinch of Himalayan salt
1 tablespoon pure vanilla extract

### Directions

Place all the ingredients in the bowl of your food processor or high-speed blender.
Blitz the ingredients until creamy, uniform and smooth.

Place your ice cream in the freezer for at least 3 hours. Bon appétit!

**Per serving:** Calories: 205; Fat: 9.9g; Carbs: 25.2g; Protein: 4.5g

## 482. Homemade Hazelnut Candy

(Ready in about 10 minutes + chilling time | Servings 12)

### Ingredients

1 ½ cups vegan chocolate, broken into chunks
1 cup peanut butter

1/2 cup hazelnuts, roughly chopped

### Directions

Line a square baking pan with parchment paper. Microwave the chocolate until completely melted.

Mix the ingredients until everything is well incorporated.

Scrape the batter into the parchment-lined pan. Place in your freezer until ready to serve. Bon appétit!

**Per serving:** Calories: 196; Fat: 14.4g; Carbs: 13.8g; Protein: 3.6g

## 483. Almond and Banana Brownie

(Ready in about 30 minutes | Servings 8)

### Ingredients

1 ½ cups all-purpose flour
1 ½ cups brown sugar
1/2 teaspoon baking powder
1/4 teaspoon salt
1/4 teaspoon ground cinnamon
1/2 teaspoon pure vanilla extract

1/2 teaspoon pure almond extract
1/2 cup cocoa powder, unsweetened
1/2 cup almond milk
1 ripe banana, mashed
1/2 cup coconut oil, melted
1/4 cup almonds, slivered

### Directions

Start by preheating your oven to 350 degrees F.

In a mixing bowl, mix the flour, sugar, baking powder, spices and cocoa powder until well combined.

Then, gradually add in the almond milk, banana and coconut oil; fold in the almonds and mix to combine well.

Pour the batter into a lightly oiled baking pan. Bake in the preheated oven for about 25 minutes or until a tester inserted in the middle comes out clean.

Bon appétit!

**Per serving:** Calories: 402; Fat: 16.7g; Carbs: 63g; Protein: 4.6g

## 484. Pumpkin and Coconut Cupcakes

(Ready in about 30 minutes | Servings 6)

### Ingredients

1 cup all-purpose flour
1 teaspoon of baking powder
1/4 teaspoon coarse sea salt
1 teaspoon pumpkin pie spice
1/2 cup brown sugar

1/2 cup coconut milk
1/2 cup coconut, shredded
1/4 cup peanut butter
1/2 cup pumpkin puree

### Directions

Begin by preheating your oven to 350 degrees F. Brush a muffin tin with a nonstick spray.

In a mixing bowl, thoroughly combine the dry ingredients. In another bowl, mix the wet ingredients until well combined.

Add the wet ingredients to the dry mixture and stir to combine well.

Now, scrape the batter into the prepared muffin tin.

Bake for about 23 minutes or until a toothpick inserted in the middle comes out dry and clean. Bon appétit!

**Per serving:** Calories: 218; Fat: 9.2g; Carbs: 30.8g; Protein: 3.8g

## 485. Country-Style Apricot Dump Cake

(Ready in about 10 minutes + chilling time | Servings 8)

### Ingredients

10 apricots, pitted and halved
1 tablespoon crystallized ginger
1/4 cup brown sugar
1 cup all-purpose flour
1 teaspoon baking powder
1/2 teaspoon ground cinnamon

4 tablespoons agave syrup
A pinch of kosher salt
A pinch of grated nutmeg
1/4 cup coconut oil, room temperature
1/2 cup almond milk

### Directions

Arrange the apricots on the bottom of a lightly oiled baking pan. Sprinkle ginger and brown sugar over them.

In a mixing bowl, thoroughly combine the flour, baking powder, cinnamon, agave syrup, salt and nutmeg.

Add in the coconut oil and almond milk and mix until everything is well incorporated. Spread the topping mixture over the fruit layer.

Bake your cake at 360 degrees F for about 40 minutes or until the top is golden brown. Bon appétit!

**Per serving:** Calories: 226; Fat: 7.5g; Carbs: 38.8g; Protein: 2.4g

# 486. Apricot and Pecan Crumb Pie

(Ready in about 45 minutes | Servings 9)

## Ingredients

1 pound apricots, pitted and halved
1 tablespoon fresh lemon juice
1 tablespoon crystallized ginger
1 cup brown sugar
1/2 cup rolled oats
1 cup all-purpose flour
1 teaspoon baking powder
1/2 teaspoon baking soda
1/2 teaspoon ground cloves
1/2 teaspoon ground anise
1/2 teaspoon ground cinnamon
1 teaspoon vanilla essence
1/4 teaspoon kosher salt
1/2 cup coconut oil, softened
1/3 cup pecans, roughly chopped

## Directions

Start by preheating your oven to 350 degrees F.

Arrange the apricots on the bottom of a lightly oiled baking pan. Sprinkle lemon juice, crystallized ginger and 1/2 cup of brown sugar over them.

In a mixing bowl, thoroughly combine the oats, all-purpose flour, baking powder, baking soda, 1/2 cup of brown sugar, ground cloves, anise, cinnamon, vanilla, salt and coconut oil.

Fold in the pecans and stir to combine. Spread the topping mixture over the apricot layer.

Bake in the preheated oven for about 45 minutes or until golden brown. Bon appétit!

**Per serving:** Calories: 322; Fat: 15.5g; Carbs: 44.8g; Protein: 3.5g

# 487. Tropical Bread Pudding

(Ready in about 2 hours | Servings 5)

## Ingredients

6 cups stale bread, cut into cubes
2 cups rice milk, sweetened
1/2 cup agave syrup
1 teaspoon vanilla extract
1/2 teaspoon ground cloves
1 teaspoon ground cinnamon
1/4 teaspoon coarse sea salt
5 tablespoons pineapple, crushed and drained
1 firm banana, sliced

## Directions

Place the bread cubes in a lightly oiled baking dish.

Now, blend the milk, agave syrup, vanilla, ground cloves, cinnamon and coarse sea salt until creamy and uniform.

Fold in the pineapple and banana and mix to combine well.

Spoon the mixture all over the bread cubes; press down slightly and set aside for about 1 hour.

Bake in the preheated oven at 350 degrees F for about 1 hour or until the top of your pudding is golden brown.

Bon appétit!

**Per serving:** Calories: 443; Fat: 4.9g; Carbs: 96.2g; Protein: 8.2g

# 488. Raspberry Cream Pie

(Ready in about 10 minutes + chilling time | Servings 10)

## Ingredients

Crust:
2 cups almonds
2 cups dates
A pinch of sea salt
A pinch of ground cloves
1/4 teaspoon ground anise
2 tablespoons coconut oil, softened

Filling:
2 ripe bananas
2 frozen bananas
2 cups raspberries
1 tablespoon agave syrup
2 tablespoons coconut oil, softened

## Directions

In your food processor, blend the crust ingredients until the mixture comes together; press the crust into a lightly oiled springform pan.

Then, blend the filling layer. Spoon the filling onto the crust, creating a flat surface with a spatula.

Transfer the cake to your freezer for about 3 hours. Store in your freezer.

Bon appétit!

**Per serving:** Calories: 225; Fat: 5.8g; Carbs: 44.8g; Protein: 1.7g

# OTHER FAVORITES

## 489. Spiced Cauliflower Bites

(Ready in about 25 minutes | Servings 4)

### Ingredients

1 pound cauliflower florets
1 cup all-purpose flour
1 tablespoon olive oil
1 tablespoon tomato paste
1 teaspoon onion powder

1 teaspoon garlic powder
1 teaspoon smoked paprika
1/2 teaspoon dried oregano
1/2 teaspoon dried basil
1/4 cup hot sauce

### Directions

Begin by preheating your oven to 450 degrees F. Pat the cauliflower florets dry using a kitchen towel.

Mix the remaining ingredients until well combined. Dip the cauliflower florets in the batter until well coated on all sides.

Place the cauliflower florets in a parchment-lined baking pan.

Roast for about 25 minutes or until cooked through. Bon appétit!

Per serving: Calories: 187; Fat: 4.1g; Carbs: 32.8g; Protein: 6.2g

## 490. Swiss-Style Potato Cake (Rösti)

(Ready in about 25 minutes | Servings 5)

### Ingredients

1 ½ pounds russets potatoes, peeled, grated and squeezed
1 teaspoon coarse sea salt
1/2 teaspoon red pepper flakes, crushed

1/2 teaspoon freshly ground black pepper
4 tablespoons olive oil

### Directions

Mix the grated potatoes, salt, red pepper and ground black pepper.

Heat the oil in a cast-iron skillet.

Drop handfuls of the potato mixture into the skillet.

Cook your potato cake over medium for about 10 minutes. Cover the potatoes and cook for another 10 minutes until the bottom of the potato cake is golden brown. Bon appétit!

Per serving: Calories: 204; Fat: 11g; Carbs: 24.6g; Protein: 2.9g

## 491. Creamed Vegan "Tuna" Salad

(Ready in about 10 minutes | Servings 8)

### Ingredients

2 (15-ounce) cans chickpeas, rinsed
3/4 cup vegan mayonnaise
1 teaspoon brown mustard
1 small red onion, chopped
2 pickles, chopped
1 teaspoon capers, drained

1 tablespoon fresh parsley, chopped
1 tablespoon fresh coriander, chopped
Sea salt and ground black pepper, to taste
2 tablespoons sunflower seeds, roasted

### Directions

Mix all the ingredients until everything is well incorporated.

Place your salad in the refrigerator until ready to serve.

Bon appétit!

Per serving: Calories: 252; Fat: 18.4g; Carbs: 17.1g; Protein: 5.5g

## 492. Traditional Hanukkah Latkes

(Ready in about 30 minutes | Servings 6)

### Ingredients

1 ½ pounds potatoes, peeled, grated and drained
3 tablespoons green onions, sliced
1/3 cup all-purpose flour
1/2 teaspoon baking powder
1/2 teaspoon sea salt, preferably kala namak

1/4 teaspoon ground black pepper
1/2 olive oil
5 tablespoons applesauce
1 tablespoon fresh dill, roughly chopped

### Directions

Thoroughly combine the grated potato, green onion, flour, baking powder, salt and black pepper.

Preheat the olive oil in a frying pan over a moderate heat.

Spoon 1/4 cup of potato mixture into the pan and cook your latkes until golden brown on both sides. Repeat with the remaining batter.

Serve with applesauce and fresh dill. Bon appétit!

Per serving: Calories: 283; Fat: 18.4g; Carbs: 27.3g; Protein: 3.2g

## 493. Thanksgiving Herb Gravy

(Ready in about 20 minutes | Servings 6)

### Ingredients

3 cups vegetable broth
1 ½ cups brown rice, cooked
6 ounces Cremini mushrooms, chopped
1 teaspoon dried basil
1 teaspoon dried oregano
1/2 teaspoon dried rosemary

1/2 teaspoon dried thyme
1/2 teaspoon garlic, minced
1/4 cup unsweetened plain almond milk
Sea salt and freshly ground black pepper

### Directions

Bring the vegetable broth to a boil over medium-high heat; add in the rice and mushrooms and reduce the heat to a simmer.

Let it simmer for about 12 minutes, until the mushrooms have softened. Remove from the heat.

Then, blend the mixture until creamy and uniform.

Add the remaining ingredients and heat your gravy over medium heat until everything is cooked through.

Serve with mashed potatoes or vegetables of choice. Bon appétit!

Per serving: Calories: 165; Fat: 1.6g; Carbs: 33.8g; Protein: 6.8g

## 494. Grandma's Cornichon Relish

(Ready in about 15 minutes + chilling time | Servings 9)

### Ingredients

3 cups cornichon, finely chopped
1 cup white onion, finely chopped
1 teaspoon sea salt
1/3 cup distilled white vinegar
1/4 teaspoon mustard seeds
1/3 cup sugar
1 tablespoon arrowroot powder, dissolved in 1 tablespoon water

### Directions

Place the cornichon, onion and salt in a sieve set over a bowl; drain for a few hours. Squeeze out as much liquid as possible.

Bring the vinegar, mustard seeds and sugar to a boil; add in the 1/3 teaspoon of the sea salt and let it boil until the sugar has dissolved.

Add in the cornichon-onion mixture and continue to simmer for 2 to 3 minutes more. Stir in the arrowroot powder mixture and continue to simmer for 1 to 2 minutes more.

Transfer the relish to a bowl and place, uncovered, in your refrigerator for about 2 hours. Bon appétit!

Per serving: Calories: 45; Fat: 0g; Carbs: 10.2g; Protein: 0.3g

## 495. Apple and Cranberry Chutney

(Ready in about 1 hour | Servings 7)

### Ingredients

1 ½ pounds cooking apples, peeled, cored and diced
1/2 cup sweet onion, chopped
1/2 cup apple cider vinegar
1 large orange, freshly squeezed
1 cup brown sugar
1 teaspoon fennel seeds
1 tablespoon fresh ginger, peeled and grated
1 teaspoon sea salt
1/2 cup dried cranberries

### Directions

In a saucepan, place the apples, sweet onion, vinegar, orange juice, brown sugar, fennel seeds, ginger and salt. Bring the mixture to a boil.

Immediately turn the heat to simmer; continue to simmer, stirring occasionally, for approximately 55 minutes, until most of the liquid has absorbed.

Set aside to cool and add in the dried cranberries. Store in your refrigerator for up to 2 weeks.

Bon appétit!

Per serving: Calories: 208; Fat: 0.3g; Carbs: 53g; Protein: 0.6g

## 496. Homemade Apple Butter

(Ready in about 35 minutes | Servings 16)

### Ingredients

5 pounds apples, peeled, cored and diced
1 cup water
2/3 cup granulated brown sugar
1 tablespoon ground cinnamon
1 teaspoon ground cloves
1 tablespoon vanilla essence
A pinch of freshly grated nutmeg
A pinch of salt

### Directions

Add the apples and water to a heavy-bottomed pot and cook for about 20 minutes.

Then, mash the cooked apples with a potato masher; stir the sugar, cinnamon, cloves, vanilla, nutmeg and salt into the mashed apples; stir to combine well.

Continue to simmer until the butter has thickened to your desired consistency.

Bon appétit!

Per serving: Calories: 106; Fat: 0.3g; Carbs: 27.3g; Protein: 0.4g

## 497. Homemade Peanut Butter

(Ready in about 5 minutes | Servings 16)

### Ingredients

1 ½ cups peanuts, blanched
A pinch of coarse salt
1 tablespoons agave syrup

### Directions

In your food processor or a high-speed blender, pulse the peanuts until ground. Then, process for 2 minutes more, scraping down the sides and bottom of the bowl.

Add in the salt and agave syrup.

Run your machine for another 2 minutes or until your butter is completely creamy and smooth.

Bon appétit!

Per serving: Calories: 144; Fat: 9.1g; Carbs: 10.6g; Protein: 6.9g

## 498. Roasted Pepper Spread

(Ready in about 10 minutes | Servings 10)

### Ingredients

2 red bell peppers, roasted and seeded
1 jalapeno pepper, roasted and seeded
4 ounces sun-dried tomatoes in oil, drained
2/3 cup sunflower seeds
2 tablespoons onion, chopped
1 garlic clove
1 tablespoon Mediterranean herb mix
Sea salt and ground black pepper, to taste
1/2 teaspoon turmeric powder
1 teaspoon ground cumin
2 tablespoons tahini

### Directions

Place all the ingredients in the bowl of your blender or food processor.

Process until creamy, uniform and smooth.

Store in an airtight container in your refrigerator for up to 2 weeks. Bon appétit!

Per serving: Calories: 111; Fat: 6.8g; Carbs: 10.8g; Protein: 4.4g

## 499. Classic Vegan Butter

(Ready in about 10 minutes | Servings 16)

### Ingredients

2/3 cup refined coconut oil, melted
1 tablespoon sunflower oil
1/4 cup soy milk
1/2 teaspoon malt vinegar
1/3 teaspoon coarse sea salt

### Directions

Add the coconut oil, sunflower oil, milk and vinegar to the bowl of your blender. Blitz to combine well.

Add in the sea salt and continue to blend until creamy and smooth; refrigerate until set. Bon appétit!

Per serving: Calories: 89; Fat: 10.1g; Carbs: 0.2g; Protein: 0.1g

## 500. Mediterranean-Style Zucchini Pancakes

(Ready in about 20 minutes | Servings 4)

### Ingredients

1 cup all-purpose flour
1/2 teaspoon baking powder
1/2 teaspoon dried oregano
1/2 teaspoon dried basil
1/2 teaspoon dried rosemary
Sea salt and ground black pepper, to taste
1 ½ cups zucchini, grated
1 chia egg
1/2 cup rice milk
1 teaspoon garlic, minced
2 tablespoons scallions, sliced
4 tablespoons olive oil

### Directions

Thoroughly combine the flour, baking powder and spices. In a separate bowl, combine the zucchini, chia egg, milk, garlic and scallions.

Add the zucchini mixture to the dry flour mixture; stir to combine well.

Then, heat the olive oil in a frying pan over a moderate flame. Cook your pancakes for 2 to 3 minutes per side until golden brown.

Bon appétit!

Per serving: Calories: 260; Fat: 14.1g; Carbs: 27.1g; Protein: 4.6g

## 501. Traditional Norwegian Flatbread (Lefse)

(Ready in about 20 minutes | Servings 7)

### Ingredients

3 medium-sized potatoes
1/2 cup all-purpose flour
1/2 cup besan
Sea salt, to taste
1/4 teaspoon ground black pepper
1/2 teaspoon cayenne pepper
2 tablespoons olive oil

### Directions

Boil the potatoes in a lightly salted water until they've softened.

Peel and mash the potatoes and then, add in the flour, besan and spices.

Divide the dough into 7 equal balls. Roll out each ball on a little floured work surface.

Heat the olive oil in a frying pan over medium-low heat and cook each flatbread for 2 to 3 minutes. Serve immediately. Bon appétit!

Per serving: Calories: 215; Fat: 4.5g; Carbs: 38.3g; Protein: 5.6g

## 502. Basic Cashew Butter

(Ready in about 20 minutes | Servings 12)

### Ingredients

3 cups raw cashew nuts
1 tablespoon coconut oil

### Directions

In your food processor or a high-speed blender, pulse the cashew nuts until ground. Then, process them for 5 minutes more, scraping down the sides and bottom of the bowl.

Add in the coconut oil.

Run your machine for another 10 minutes or until your butter is completely creamy and smooth. Enjoy!

Per serving: Calories: 130; Fat: 10.1g; Carbs: 6.8g; Protein: 3.8g

## 503. Apple and Almond Butter Balls

(Ready in about 15 minutes | Servings 12)

### Ingredients

1/2 cup almond butter
1 cup apple butter
1/3 cup almonds
1 cup fresh dates, pitted
1/2 teaspoon ground cinnamon
1/4 teaspoon ground cardamom
1/2 teaspoon almond extract
1/2 teaspoon rum extract
2 ½ cups old-fashioned oats

### Directions

Place the almond butter, apple butter, almonds, dates and spices in the bowl of your blender or food processor.

Process the mixture until you get a thick paste.

Stir in the oats and pulse a few more times to blend well. Roll the mixture into balls and serve well-chilled.

Per serving: Calories: 134; Fat: 2.4g; Carbs: 27.6g; Protein: 2.3g

## 504. Raw Mixed Berry Jam

(Ready in about 1 hour 5 minutes | Servings 10)

### Ingredients

1/4 pound fresh raspberries
1/4 pound fresh strawberries, hulled
1/4 pound fresh blackberries
2 tablespoons lemon juice, freshly squeezed
10 dates, pitted
3 tablespoons chia seeds

### Directions

Puree all the ingredients in your blender or food processor.

Let it sit for about 1 hour, stirring periodically.

Store your jam in sterilized jars in your refrigerator for up to 4 days. Bon appétit!

Per serving: Calories: 57; Fat: 1.6g; Carbs: 10.7g; Protein: 1.3g

## 505. Basic Homemade Tahini

(Ready in about 10 minutes | Servings 16)

### Ingredients

10 ounces sesame seeds, hulled

3 tablespoons canola oil

1/4 teaspoon kosher salt

### Directions

Toast the sesame seeds in a nonstick skillet for about 4 minutes, stirring continuously. Cool the sesame seeds completely.

Transfer the sesame seeds to the bowl of your food processor. Process for about 1 minute.

Add in the oil and salt and process for a further 4 minutes, scraping down the bottom and sides of the bowl.

Store your tahini in the refrigerator for up to 1 month. Bon appétit!

**Per serving:** Calories: 135; Fat: 13.4g; Carbs: 2.2g; Protein: 3.6g

## 506. Homemade Vegetable Stock

(Ready in about 55 minutes | Servings 6)

### Ingredients

2 tablespoons olive oil
1 cup onion, chopped
2 cup carrots, chopped
1 cup celery, chopped
4 cloves garlic, minced
2 sprigs rosemary, chopped

2 sprigs thyme, chopped
1 bay laurel
1 teaspoon mixed peppercorns
Sea salt, to taste
6 cups water

### Directions

In a heavy-bottomed pot, heat the oil over medium-high heat. Now, sauté the vegetables for about 10 minutes, stirring periodically to ensure even cooking.

Add in the garlic and spices and continue sautéing for 1 minute or until aromatic.

Add in the water, turn the heat to a simmer and let it cook for a further 40 minutes.

Set a strainer over a big bowl and line it with cheesecloth. Pour the stock through and discard the solids.

Bon appétit!

**Per serving:** Calories: 68; Fat: 4.4g; Carbs: 6.2g; Protein: 0.8g

## 507. 10-Minute Basic Caramel

(Ready in about 10 minutes | Servings 10)

### Ingredients

1/4 cup coconut oil
1 ½ cups granulated sugar
1/3 teaspoon coarse sea salt

1/3 cup water
2 tablespoons almond butter

### Directions

Melt the coconut oil and sugar in a saucepan for 1 minute.

Whisk in the remaining ingredients and continue to cook until everything is fully incorporated and your caramel is deeply golden.

Bon appétit!

**Per serving:** Calories: 183; Fat: 7.7g; Carbs: 30g; Protein: 0g

## 508. Nutty Chocolate Fudge Spread

(Ready in about 25 minutes | Servings 16)

### Ingredients

1 pound walnuts
1 ounce coconut oil, melted
2 tablespoons corn flour
4 tablespoons cocoa powder

A pinch of grated nutmeg
1/3 teaspoon ground cinnamon
A pinch of salt

### Directions

Roast the walnuts in the preheated oven at 350 degrees F for approximately 10 minutes until your walnuts are fragrant and lightly browned.

In your food processor or a high-speed blender, pulse the walnuts until ground. Then, process them for 5 minutes more, scraping down the sides and bottom of the bowl; reserve.

Melt the coconut oil over medium heat. Add in the corn flour and continue to cook until the mixture starts to boil.

Turn the heat to a simmer, add in the cocoa powder, nutmeg, cinnamon and salt; continue to cook, stirring occasionally, for about 10 minutes.

Fold in the ground walnuts, stir to combine and store in a glass jar. Enjoy!

**Per serving:** Calories: 207; Fat: 20.4g; Carbs: 5.4g; Protein: 4.6g

## 509. Cashew Cream Cheese

(Ready in about 10 minutes | Servings 6)

### Ingredients

1 ½ cups cashews, soaked overnight and drained
1/3 cup water
1/4 teaspoon coarse sea salt

1/4 teaspoon dried dill weed
1/4 teaspoon garlic powder
2 tablespoons nutritional yeast
2 probiotic capsules

### Directions

Process the cashews and water in your blender until creamy and uniform.

Add in the salt, dill, garlic powder and nutritional yeast; continue to blend until everything is well incorporated.

Spoon the mixture into a sterilized glass jar. Add in the probiotic powder and combine with a wooden spoon (not metal!)

Cover the jar with a clean kitchen towel and let it stand on the kitchen counter to ferment for 24-48 hours.

Keep in your refrigerator for up to a week. Bon appétit!

**Per serving:** Calories: 197; Fat: 14.4g; Carbs: 11.4g; Protein: 7.4g

## 510. Homemade Chocolate Milk

(Ready in about 10 minutes | Servings 4)

### Ingredients

4 teaspoons cashew butter
4 cups water
1/2 teaspoon vanilla paste

4 teaspoons cocoa powder
8 dates, pitted

### Directions

Place all the ingredients in the bowl of your high-speed blender.

Process until creamy, uniform and smooth.

Keep in a glass bottle in your refrigerator for up to 4 days. Enjoy!

**Per serving:** Calories: 79; Fat: 3.1g; Carbs: 13.3g; Protein: 1.3g

## 511. Traditional Korean Buchimgae

(Ready in about 20 minutes | Servings 4)

### Ingredients

1/2 cup all-purpose flour
1/2 cup chickpea flour
1/2 teaspoon baking powder
1 teaspoon garlic powder
1/4 teaspoon ground cumin
1/2 teaspoon sea salt
1 carrot, trimmed and grated

1 small onion, finely chopped
1 cup Kimchi
1 green chili, minced
1 flax egg
1 tablespoon bean paste
1 cup rice milk
4 tablespoons canola oil

### Directions

Thoroughly combine the flour, baking powder and spices. In a separate bowl, combine the carrot, onion, Kimchi, green chili, flax egg, bean paste and rice milk.

Add the vegetable mixture to the dry flour mixture; stir to combine well.

Then, heat the oil in a frying pan over a moderate flame. Cook the Korean pancakes for 2 to 3 minutes per side until crispy.

Bon appétit!

Per serving: Calories: 315; Fat: 19g; Carbs: 26.1g; Protein: 9.5g

## 512. Easy Homemade Nutella

(Ready in about 25 minutes | Servings 20)

### Ingredients

3 ½ cups hazelnuts
1 teaspoon vanilla seeds
A pinch of coarse sea salt
A pinch of grated nutmeg

1/2 teaspoon ground cinnamon
1/2 teaspoon ground cardamom
1 cup dark chocolate chips

### Directions

Roast the hazelnuts in the preheated oven at 350 degrees F for approximately 13 minutes until your hazelnuts are fragrant and lightly browned.

In your food processor or a high-speed blender, pulse the hazelnuts until ground. Then, process the mixture for 5 minutes more, scraping down the sides and bottom of the bowl.

Add in the remaining ingredients.

Run your machine for a further 4 to 5 minutes or until the mixture is completely creamy and smooth. Enjoy!

Per serving: Calories: 187; Fat: 17.1g; Carbs: 7g; Protein: 4g

## 513. Delicious Lemon Butter

(Ready in about 10 minutes | Servings 8)

### Ingredients

1/2 cup granulated sugar
2 tablespoons cornstarch
1/2 teaspoon lemon zest, grated

1 cup water
2 tablespoons fresh lemon juice
2 tablespoons coconut oil

### Directions

In a saucepan, combine the sugar, cornstarch and lemon zest over a moderate heat.

Stir in the water and lemon juice and continue to cook until the mixture has thickened. Heat off.

Stir in the coconut oil. Bon appétit!

Per serving: Calories: 87; Fat: 3.4g; Carbs: 14.6g; Protein: 0g

## 514. Mom's Blueberry Jam

(Ready in about 40 minutes | Servings 20)

### Ingredients

1 ½ pounds fresh blueberries
1 pound granulated sugar
1 cinnamon stick

5-6 cloves
1 vanilla pod, split lengthways
1 lemon, juiced

### Directions

Mix all the ingredients in a saucepan.

Continue to cook over medium heat, stirring constantly, until the sauce has reduced and thickened for about 30 minutes.

Remove from the heat. Leave your jam to sit for 10 minutes. Ladle into sterilized jars and cover with the lids. Let it cool completely.

Bon appétit!

Per serving: Calories: 108; Fat: 0.1g; Carbs: 27.6g; Protein: 0.2g

## 515. Authentic Spanish Tortilla

(Ready in about 30 minutes | Servings 4)

### Ingredients

2 tablespoons olive oil
1 ½ pounds russet potatoes, peeled and sliced
1 onion, chopped
Sea salt and ground black pepper, to taste
1/4 cup rice milk

8 ounces tofu, pressed and drained
1/2 cup besan
2 tablespoons cornstarch
1/2 teaspoon ground cumin
1/4 teaspoon ground allspice

### Directions

Heat 1 tablespoon of the olive oil in a frying pan. Then, add the potatoes, onion, salt and black pepper to the frying pan.

Cook for about 20 minutes or until the potatoes have softened.

In a mixing bowl, thoroughly combine the remaining ingredients. Add in the potato mixture and stir to combine.

Heat the remaining 1 tablespoon of the olive oil in a frying pan over medium-low heat. Cook your tortilla for 5 minutes per side. Serve warm.

Bon appétit!

Per serving: Calories: 365; Fat: 13.9g; Carbs: 48.1g; Protein: 14.5g

## 516. Traditional Belarusian Draniki

(Ready in about 30 minutes | Servings 4)

### Ingredients

4 waxy potatoes, peeled, grated and squeezed
4 tablespoons scallions, chopped
1 green chili pepper, chopped
1 red chili pepper, chopped
1/3 cup besan
1/2 teaspoon baking powder
1 teaspoon paprika
Sea salt and red pepper, to taste
1/4 cup canola oil
2 tablespoons fresh cilantro, chopped

### Directions

Thoroughly combine the grated potatoes, scallions, pepper, besan, baking powder, paprika, salt and red pepper.

Preheat the oil in a frying pan over a moderate heat.

Spoon 1/4 cup of potato mixture into the pan and cook your draniki until golden brown on both sides. Repeat with the remaining batter.

Serve with fresh cilantro. Bon appétit!

**Per serving:** Calories: 350; Fat: 14.4g; Carbs: 45.6g; Protein: 6.8g

## 517. Mediterranean Tomato Gravy

(Ready in about 20 minutes | Servings 6)

### Ingredients

3 tablespoons olive oil
1 red onion, chopped
3 cloves garlic, crushed
4 tablespoons cornstarch
1 can (14 ½-ounce) tomatoes, crushed
1/2 teaspoon dried basil
1/2 teaspoon dried oregano
1/2 teaspoon dried thyme
1 teaspoon dried parsley flakes
Sea salt and black pepper, to taste

### Directions

Heat the olive oil in a large saucepan over medium-high heat. Once hot, sauté the onion and garlic until tender and fragrant.

Add in the cornstarch and continue to cook for 1 minute more.

Add in the canned tomatoes and bring to a boil over medium-high heat; stir in the spices and turn the heat to a simmer.

Let it simmer for about 10 minutes until everything is cooked through.

Serve with vegetables of choice. Bon appétit!

**Per serving:** Calories: 106; Fat: 6.6g; Carbs: 9.6g; Protein: 0.8g

## 518. Pepper and Cucumber Relish

(Ready in about 20 minutes + chilling time | Servings 10)

### Ingredients

6 cucumbers, chopped
1 red bell pepper, seeded and chopped
1 green bell pepper, seeded and chopped
2 tablespoons coarse sea salt
1/2 cup wine vinegar
2/3 cup granulated sugar
1/2 teaspoon fennel seeds
1/4 teaspoon mustard seeds
1/4 teaspoon ground turmeric
1/2 teaspoon ground allspice
1 tablespoon mixed peppercorns
4 teaspoons cornstarch

### Directions

Place the cucumber, bell pepper and salt in a sieve set over a bowl; drain for a few hours. Squeeze out as much liquid as possible.

Bring the vinegar and sugar to a boil; add in the 1/3 teaspoon of the sea salt and let it boil until the sugar has dissolved.

Add in the cucumber-pepper mixture and continue to simmer for 2 to 3 minutes more. Stir in the spices and cornstarch; continue to simmer for 1 to 2 minutes more.

Transfer the relish to a bowl and place, uncovered, in your refrigerator for about 2 hours. Bon appétit!

**Per serving:** Calories: 66; Fat: 0.3g; Carbs: 15.3g; Protein: 1.5g

## 519. Homemade Almond Butter

(Ready in about 20 minutes | Servings 20)

### Ingredients

1 pound almonds
A pinch of sea salt
A pinch of grated nutmeg

### Directions

Roast the almonds in the preheated oven at 350 degrees F for approximately 9 minutes until your nuts are fragrant and lightly browned.

In your food processor or a high-speed blender, pulse the almonds until ground. Then, process the mixture for 5 minutes more, scraping down the sides and bottom of the bowl.

Add in the salt and nutmeg.

Run your machine for another 10 minutes or until your butter is completely creamy and smooth. Enjoy!

**Per serving:** Calories: 131; Fat: 11.3g; Carbs: 4.8g; Protein: 4.8g

## 520. Indian-Style Mango Chutney

(Ready in about 1 hour | Servings 7)

### Ingredients

5 mangoes, peeled and diced
1 yellow onion, chopped
2 red chilies, chopped
3/4 cup balsamic vinegar
1 ½ cups granulated sugar
1 teaspoon coriander seeds
1 tablespoon chana dal
1/2 teaspoon jeera
1/4 teaspoon turmeric powder
1/4 teaspoon Himalayan salt
1/2 cup currants

### Directions

In a saucepan, place the mangoes, onion, red chilies, vinegar, granulated sugar, coriander seeds, chana dal, jeera, turmeric powder and salt. Bring the mixture to a boil.

Immediately turn the heat to simmer; continue to simmer, stirring occasionally, for approximately 55 minutes, until most of the liquid has absorbed.

Set aside to cool and add in the currants. Store in your refrigerator for up to 2 weeks.

Bon appétit!

**Per serving:** Calories: 273; Fat: 2.3g; Carbs: 64.3g; Protein: 2.4g

# 521. Easy Vegetable Pajeon

(Ready in about 20 minutes | Servings 4)

## Ingredients

1/2 cup all-purpose flour
1/2 cup potato starch
1 teaspoon baking powder
1/3 teaspoon Himalayan salt
1/2 cup kimchi, finely chopped
4 scallions, chopped
1 carrot, trimmed and chopped
2 bell peppers, chopped
1 green chili pepper, chopped
1 cup kimchi liquid
2 tablespoons olive oil
Dipping sauce:
2 tablespoons soy sauce
2 teaspoons rice vinegar
1 teaspoon fresh ginger, finely grated

## Directions

Thoroughly combine the flour, potato starch, baking powder and salt. In a separate bowl, combine the vegetables and kimchi liquid.

Add the vegetable mixture to the dry flour mixture; stir to combine well.

Then, heat the oil in a frying pan over a moderate flame. Cook the Pajeon for 2 to 3 minutes per side until crispy.

Meanwhile, mix the sauce ingredients. Serve your Pajeon with the sauce for dipping. Bon appétit!

**Per serving:** Calories: 255; Fat: 10.6g; Carbs: 33.3g; Protein: 6.2g

# 522. Healthy Chocolate Peanut Butter

(Ready in about 15 minutes | Servings 20)

## Ingredients

2 ½ cups peanuts
1/2 teaspoon coarse sea salt
1/2 teaspoon cinnamon powder
1/2 cup cocoa powder
10 dates, pitted

## Directions

Roast the peanuts in the preheated oven at 350 degrees F for approximately 7 minutes until the peanuts are fragrant and lightly browned.

In your food processor or a high-speed blender, pulse the peanuts until ground. Then, process the mixture for 2 minutes more, scraping down the sides and bottom of the bowl.

Add in the salt, cinnamon, cocoa powder and dates.

Run your machine for another 2 minutes or until your butter is completely creamy and smooth. Enjoy!

**Per serving:** Calories: 118; Fat: 9.2g; Carbs: 6.9g; Protein: 5.1g

# 523. Chocolate Walnut Spread

(Ready in about 20 minutes | Servings 15)

## Ingredients

1 cup walnuts
1 teaspoon pure vanilla extract
1/2 cup agave nectar
4 tablespoons cocoa powder
A pinch of ground cinnamon
A pinch of grated nutmeg
A pinch of sea salt
4 tablespoons almond milk

## Directions

Roast the walnuts in the preheated oven at 350 degrees F for approximately 10 minutes until they are fragrant and lightly browned.

In your food processor or a high-speed blender, pulse the walnuts until ground. Then, process the mixture for 5 minutes more, scraping down the sides and bottom of the bowl.

Add in the remaining ingredients.

Run your machine for a further 5 minutes or until the mixture is completely creamy and smooth. Enjoy!

**Per serving:** Calories: 78; Fat: 4.7g; Carbs: 9g; Protein: 1.5g

# 524. Pecan and Apricot Butter

(Ready in about 15 minutes | Servings 16)

## Ingredients

2 ½ cups pecans
1/2 cup dried apricots, chopped
1/2 cup sunflower oil
1 teaspoon bourbon vanilla
1/4 teaspoon ground anise
1/2 teaspoon cinnamon
1/8 teaspoon grated nutmeg
1/8 teaspoon salt

## Directions

In your food processor or a high-speed blender, pulse the pecans until ground. Then, process the pecans for 5 minutes more, scraping down the sides and bottom of the bowl.

Add in the remaining ingredients.

Run your machine for a further 5 minutes or until the mixture is completely creamy and smooth. Enjoy!

**Per serving:** Calories: 163; Fat: 17g; Carbs: 2.5g; Protein: 1.4g

# 525. Cinnamon Plum Preserves

(Ready in about 40 minutes | Servings 20)

## Ingredients

5 pounds ripe plums rinsed
2 pounds granulated sugar
2 tablespoons lemon juice
3 cinnamon sticks

## Directions

Mix all the ingredients in a saucepan.

Continue to cook over medium heat, stirring constantly, until the sauce has reduced and thickened for about 30 minutes.

Remove from the heat. Leave your jam to sit for 10 minutes. Ladle into sterilized jars and cover with the lids. Let it cool completely.

Bon appétit!

**Per serving:** Calories: 223; Fat: 0.3g; Carbs: 58.1g; Protein: 0.8g

## 526. Middle-Eastern Tahini Spread

(Ready in about 10 minutes | Servings 16)

### Ingredients

10 ounces sesame seeds
3 tablespoons cocoa powder
1 teaspoon vanilla seeds

1/4 teaspoon kosher salt
1/2 cup fresh dates, pitted
3 tablespoons coconut oil

### Directions

Toast the sesame seeds in a nonstick skillet for about 4 minutes, stirring continuously. Cool the sesame seeds completely.

Transfer the sesame seeds to the bowl of your food processor. Process for about 1 minute.

Add in the remaining ingredients and process for a further 4 minutes, scraping down the bottom and sides of the bowl.

Store your tahini spread in the refrigerator for up to 1 month. Bon appétit!

**Per serving:** Calories: 143; Fat: 13.3g; Carbs: 6.2g; Protein: 3.9g

## 527. Vegan Ricotta Cheese

(Ready in about 10 minutes | Servings 12)

### Ingredients

1/2 cup raw cashew nuts, soaked overnight and drained
1/2 cup raw sunflower seeds, soaked overnight and drained
1/4 cup water
1 heaping tablespoon coconut oil, melted

1 tablespoon lime juice, freshly squeezed
1 tablespoon white vinegar
1/4 teaspoon Dijon mustard
2 tablespoons nutritional yeast
1/2 teaspoon garlic powder
1/2 teaspoon turmeric powder
1/2 teaspoon salt

### Directions

Process the cashews, sunflower seeds and water in your blender until creamy and uniform.

Add in the remaining ingredients; continue to blend until everything is well incorporated.

Keep in your refrigerator for up to a week. Bon appétit!

**Per serving:** Calories: 74; Fat: 6.3g; Carbs: 3.3g; Protein: 2.7g

## 528. Super Easy Almond Milk

(Ready in about 10 minutes | Servings 6)

### Ingredients

1 cup raw almonds, soaked overnight and drained
6 cups water
1 tablespoon maple syrup

A pinch of grated nutmeg
A pinch of salt
A pinch of ground cinnamon
1 teaspoon vanilla extract

### Directions

Place all the ingredients in the bowl of your high-speed blender.

Process until creamy, uniform and smooth.

Strain the liquid using a nut milk bag; squeeze until all of the liquid is extracted.

Keep in a glass bottle in your refrigerator for up to 4 days. Enjoy!

**Per serving:** Calories: 78; Fat: 6g; Carbs: 4.8g; Protein: 2.5g

## 529. Homemade Vegan Yogurt

(Ready in about 10 minutes | Servings 6)

### Ingredients

1 ½ cups full-fat coconut milk
1 teaspoon maple syrup

A pinch of coarse sea salt
2 capsules vegan probiotic

### Directions

Spoon the coconut milk into a sterilized glass jar. Add in the maple syrup and salt.

Empty your probiotic capsules and stir with a wooden spoon (not metal!)

Cover the jar with a clean kitchen towel and let it stand on the kitchen counter to ferment for 24-48 hours.

Keep in your refrigerator for up to a week. Bon appétit!

**Per serving:** Calories: 141; Fat: 14.2g; Carbs: 4g; Protein: 1.3g

## 530. South Asian Masala Paratha

(Ready in about 20 minutes | Servings 5)

### Ingredients

2 cups all-purpose flour
1 teaspoon Kala namak salt
1/2 teaspoon garam masala
1/2 cup warm water

1 tablespoon canola oil
10 tablespoons coconut oil, softened

### Directions

In a mixing bowl, thoroughly combine the flour, salt and garam masala. Make a well in the flour mixture and gradually add in the water and canola oil; mix to combine.

Knead the dough until it forms a sticky ball. Let it rest in your refrigerator overnight.

Divide the dough into 5 equal balls and roll them out on a clean surface. Spread the coconut oil all over the paratha and fold it in half. Spread the coconut oil over it and fold it again.

Roll each paratha into a circle approximately 8 inches in diameter.

Heat a griddle until hot. Cook each paratha for about 3 minutes or until bubbles form on the surface. Turn over and cook on the other side for 3 minutes longer. Serve warm.

**Per serving:** Calories: 441; Fat: 30.4g; Carbs: 38.1g; Protein: 5.2g

## 531. Traditional Swedish Raggmunk

(Ready in about 30 minutes | Servings 5)

### Ingredients

1 ½ pounds waxy potatoes, peeled, grated and squeezed
3 tablespoons shallots, chopped
2 chia eggs
1/2 cup all-purpose flour

1 teaspoon baking powder
Sea salt and ground black, to season
1 teaspoon cayenne pepper
1/2 cup canola oil
6 tablespoons applesauce

### Directions

Thoroughly combine the grated potatoes, shallots, chia eggs, flour, baking powder, salt, black pepper and cayenne pepper.

Preheat the oil in a frying pan over a moderate heat.

Spoon 1/4 cup of the potato mixture into the pan and cook the potato cakes for about 5 minutes per side. Repeat with the remaining batter.

Serve with applesauce and enjoy!

**Per serving:** Calories: 356; Fat: 22.1g; Carbs: 36.5g; Protein: 4.3g

# 532. Buffalo Gravy with Beer

(Ready in about 30 minutes | Servings 5)

## Ingredients

3 tablespoons olive oil
1 small red onion, chopped
1 teaspoon garlic, minced
1/3 cup whole wheat flour
3 cups vegetable broth
1/2 teaspoon dried rosemary
1/2 teaspoon dried oregano

1/2 teaspoon dried parsley
flakes
1/2 teaspoon dried sage
1 teaspoon hot paprika
Sea salt and freshly cracked
black peppercorns, to taste
1 cup beer

## Directions

Heat the olive oil in a large saucepan over medium-high heat. Once hot, sauté the onion and garlic until tender and fragrant.

Add in the flour and continue to cook for 1 minute more.

Pour in the vegetable broth and bring to a boil over medium-high heat; stir in the spices and turn the heat to a simmer.

Pour in the beer and let it simmer, partially covered, for about 10 minutes until everything is cooked through.

Serve with mashed potatoes or cauliflower. Bon appétit!

**Per serving:** Calories: 222; Fat: 16.8g; Carbs: 11.2g; Protein: 7.3g

# 533. Spicy Cilantro and Mint Chutney

(Ready in about 10 minutes | Servings 9)

## Ingredients

1 ½ bunches fresh cilantro
6 tablespoons scallions, sliced
3 tablespoons fresh mint
leaves

2 jalapeno peppers, seeded
1/2 teaspoon kosher salt
2 tablespoons fresh lime juice
1/3 cup water

## Directions

Place all the ingredients in the bowl of your blender or food processor.

Then, combine the ingredients until your desired consistency has been reached.

Bon appétit!

**Per serving:** Calories: 15; Fat: 0g; Carbs: 0.9g; Protein: 0.1g

# 534. Cinnamon Almond Butter

Ready in about 30 minutes | Servings 16)

## Ingredients

2 cups almonds
1 tablespoon cinnamon,
ground
1 teaspoon pure vanilla extract

3 tablespoons agave syrup
A pinch of sea salt
A pinch of grated nutmeg

## Directions

Roast the almonds in the preheated oven at 350 degrees F for approximately 9 minutes until your nuts are fragrant and lightly browned.

In your food processor or a high-speed blender, pulse the almonds until ground. Then, process the mixture for 10 minutes more, scraping down the sides and bottom of the bowl.

Add in the cinnamon, vanilla, agave syrup, salt and nutmeg.

Run your machine for another 10 minutes or until your butter is completely creamy and smooth. Enjoy!

**Per serving:** Calories: 118; Fat: 8.9g; Carbs: 7.5g; Protein: 3.8g

# 535. Rainbow Vegetable Pancakes

(Ready in about 20 minutes | Servings 4)

## Ingredients

1 cup all-purpose flour
1 teaspoon baking powder
Sea salt and ground black
pepper, to taste
1 teaspoon paprika
1 cup zucchini, grated
1 cup button mushrooms,
chopped

2 medium carrots, trimmed
and grated
1 red onion, finely chopped
1 garlic clove, minced
1 cup spinach, torn into pieces
1/4 cup water
1 teaspoon hot sauce
2 chia eggs

## Directions

Thoroughly combine the flour, baking powder, salt, black pepper and paprika. In a separate bowl, combine the vegetables and water.

Add in the hot sauce and chia eggs and mix to combine well. Add the vegetable mixture to the dry flour mixture; stir to combine well.

Then, heat the oil in a frying pan over a moderate flame. Cook the pancakes for 2 to 3 minutes per side until crispy and golden brown.

Bon appétit!

**Per serving:** Calories: 222; Fat: 4.9g; Carbs: 38.1g; Protein: 7.5g

# 536. Garden Tomato Relish

(Ready in about 10 minutes + chilling time | Servings 10)

## Ingredients

1 pound tomatoes, chopped
1 red onion, chopped
1 garlic clove, minced
1 cup extra-virgin olive oil
2 tablespoons capers

1 teaspoon chili powder
1 tablespoon curry powder
2 tablespoons cilantro,
chopped
2 tablespoons malt vinegar

## Directions

Thoroughly combine the tomatoes, onion, garlic and olive oil. Grill for about 8 minutes.

Add in the remaining ingredients and stir to combine well.

Transfer the relish to a bowl and place, uncovered, in your refrigerator for about 2 hours. Bon appétit!

**Per serving:** Calories: 208; Fat: 21.8g; Carbs: 3.5g; Protein: 0.7g

## 537. Crunchy Peanut Butter

(Ready in about 10 minutes | Servings 20)

### Ingredients

2 ½ cups peanuts
1/2 teaspoon coarse sea salt
1/2 teaspoon cinnamon powder
10 dates, pitted

### Directions

Roast the peanuts in the preheated oven at 350 degrees F for approximately 7 minutes until the peanuts are fragrant and lightly browned.

In your food processor or a high-speed blender, pulse the peanuts until ground. Reserve for about 1/2 cup of the mixture.

Then, process the mixture for 2 minutes more, scraping down the sides and bottom of the bowl.

Add in the salt, cinnamon and dates.

Run your machine for another 2 minutes or until your butter is smooth. Add in the reserved peanuts and stir with a spoon. Enjoy!

**Per serving:** Calories: 114; Fat: 9g; Carbs: 5.6g; Protein: 4.8g

## 538. Easy Orange Butter

(Ready in about 10 minutes | Servings 7)

### Ingredients

2 tablespoons granulated sugar
2 tablespoons cornstarch
1 teaspoon orange zest
1 teaspoon fresh ginger, peeled and minced
2 tablespoons orange juice
1/2 cup water
A pinch of grated nutmeg
A pinch of grated kosher salt
7 tablespoons coconut oil, softened

### Directions

In a saucepan, combine the sugar, cornstarch, orange zest and ginger over a moderate heat.

Stir in the orange juice, water, nutmeg and salt; continue to cook until the mixture has thickened. Heat off.

Stir in the coconut oil. Bon appétit!

**Per serving:** Calories: 140; Fat: 13.6g; Carbs: 6.3g; Protein: 0g

## 539. Cinnamon Cashew Butter

(Ready in about 15 minutes | Servings 9)

### Ingredients

2 cups raw cashew nuts
A pinch of sea salt
A pinch of grated nutmeg
1 teaspoon ground cinnamon
4 tablespoons agave syrup
2 tablespoons peanut oil

### Directions

Roast the cashew nuts in the preheated oven at 350 degrees F for approximately 8 minutes until the peanuts are fragrant and lightly browned.

In your food processor or a high-speed blender, pulse the cashew nuts until ground. Then, process the nuts for 2 minutes more, scraping down the sides and bottom of the bowl.

Add in the salt, nutmeg, cinnamon, agave syrup and oil.

Run your machine for another 2 minutes or until your butter is completely creamy and smooth. Enjoy!

**Per serving:** Calories: 162; Fat: 11.1g; Carbs: 13.7g; Protein: 3.3g

## 540. Easy Ukrainian Deruny

(Ready in about 30 minutes | Servings 4)

### Ingredients

4 medium-sized potatoes, peeled and diced
1/2 cup all-purpose flour
1/2 cup besan flour
1/2 teaspoon baking powder
1 sweet onion, peeled and chopped
1 flax egg
Sea salt and ground black pepper, to taste
1 teaspoon paprika
1/4 cup olive oil, or as needed

### Directions

Boil the potatoes in a lightly salted water until they've softened.

Peel and mash the potatoes in a mixing bowl.

Then, add in the flour, besan, baking powder, sweet onion, flax egg, salt, black pepper and paprika.

Then, heat the oil in a frying pan over a moderate flame. Cook the potato cakes for about 3 minutes per side until crispy and golden brown. Bon appétit!

**Per serving:** Calories: 420; Fat: 14.9g; Carbs: 63.4g; Protein: 9.5g

## 541. Decadent Pickled Peaches

(Ready in about 1 hour 30 minutes | Servings 10)

### Ingredients

6 peaches, peeled, pitted and diced
6 Roma tomatoes, peeled and diced
2 sweet onions, diced
2 stalks celery, diced
1 teaspoon English mustard powder
1 teaspoon cumin seeds
1 teaspoon sea salt
1 cups malt vinegar
1/4 cup agave syrup

### Directions

In a large saucepan, place the peaches, tomatoes, sweet onions, celery, spices, vinegar and agave syrup. Bring to a boil over medium-high heat.

Now, turn the heat to a simmer and continue to cook for 1 hour 30 minutes or until the sauce has thickened and reduced.

Store in glass jars in your refrigerator. Bon appétit!

**Per serving:** Calories: 102; Fat: 0.5g; Carbs: 23.4g; Protein: 2g

## 542. Classic Pear Butter

(Ready in about 30 minutes | Servings 10)

### Ingredients

2 pounds ripe pears, peeled, cored and diced
1/4 cup water
1 tablespoon fresh lemon juice
2 tablespoons maple syrup
1 teaspoon ground cinnamon
1/4 teaspoon nutmeg
4-5 whole cloves
1/2 teaspoon vanilla beans
A pinch of coarse salt

### Directions

Add the pears and water to a heavy-bottomed pot and cook for about 20 minutes.

Then, mash the cooked pears with a potato masher; stir in the remaining ingredients; stir to combine well.

Continue to simmer until the pear butter has thickened to your desired consistency. Bon appétit!

**Per serving:** Calories: 51; Fat: 0.3g; Carbs: 12.6g; Protein: 0.5g

# 543. Old-Fashioned Pecan Spread

(Ready in about 10 minutes | Servings 16)

## Ingredients

2 cups pecan, soaked and drained

5 tablespoons coconut oil

4 tablespoons orange juice

1 cup dates, pitted

## Directions

In your food processor or a high-speed blender, pulse the pecans until ground.

Then, process the nuts for 2 minutes more, scraping down the sides and bottom of the bowl.

Add in the coconut oil, orange juice and dates. Continue to blend until your desired consistency is achieved.

Bon appétit!

**Per serving:** Calories: 125; Fat: 13.1g; Carbs: 2.5g; Protein: 1.1g

# 544. Raspberry Star Anise Jelly

(Ready in about 35 minutes | Servings 20)

## Ingredients

2 pounds fresh raspberries

2 pounds granulated sugar

1 heaping teaspoon anise star

1 vanilla bean, split lengthwise

## Directions

Mix all the ingredients in a saucepan.

Continue to cook over medium heat, stirring constantly, until the sauce has reduced and thickened for about 25 minutes.

Remove from the heat. Leave your jam to sit for 10 minutes. Ladle into sterilized jars and cover with the lids. Let it cool completely.

Store in the cupboard for a few months. Bon appétit!

**Per serving:** Calories: 201; Fat: 0.3g; Carbs: 50g; Protein: 0.5g

# 545. Mediterranean-Style Tahini Spread

(Ready in about 10 minutes | Servings 16)

## Ingredients

10 ounces sesame seeds

A pinch of sea salt

1/4 teaspoon ground black pepper, or more to taste

1 tablespoon fresh parsley leaves

1 tablespoon fresh basil

1 tablespoon fresh chives

1 tablespoon lime juice

2 garlic cloves

2 tablespoons grapeseed oil

## Directions

Toast the sesame seeds in a nonstick skillet for about 4 minutes, stirring continuously. Cool the sesame seeds completely.

Transfer the sesame seeds to the bowl of your food processor. Process for about 1 minute.

Add in the remaining ingredients and process for a further 4 minutes, scraping down the bottom and sides of the bowl.

Store your spread in the refrigerator for up to 1 month. Bon appétit!

**Per serving:** Calories: 128; Fat: 12.5g; Carbs: 2.3g; Protein: 3.6g

# 546. Sweet Cinnamon Walnut Spread

(Ready in about 20 minutes | Servings 16)

## Ingredients

1 ½ cups raw walnuts

2 ounces dark chocolate, broken into chunks

1 teaspoon ground cinnamon

A pinch of sea salt

A pinch of grated nutmeg

1/3 cup agave syrup

## Directions

Roast the walnuts in the preheated oven at 350 degrees F for approximately 10 minutes until they are fragrant and lightly browned.

In your food processor or a high-speed blender, pulse the walnuts until ground. Then, process the mixture for 5 minutes more, scraping down the sides and bottom of the bowl.

Add in the remaining ingredients.

Run your machine for a further 5 minutes or until the mixture is completely creamy and smooth. Enjoy!

**Per serving:** Calories: 100; Fat: 7.6g; Carbs: 7.4g; Protein: 1.6g

# 547. Coconut "Feta" Cheese

(Ready in about 30 minutes + chilling time | Servings 12)

## Ingredients

1 ½ cups full-fat coconut milk

1/2 cup hot water

1 teaspoon Himalayan salt

1/2 teaspoon garlic powder

1/4 teaspoon dried dill weed

1 tablespoon coconut oil

2 tablespoons nutritional yeast

4 teaspoons agar agar powder

1 tablespoon white vinegar

## Directions

In a saucepan, place the milk and water.

Add in the salt, garlic powder, dill, coconut oil, nutritional yeast and agar agar powder and whisk to combine well.

Heat the mixture over medium heat, stirring continuously; bring to a rapid boil. Add in the vinegar and stir to combine well.

Turn the heat to a simmer and continue to whisk for 6 to 7 minutes more or until the mixture is uniform and smooth.

Spoon the mixture into lightly greased molds. Let it stand for 20 minutes at room temperature. Place in your refrigerator for at least 2 hours or until set.

Store in your refrigerator for up to a week. Enjoy!

**Per serving:** Calories: 72; Fat: 7.2g; Carbs: 1.5g; Protein: 1.3g

# 548. Classic Onion Relish

(Ready in about 35 minutes | Servings 6)

## Ingredients

4 tablespoons vegan butter
1 pound red onions, peeled and sliced
4 tablespoons granulated sugar
4 tablespoons white vinegar
1 ½ cups boiling water
1 teaspoon sea salt
1 teaspoon mustard seeds
1 teaspoon celery seeds

## Directions

In a frying pan, melt the butter over medium-high heat. Then, sauté the onions for about 8 minutes, stirring frequently to ensure even cooking.

Add in the sugar and continue sautéing for 5 to 6 minutes more. Add in the vinegar, boiling water, salt, mustard seeds and celery seeds.

Turn the heat to a simmer and continue to cook, covered, for about 20 minutes.

Remove the lid and continue to simmer until all the liquid has evaporated. Bon appétit!

**Per serving:** Calories: 118; Fat: 7.9g; Carbs: 11.3g; Protein: 0.9g

# 549. Hot and Spicy Gravy

(Ready in about 25 minutes | Servings 6)

## Ingredients

6 tablespoons vegan butter
1 shallot, chopped
1 teaspoon garlic, minced
1/3 cup whole-wheat flour
3 cups vegetable stock
1 cup oat milk, unsweetened
2 tablespoons vegan Worcestershire sauce
3 tablespoons hot pepper sauce
1/2 teaspoon cayenne pepper
Kosher salt and ground black pepper, to taste

## Directions

Heat the olive oil in a large saucepan over medium-high heat. Once hot, sauté the shallot and garlic until tender and fragrant or about 2 minutes.

Add in the flour and continue to cook for 1 minute more.

Pour in the vegetable stock and bring to a boil over medium-high heat; stir in the spices and turn the heat to a simmer.

Add in the remaining ingredients and let it simmer, partially covered, for about 10 minutes until cooked through.

Serve with mashed potatoes or cauliflower. Bon appétit!

**Per serving:** Calories: 174; Fat: 13.9g; Carbs: 8.2g; Protein: 4.9g

# 550. Old-Fashioned Sweet Potato Cakes

(Ready in about 30 minutes | Servings 5)

## Ingredients

1 ½ pounds sweet potatoes, peeled, grated and squeezed
1 Vidalia onion, chopped
2 cloves garlic, minced
1 cup all-purpose flour
1/4 cup cornstarch
1 teaspoon baking powder
2 flax eggs
Sea salt and freshly ground black pepper, to taste
1 teaspoon Za'atar spice
1/3 cup olive oil

## Directions

In a mixing bowl, thoroughly combine the sweet potatoes, Vidalia onion, garlic, flour, cornstarch, baking powder, flax eggs, salt, black pepper and Za'atar spice.

Preheat the oil in a frying pan over a moderate heat.

Spoon 1/4 cup of the potato mixture into the pan and cook the potato cakes until golden brown on both sides or about 10 minutes. Repeat with the remaining batter.

Serve with toppings of choice. Bon appétit!

**Per serving:** Calories: 391; Fat: 16.4g; Carbs: 55.7g; Protein: 5.8g

Made in the USA
Monee, IL
21 September 2020